GRAHAM GREENE: ON THE FRONTIER

Graham Greene: On the Frontier

Politics and Religion in the Novels

Maria Couto

St. Martin's Press   New York

First published in the United States of America in 1988

Printed in Hong Kong

ISBN 0–312–01356–6

Library of Congress Cataloging-in-Publication Data
Couto, Maria.
Graham Greene : on the frontier : politics and religion in the
novels / Maria Couto.
p.   cm.
Bibliography: p.
Includes index.
ISBN 0–312–01356–6 : $29.95
1. Greene, Graham, 1904–   —Political and social views.
2. Greene, Graham, 1904–   —Religion.   3. Politics in
literature.
4. Religion in literature.   I. Title.
PR6013.R44Z63188 1986
823′.912–dc 19   87–18759
                                                              CIP

For my mother and father

'He had a keen insight into abstract truth; but he was an Englishman to the backbone in his severe adherence to the real and the concrete. He had a most classical taste, and a genius for the philosophy of art; and he was fond of historical inquiry, and the politics of religion. He had no turn for theology as such . . . He took an eager, courageous view of things.'

Cardinal Newman, *Apologia Pro Vita Sua*

Contents

Acknowledgements   ix

    Introduction   1

1   **Explorations**   10

2   **The Intimate Enemy**   30

3   **The Religious Sense**   62

4   **England, My England**   91

5   *Colons*, **Intermediaries and Exiles**   111

6   **Hegemonies**   145

    Conclusion: Face to Face   197

Interview with Graham Greene   206
Appendix: Letters to the Press   222
Notes   230
Bibliography   241
Index   246

Acknowledgements

This book owes much to the advice, criticism and knowledge of friends and colleagues. No acknowledgement can adequately express my debt to them. At the top of a long list of those whom I must thank are my students at Lady Shri Ram College, Delhi University, where some of the interpretations in this book were developed during discussion. Graham Greene was generous with his time and patience. It has been a privilege to listen to this 'traveller', so rooted in his own tradition and yet at home everywhere. His clear-eyed honesty about life and world affairs and his compassion have enriched me. His practical help too was invaluable. I thank him specially for access to material he holds personally, and for permission to quote extensively from his work. I would like to record my particular obligation to Elisabeth Dennys, who put up with intrusions on her peace. As a dedicated custodian of important material she has contributed to the final shape of this book. The support of Samuel Hynes (Princeton University) has been crucial to the publication of this book. He read the work at various stages, and gave me the benefit of his knowledge and experience. Marina Warner and Salman Rushdie generously found the time to read the finished draft. Their perceptions have helped in important final revisions. I cannot express fully my gratitude to them and to Chinua Achebe, Ngũgĩ Wa Thiong'O and Dr Davidson Nicol of Sierra Leone and Christ College, Cambridge, who helped me with insights into Greene's Africa. The flaws are my own as also all responsibility for interpretation of the material I have used. Deep too and unbounded is my gratitude to Michael Thomas for his unfailing encouragement and to my sister, Emma Martin, who transcribed with patient care the record of conversations with Graham Greene.

But for all this help, the book would not have reached its present form nor would I have been able to write it without the support of an extended family all of whom I cannot possibly name individually nor thank enough. However, I would like to express my special gratitude to Sarah Joseph, friend and colleague in Delhi, whose incisive comments sparked off some directions of the work; Krishna Basrur, who shares a lifetime's enthusiasms; M. S. Prabhakar, for intimations and a humane understanding of literature and politics;

ix

K. J. Mahale, Leela Kasturi, Jennifer McKay, Manju Jain, Girish Karnad, Leela and Moni Malhoutra, Jayanthi Belliapa, Uma Ram Nath, Maya Kak and Peter O'Neill who have helped with constructive and practical advice; Victor Couto and Olga Judson who with their discipline, tenacity and sense of history taught me more than they would be willing to acknowledge; the staff of the London Library and the Commonwealth Institute Library.

I am greatly indebted to them all and to my children, Vinay, Veena and Vivek for cheerful collaboration. Finally and most of all to Alban, as always, for everything, including cross-examinations that clarified many of my thoughts with his creative and vigorous dissent as the devil's advocate.

MARIA COUTO

Introduction

Graham Greene has often declared himself to be a political novelist, not a Catholic novelist but a novelist who happens to be a Catholic. This is not to say that he is comfortable with the word 'politics' in relation to art and indeed prefers not to be drawn into any discussion of the politics of his novels.[1] Greene is neither a polemicist nor a political activist. The politics of his fiction is the politics of life itself in the Lukácsian sense: 'everything in man's life is politics, whether man is conscious of it, unconscious of it, or even trying to escape from it'.[2] The novels do not offer a system but life as it is lived in our world with contradictions and complexities that characterise human relations. The incoherence and inconsistency of behaviour and thought are emphasised in order to arrive at the possibility of truth.

Critical estimates of Graham Greene centre on the obsessions and fixations attached to Catholicism, the theme of betrayal, lost innocence, corrupt human nature.[3] They illustrate the skill of the craftsman, the sensibility of a writer of his time influenced by the popular form of the thriller and film. All these reveal the art of the writer without comprehending his vision. My interpretation of Greene's work recognises the religious and political bases of his novels to trace the development of a vision in which the topical and the contemporary accentuate the fundamental and the enduring. Both aspects are seen to combine creatively so that a sense of the eternal permeates the human and the 'now' to contribute to the complexity of experience.

My discussion of the novels of Graham Greene proceeds from an interpretation of Catholicism as a structure of signification in which the fiction mediates between the polarities of natural–supernatural, temporal–eternal, secular–sacred, human–Christian to reveal that life cannot be thus compartmentalised if it is to be lived morally. Religion does not have to do with some 'eternal' deprived of temporal roots, nor has politics to do with a 'temporal' stripped of transcendental significance. Reality is not cut in two nor is Man temporal on the one hand and eternal on the other.[4]

Greene's fictional man hovers between damnation and salvation,

1

an ambivalent idea which can be interpreted either as religious 'well being' or as social 'welfare', as religious liberation or political liberty. The novels present characters often in close-up, in extreme situations, at dramatic moments, to accentuate that there is no true religion, nor the moral life without its embodiment in politics, and there is no true politics without religious underpinning.

The frontiers of experience explored in the novels cannot be ignored and have to be confronted to unravel the significance of Greene's achievement. The fact that the fiction does not follow any political idea through to its ideological conclusion has been responsible for the general neglect of this area of study. But it is this fact that they do not conform to an ideological mould which accounts for the freedom, humanism and perhaps the permanence of his achievement. Graham Greene's novels illuminate the moral sense by structuring the narrative within a framework of political consciousness and the religious sense. They illustrate that religion and politics, traditionally seen as antagonistic forces, Church and State, sacred and secular, God and Caesar, are elements of the same reality.

Before entering into a discussion of the novels it is important to recognise Greene's use of 'religion' and 'politics' to construct reality. His work attempts to capture myths from a world lost as much in the devastations of the First World War as in the slow erosion of the certitudes of religious belief. The old paradigms of patriotism, nationalism, the once revered codes of valour, honour, and gallantry had failed. As Claud Cockburn writes, of his childhood and youth, he had once been encouraged to play Germans and English with tin soldiers but when he demanded to be taught the War Game that engaged the leisure hours and the imagination of his elders he was disappointed: 'Neither my father nor my uncles would teach it to me. They had given up playing it themselves. They said that to learn it now would be not only pointless but actually misleading because very soon now there would be a new war which would make all strategy, tactics and rules of the War Game obsolete.'[5]

The new god of Communism did not appeal to Greene. His work takes as its starting point the construction of myths for a changing world. It encodes the truths of tradition, the essence of spirituality as inner life and experience of a new world order in human terms. The fact that the paradigm developed encompasses religious faith should not be misinterpreted as a simple desire for the old certainties destroyed by rationalism. The power of Greene's work indeed rests on its underpinnings: a recognition of historical process, of the need for and validity of change.

The early stages of Greene's literary career coincided with a time of radical movements in the world order that began to be felt after the First World War and had more powerful reverberations after the Second World War. The need to reconstruct and recover in the Western world sprang into being simultaneously with the birth of new nation states that transmitted vibrant expressions of humanity, and life. These cultures, hitherto concealed under the weight of colonial assumptions, were spaces once peripheral and 'silent'. Greene's exploration of these frontiers reveals a world of divergences, heterogeneity, multiple voices. Since those years in the 1930s he has consistently displayed a capacity to listen and to comprehend the experience of a shared humanity which is also the global reality of geopolitical power. Greene's gifts as a story-teller have concealed a more significant element in his work; his curiosity about men and the world, and his ability to see the world changing about him in many different ways. These varying directions are woven into his work within a structure of complex human experience rather than as an expression of idea and history.

It is possible to argue that Greene is, perhaps, the only English writer to have recognised a larger human reality in this sense. Following these perceptions he moved the focus of his fiction from England and Europe, the 'dead' centres, to new centres of life and movement which he presents in configurations that make up the modern system, arguably no less exploitative and some would say more insidious than the empires of old. E. M. Forster's *A Passage to India* shifted the focus as well in its exploration of the Hindu way of life.[6] Greene's emphasis, however, has been less metaphysical than mundane, less concerned with refinements of sensibility than with the nitty gritty of life. He may be said to have contributed greatly to world literature as we now know it by developing within his own oeuvre a paradigm that encompasses alternative world views. His extensive readership particularly in areas outside the Anglo-American world may have less to do with the 'popular' form of his fiction and its accessibility than with the reality explored. Some of these aspects need to be discussed and if this has not yet been undertaken it is because his tales beguile and entertain, his Catholicism and craftsmanship provide much material for critical analysis, and he has himself diverted our minds with confessions, hints and explanations – a fascination for the dangerous edge of things, the

revolver in the corner cupboard, boredom, manic depression –
which are, perhaps, ways of escape, even disguises which the
author adopts to suit his own needs.

The discussion that follows proceeds from an understanding of
Greene's novels within this framework of society and history in an
attempt to illustrate that religion and politics are modes of human
experience. The fact that Greene has worked within the structure of
dogma and orthodoxy more fully than with ideology leads, not
unreasonably, to an emphasis on the religious element in all appreciation of his work. It is important to examine at this stage why the
term political writer may not have seemed apt. He took, for instance,
a path far removed from that of George Orwell although their
writing illustrates a dream shared: England between 1830 and 1914 –
a peaceful and ordered life; its combination of Christian, liberal
virtues; a well established code of conduct and the recognition,
however inadequately realised, of liberty as a natural birthright.
They also share, more importantly, a revulsion of the modern world
of mechanical living and urban development, a suspicion of the
'smelly little orthodoxies which are now contending for our souls.'[7]

In the context of political action at a time when writers went to
Spain, Greene reveals a sceptical and honest appreciation of the
writer's role, not least his own. Since he did not take sides the
popular, albeit often justifiable, link between Catholic and Conservative, is somehow attached to Graham Greene less by his
readers than by critical and journalistic assessments which have
rarely paused to consider that conversion to Catholicism did not
mean for Greene as it did for many Englishmen, a conversion to
conservatism. And yet this idea did take shape so firmly that even
the cartoonist, David Low, appears to have contributed to this
popular myth. In 1953 Evelyn Waugh protested against the projected
visit to England by Marshall Tito. Low's cartoon on the occasion
shows a group of Catholic priests and laymen of whom only Waugh
and Greene are identified by name remonstrating: 'For shame! Now
if it were for some sturdy upholder of democracy – like Franco. . . '.[8]
For students approaching this period of social history from the
outside, as it were, the whole phenomenon seems strange particularly
since, of all the writers of the 1930s, Greene remains consistent in his
concerns, unswerving in his loyalties, and as radical as he always
has been.

Since the 1930s were a period when writers were active in political
action and political parties which included political journalism,

Greene's 'separateness' in this regard seems to have been mistaken for an essential conservatism, even subversive in intent. His refusal to join the strike at *The Times* may have added to this impression.[9] *The Times* was the only national daily to print throughout the 1926 General Strike and Greene, then working as sub-editor helped in the crisis: 'it was to prevent Churchill's *British Gazette* from being the only voice to be heard. It was important to have a non-official newspaper and so I helped to load the vans. I was criticised for that, of course, by the Left but Orwell defended me at the time.'[10] Bernard Bergonzi's assessment of Greene's work in *Reading the Thirties* comes up with a contradiction: he discusses the work as influenced by Auden but finds Greene right-wing.[11] The early novels are usually categorised as thrillers, evocative of mood and atmosphere, political but revealing a pessimism that later found expression in what are called the 'Catholic' novels and it is generally assumed that Greene turned 'political' after his experience in Vietnam with the publication of *The Quiet American* (1955). Since the main directions of writers in the 1930s – those for and those against Franco – were so clearly drawn it is quite possible that Greene's refusal to join the group contributed to the description of his novels as good but popular, serious but 'Catholic'. The distinction he introduced between novels and 'entertainment' further diverted attention from the sociopolitical context of his work.

Perhaps Greene's commitment has always been suspect because at a time when political activism was almost the *sine qua non* of the vocation of writing Greene joined no political party except, briefly, the Communist Party as a probationary member in Oxford along with Claud Cockburn who stayed the course, and later the Independent Labour Party (ILP) for a few months. He was a friend of Claud Cockburn, and writes in *A Sort of Life* of the influence of T. S. Eliot, as also of his friendship, later, with Herbert Read and Evelyn Waugh. Contradictions and apparent evasions made it difficult to find him a label and Catholicism was the one most obviously and readily available. This has been unfortunate since Catholicism has resulted in his being categorised with writers with whose work his own has little in common.

It is true that he was provoked by the inflated rhetoric of the time and commented scathingly on 'the sweeping statements, the safe marble gestures, the self-importance' of the lofty idealism of those years.[12] Unlike Waugh, who expressed his conservative ideology, he did not contribute to 'Authors Take Sides on the Spanish War'.[13]

A similar publication during the Vietnam war, however, has his contribution.[14] Here the loyalties seemed to be more clear although his consciousness of being a sympathetic outsider in struggles, with the advantage of what Greene half in jest calls 'the safety of a return ticket', has saved his work from ideological rhetoric and moral complacency. He broods over the fact of death to reveal meanings and codes for life; war provokes a reflection on violence, not on Nazism and Fascism; he sifts human motives for political action with candour. In an essay entitled *At Home* written in 1940, for instance, he links the timely with the timeless, and his insights carry intimations of the subsequent disillusion of those who were most politically articulate:

> I think it was a sense of impatience because the violence was delayed rather than a masochistic enjoyment of discomfort that made many writers of recent years go abroad to try and meet it half-way: some went to Spain and others to China. Less ideological, perhaps less courageous, writers chose corners where the violence was more moderate; but the hint of it had to be there to satisfy that moral craving for the just and reasonable expression of human nature left without belief. The craving wasn't quite satisfied because we all bought two way tickets . . . The moral sense was tickled; that was all. One came home and wrote a book, leaving the condemned behind in the back rooms of hotels where the heating was permanently off or eking out a miserable living in little tropical towns. We were sometimes – God forgive us – amusing at their expense, even though we guessed all the time that we should be joining them soon for ever.[15]

He did not quite follow his contemporaries in any of their overt commitments or actions, but confined himself to story-telling with a clarity of mind and intensity of feeling that make his novels parables of our time of changes affecting the world order and individual life during the 1930s and in the successive decades of increasing super-power confrontation. What needs to be recognised along with the religious intensity of his work is that since the 1930s when writers first defined the language of literature as a form of political action, Greene has extended and perfected this development. His work reveals that the act of writing is in itself a political act just as to ask the question 'What is the purpose of life?' is a religious question, and if the answer to that is 'Nothing' it constitutes a religious answer.

This is an aspect of his work that has not received much attention perhaps because the Catholic structure of some of the novels began to overwhelm the reader.

In one of his columns for *The Tribune* in 1943 George Orwell discusses what he regards as the dangerous mistake that the Socialist movement makes in ignoring 'what one might call the neo-reactionary school of writers'. There is, he states, a considerable number of these writers, intellectually distinguished, 'influential in a quiet way and their criticisms of the Left are much more damaging than anything that issues from the Individualist League or the Conservative Central Office'. The writers named by Orwell as belonging to a group round the *Criterion* in the 1920s and 1930s are Wyndham Lewis, T. S. Eliot, Aldous Huxley, Malcolm Muggeridge, Evelyn Waugh and Graham Greene.[16]

Orwell describes the group as being influenced by T. E. Hulme and the revival of pessimism: 'the new pessimism has queerer affiliations. It links up not only with Catholicism, Conservatism and Fascism but also with Pacifism (California brand especially) and Anarchism.' Otherworldliness, says Orwell, is the best alibi a rich man can have.[17] Greene's novels do indeed present solutions and hope only in terms of an after-life but there is always a validation of struggle and responsibility as an expression of humanity, in fact, as the imperatives of the moral life. Some of these attacks may have been prompted by the fact that Greene's early novels, particularly *Brighton Rock* published in 1938, were found to be anti-Semitic in tone, a point discussed more fully later in this book.

> During those years [says Greene in response] we did not think in those terms and I meant the term 'Jew' to be descriptive. When I reread it later because the anti-Semitic idea was pointed out to me I could see that it could be regarded as anti-Semitic and I replaced it by 'tycoon'. But it was not meant to be anti-Semitic and I was given the Jerusalem prize in 1981.[18]

Orwell seems to have been always put off by Greene's Catholicism. His attitude is suggested in his correspondence. After the publication of *The Heart of the Matter* in 1948, a novel he disliked intensely, he wrote to Julyan Symons discussing various Catholic writers 'I think it is about time to do a counterattack against these Catholic writers.'[19] Yet in 1949 in a letter written to T. R. Fyvel he responds to Fyvel's articles and one of the points raised is in defence of Graham Greene:

You keep referring to him as an extreme conservative, the usual reactionary type. This isn't so at all, either in his books or privately. Of course he is a Catholic, and in some issues has to take sides politically with the church, but in outlook he is just a mild Left with faint CP leanings. I have even thought that he might become our first Catholic fellow-traveller, a thing that doesn't exist in England, but does in France . . . If you look at books like *A Gun for Sale, England Made Me, The Confidential Agent,* and others you will see that there is the usual left-wing scenery. The bad men are millionaires, armament manufacturers etc and the good man is sometimes a Communist.[20]

Graham Greene's novels, however, cannot be discussed in terms of bad men and good Communists, as very perceptively revealed by Angus Wilson who said that *Brighton Rock* was published at a time when it was 'important to feel something deeper than just right and wrong, good guys and rotten eggs . . . a realisation that jog-along decency, human justice, right and wrong as being enough just couldn't satisfy.'[21] The old scheme was disintegrating and new forms of experience needed a deeper comprehension than rationality and human justice could offer, nor was religious absolutism of much help.

Greene's quest for a language that could translate moral imperatives and modern experience led him into orthodoxy which in perspective does not seem like evasion but at the time of publication disturbed both Catholics and Socialists. The literary and academic establishment has inherited these perceptions. In subsequent years Greene's stature as 'the greatest living English novelist' is often reiterated without quite coming to grips with the reality of his fiction: the material and the spiritual; politics and faith; old forms and new worlds; a language of radical wit and wisdom that is unmistakably his own. It is neither Catholic nor Communist but essentially Christian and humanist encompassing the ideals and values of both.

My reading of Greene's work occasionally breaks chronological sequence of the publication of the novels to emphasise themes; the idea of conscience and the religious sense is followed by analysis of the idea of empire and post-Empire that informs his work. Novels, travelogues and despatches are discussed to illustrate a vision that has developed after much travel and deliberate exposure to changes affecting the world order and individual experience. The early novels illustrate a sensitivity to the social and psychological consequences of the First World War, to the realities of Hunger Marches, Franco's Spain, and the threat of the Second World War. The later novels open out to wider questions relating to the loss of an empire, the birth of new hegemonies, the links between all these events and the quality of human life.

A framework of moral values deepens issues that deal with the State and the functioning of a world order and survival at these various levels defines what is meant by the religious sense. The overt use of Catholicism in some novels intensifies the discourse on human affairs so that the human act is given meaning within man's being in time and in the eternal dimension which is always present within the visible and finite landscape. The total oeuvre is more than the expression of religious belief, of the realities of the postwar world and of the end of the empire: it embodies a demystification of the modern system. This is a complex and intricate exercise since the novels also confront the reality of death to express faith in life.

1

Explorations

Several influences compose the seed-bed of Greene's creative process – the adventure stories of his childhood, the religious, moral and aesthetic sensibilities of Cardinal Newman, Joseph Conrad and Henry James, and his travel. Like half-quarried and half-sculpted stones which reveal the mind and perceptions of the artist, Greene's travelogues offer fascinating and penetrating glimpses of elements of his fiction and of its political and spiritual constituents. It is therefore fitting that a study of his novels should begin with a discussion of these influences. The travelogues *Journey Without Maps* (1935) and *The Lawless Roads* (1939) are accounts of travel in Liberia and Mexico respectively. Politics here, as in the novels, does not express power struggles but explores justice; it is a search for models of action and for an environment consonant with human dignity. Although Greene may not have 'stared the Twentieth Century in the eye' as George Orwell did, the novels illustrate realities first perceived in the travel. It is on his journeys that Greene first sees the underside of social structures, not least the structure of the Church. The villages of Liberia and the empty churches of Mexico give the young writer a free rein to explore differences, and at the same time his own loneliness compels him to identify himself with the cultures under siege, abandoned by all except the poor and the wretched. Although the travelogues reveal a romantic view of pristine life this is balanced by a curiosity and a feel for the textures and depths of civilisations and cultures 'from granite to grass'.[1]

Writers of Greene's generation turned to travel writing and their work is striking because the travels are transmuted into interior journeys and parables of their times. Landscape and incident – the factual materials of *reportage* – do the work of symbol and myth – the materials of *fable*.[2] The important point is that Greene's accounts try to move beyond Europe as the centre of the world. The physical journey framed by exploration of an inner world is as much a private universe as an attempt to understand the Western psyche. Africa is 'the shape of the human heart' and Mexico a 'state of mind'. These

10

geographical and cultural realities are apprehended, in so far as is possible, as responses alternative to the Western metaphysic.

Greene's view of Africa is open-minded; his observations on himself and his own culture lead him to evaluate the contributions of other cultures with a discernment rare in his contemporaries. Evelyn Waugh travelled to parts of Africa, Guyana and Mexico but remained detached, cynical, and derisory although he promises otherwise:

> One does not travel, any more than one falls in love, to collect material. It is simply part of one's life. Some writers have a devotion for rural England . . . others move into society; for myself and many better than me, there is a fascination in distant and barbarous places . . . and particularly for the borderlands of conflicting cultures and states of development, where ideas, uprooted from their traditions become oddly changed in transplantation.[3]

Waugh travels with his cultural baggage intact: his unquestioning acceptance of the ideological connotations of 'barbarous' and 'development' makes his response considerably different from that of Graham Greene who pauses to reflect over the centuries of cerebration that has led his own world to barbarism.[4] Graham Greene's travels brought him to the ground level of Empire face to face with human beings in human situations of colonialism. These perceptions illuminate later fiction. Their relevance increases with each passing decade and shows that the process then recorded by the traveller has a bearing on social change in contemporary society, on international political and cultural relationships wedded to materialism. When he writes of worship the ideal of transcendence does not become with him an excuse for dogmatism but an opportunity for critical appraisal of his own tradition. The travelogues reveal the directions of a search that engages all his work.

This is not to say that *Journey Without Maps* is free from the assumptions and biases of a tradition of European writing on Africa: love and devotion in the noble savage; Africa as a sanctuary for the outcast of civilisation; an experience where 'in the emptiness of the continent it is easy to assume anonymity'[5] as S. E. Ogude suggests, or where Greene is able to excuse 'the physical ugliness of his Africans with the myth of their moral beauty'. Intellectually, says Ogude of Greene's Africa, it suggests the picture of the world as it should be, or as it was conceived. It is the nearest thing to the Paradise which Adam lost, and this to Greene, means the world of innocence, of altruistic generosity as opposed to the self-interest (enlightened or crude) that parades itself as humanitarianism or philanthropy. It is the world of disinterested friendship and warm-hearted good nature. Thus during his travels, Greene appears to be on the lookout for these warm-hearted creatures and when he sees one, he becomes poetical, almost delirious.[6]

Indeed there is much in *Journey Without Maps* that may be seen as the expression of imperial assumptions not least its idealisation of the 'noble savage' and vilification of the creole. When Greene philosophises and moralises in order to posit the pristine beauty of land and people against the corruption of the creole the writing tends to be repetitive and sentimental. Graham Greene likes to qualify his use of the term 'creole'. It refers he says, to people educated in the USA whose ancestors had left Liberia generations before. Back in Liberia these new arrivals exploited their own people with weapons of what Greene calls a creole culture: 'they had nothing of their own culture left'. It has nothing to do, he insists, with more recent uses of the word to represent an indigenous population with Western education.[7]

The text exudes disgust with colonial transplantations, even when writing of Freetown, a city to which Greene returned when working for the British Secret Service during the Second World War and came to love. But in 1934 he dislikes it: 'This was an English capital city . . . everything ugly in Freetown was European . . . if there was anything beautiful in the place it was native' (p. 38). The term 'creole' crops up here as well in the description of men: 'they had been educated to understand how they had been swindled, how they had been given the worst of two worlds . . . they had died in so far as they had once been men, inside their European clothes' (p. 39). He mourns the loss of origins and native power of expression in the 'Creole gossip writer' of the Sierra Leone *Daily Mail*.

Greene's travelogue reveals an anguished sense of loss of roots, a distrust of imitations and these insights inform the characterisation of his later fiction. The writing conveys the extent of Greene's horror at the results of slavish imitation and his search for roots: 'If they had been slaves they would have had more dignity; there is no shame in being ruled by a stranger, but these men had been given their tin shacks, their cathedral, their votes and city councils, their shadow of self-government; they were expected to play the part like white men and the more they copied white men, the more funny it was to the prefects' (p. 39).

The excesses of description are prompted by an agonising recall of the loss of the innocent beauty of undespoiled, rural England, its pagan rites, and the contrast with the soulless brashness of urban bourgeoisie in London. In Africa Greene seeks his own spiritual origins and looks for what may have existed before the corruptions of materialism set in. Alongside the meaning, the mystery, the fundamental essence of Africa are insights into socioeconomic realities. The journey into Africa, though a metaphysical journey, reconstructs in diverse and more sociopolitical dimensions than do Forster and Orwell the truths of the colonial encounter.

Much has been made of Greene's term 'seediness' first used in *Journey Without Maps*. The result has been the drawing of a map of what has been called 'Greeneland' with seediness as its most important feature. The novelist has come to regret ever having used the word. Seediness is less the seamy side of life, the physical decay and squalor it is often taken to mean than *prima materia*, the primeval slime. This source of material creation implies both the origin of mankind and the reality from which the artist creates situations to explore human anguish and vulnerability:

> I'm always slightly irritated by that phrase 'Greeneland', and I can't help wondering where these critics live, what sort of lives they live. I mean the Vietnam War is seedy . . . The rule of Batista in Cuba belonged to that seedy world – dirt, torture, people half-starved. Where do these critics live? Do they live in Kensington and listen to the traffic going past the window and then have a cocktail party with friends? That, I think, is a worse world than 'Greeneland', and less true . . . [As for the seedy] it's the same draw that a child has towards making a mud pie. Perhaps it's a certain remaining infantility in one's character. The seedy is nearer the beginning, isn't it – or nearer the end . . . No, it's not that I enjoy puddling in the mess, but if there's a mess, I feel it's our duty to look at it.[8]

Seediness is implicit in human nature, in reality itself whether in Africa and Mexico or in the London of Leicester Square, Bond Street and Tottenham Court Road.[9]

In *Journey Without Maps* the *prima materia* for the metaphysical quest is the physical journey. The objective and the subjective are expressed with descriptions of sharply observed visual detail and conversations with his carriers alternating with withdrawal into self. The fact that his cousin who accompanied him is barely mentioned and remains unnamed is sometimes taken as proof of the unreality of Greene's descriptions of what actually happened and was experienced. In *Too Late to Turn Back*, Barbara Greene's account of the journey,[10] Graham Greene plays a major role and the description of his bout of fever which she thought would kill him is not mentioned in detail by Greene himself. Greene's selection of the facts of his travel in *Journey Without Maps* is determined by an inner metaphysic which perceives both his world as well as the realities of Africa. He returns again and again to the meaning of the term 'civilisation' in order to suggest exploitation. When he describes cannibalistic societies he does so by referring to the secret societies as distinct from African society as a whole, and above all by not implying expert knowledge on the subject: 'I am not an anthropologist and I cannot pretend to remember very much of what Dr Harley told me'. The opportunity for indicting Western assumptions is not lost: 'This is the territory the United States map marks so vaguely and excitingly as "Cannibal" ' (pp. 173–4).

The choice of Liberia initially prompted by a Government report describing the economic backwardness of the interior of the region seemed the proper place to begin to understand the point at which his own civilisation had gone astray. He deliberately avoids parts of Africa 'where the white settler has been most successful in reproducing the conditions of his country, its morals and its popular art' (p. 20). In looking for an area of darkness he searches an answer to the moral decline of England but nowhere does the text suggest that the white man was corrupted by contact with 'other' peoples and cultures. In fact, he implies the reverse and all men share the quality of darkness. The difference between Conrad's and Greene's view of Africa is that the subtle questionings of the former are abandoned for an active enquiry into the operations of the imperial ideal. Conrad spared British imperialism reserving his wrath for European imperialisms – mainly the Belgian Congo – in relation to which he evokes a moral ideal for the British empire. Greene's work lacks the power of the Conradian imagery for colonial activity, but gains in compassion for the human experience of colonialism, a compassion for both parties to the encounter as individual lives trapped in a machine.

merely in relation to pristine Africa but to an old-fashioned English-ness both regrettably sharing a heroic but fast-disappearing tradition. The contrast between the past and the present is deepened in his use of the myth of knowledge and innocence, of the world and the gardens of childhood. The exploration moves from the world to the self; it is ethnocentric in orientation but seeks a paradigm for a changing world order; it crosses boundaries of ethnocentricity to arrive at the frontiers of justice, freedom, dignity and faith. The following passages from *Journey Without Maps* are integral to in-terpretation of Greene's work:

'Devil', of course, is a word used by the English-speaking native to describe something unknown in *our* theology: it has nothing to do with evil. One might equally call these big bush devils angels for they have the angelic properties of alacrity and invisibility – if that word contained no element of 'good'. In a Christian land we have grown so accustomed to the idea of a spiritual war, of God and Satan, that this supernatural world, which is neither good nor evil but simply Power, is almost beyond sympathetic compre-hension. Not quite: for those witches which haunted our child-hood were neither good nor evil. They terrified us with their power, but we knew all the time that we must not escape them. They simply demanded recognition: flight was weakness (p. 176).

Details of human suffering, disease, and death abound to empha-sise the lie of empire as civilisation. Time and again Greene differ-entiates between the men at the bar – prospectors, shipping agents, merchants, engineers – who were not guilty of the meannesses and hypocrisies of the rulers, but were 'simply out to make money', while the real rulers gave garden parties and were supposed to be there 'for the good of the ruled'. The most powerful writing is contained in the following passage:

Kailahun, in memory, has become a clean village, one of the cleanest we stayed in, but what impressed me at the time was the dirt and the disease, the children with proturberant navels reliev-ing themselves in the dust among the goats and chickens, the pock-marked women smeared about the face and legs and breasts with some white ointment they squeezed from a plant in the bush and used for beauty and for medicine. They used it for smallpox, for fever, for toothache, for indigestion; for every ailment under their bleak sun; when they were young it soothed their headaches; when they were older they smoothed it on their bellies to bring them ease in their confinement; when they were dying it lay like a sediment of salt on their dried-up breasts and in their pitted thighs. Here you could measure what civilisation was worth; looking back later to Kailahun from the villages of the Republic, where civilisation stopped within fifty miles of the coast, I could see no great difference. 'Workers of the World Unite!': I thought of the wide shallow slogans of political parties, as the thin bodies, every rib showing, with dangling, swollen elbows or pock-marked skin, went by me to the market; why should we pretend to talk in terms of the world when we mean only Europe or the white races? Neither ILP nor Communist Party urges a strike in England because the plate-layers of Sierra Leone are paid sixpence a day without their food. Civilisation here remained exploitation; we had hardly, it seemed to me, improved the natives lot at all, they were as worn out with fever as before the white man came, we had introduced new diseases and weakened their resistance to the old, they still drank from polluted water and suffered from the same worms, they were still at the mercy of their chiefs, for what could a Deputy Commissioner really know, shifted from district to district, picking up only a few words of the language, dependent on an interpreter? Civilisation so far as Sierra Leone was concerned was the railway to Pendembu, the increased export of palm-nut; civilisation, too, was Lever Brothers and the price they controlled; civilisation was the long bar in the Grand, the sixpenny wages (pp. 60–1).

These passages suggest a vision that integrates spiritual ends with values determined by a particular cultural standpoint which conflicts with received views of Empire, religion and civilisation. The juxtaposition of cultures, occasionally simplistic and superficial, reveals Greene's preoccupations and the following descriptions of the funeral of a tribal chief in *Journey Without Maps* illustrates the bare essentials Greene cherishes himself:

It was a tiny place perched on an uneven rocky mound. The grave was in the centre of the village among flat stones which marked the other graves; a mat was spread on it, and a middle-aged woman sat there, the youngest mother among the chief's wives. She was shielded from the sun by a roof of palm branches, and a pile of fuel and a cooking-pot stood there at the spirit's disposal. Christianity and paganism both marked the dead man's grave, for there was a rough cross stuck on the mound to propitiate the God whom the old chief had accepted on his deathbed, while in a pit close by, following a pagan rite, sat eight wives, naked except for a loin-cloth. Other women were spreading them with clay; it was rubbed even into their hair. The majority were old and hideous anyway, but now the pale colour of the pit in which they sat, they looked as if they had been torn half decomposed from the ground. They had lost with their colour their mark of race and might have been women of any nation who had been buried and dug up again. There was pathos in the bareness of these symbols, the cross, the clay, the youngest mother. One felt that two religions here were appealing on the simplest terms; splendour and the big battalions were on neither side. There must have been scenes very like this, I thought, in the last days of pagan England, when a story about a bird flying through a lighted hall into the dark played its part in the conversion of a king (p. 87).

Greene visited Mexico in 1938 to report on the religious persecution and brutal anti-clerical purges that began in the late 1920s with President Calles and his socialist revolution. Calles sought to limit foreign influence in the oil industry but succeeded in remaining on good terms with his American neighbours. A number of social reforms, including land redistribution and nationalisation of the oil companies, were instituted by Calles's successor, President Cardenas, during whose time Greene visited Mexico, but the postwar era ushered in increasing American investment and influence in the republic. Greene's insights into the 'phony revolution' and the relationship between the two countries are not unjustified particularly since most governments in Mexico since the Second World War have been fundamentally right wing though less overtly dictatorial than during the interwar period.

Graham Greene and Evelyn Waugh, in fact, went to Mexico within months of each other – the latter with a definite commitment to discredit the Government, an assignment he appears to have regretted for he later dismissed his book on Mexico, *Robbery Under Law* from the canon of his work. It dealt, Waugh said, 'little with travel and much with political questions'.[12] Christopher Sykes, Evelyn Waugh's biographer, discusses *Robbery Under Law* to illustrate how Greene turned his own Mexican experience to better account.

Greene 'did not attempt a political thesis or history but wrote instead a triumphant interpretation through the eyes of an artist of an unhappy place at a miserable time'.[13]

Greene's journey across the border from Texas into Mexico appears to have presented him with a dramatic juxtaposition of the landscapes of materialism and poverty, of urban development and rural deprivation which he records in *The Lawless Roads*: 'In Mexico the standard of living is appallingly low outside the great towns, but here that low standard lay next door to the American standard: the West Side hovels were mocked by the Plaza Hotel soaring yellowly up to scrape against the sky' (p. 27). It led to his understanding of faith, of the links between man's aspirations and his capacity for struggle and endurance. It is thus extremely misleading to interpret Greene's work as having assumed clearer political directions after his visit to Vietnam, or to link what is called his anti-Americanism with the Vietnam war. The insights of his novels are already evident in the travelogues; indeed it is the travel that gives form and content to his perceptions of the twin evils of industrial capitalism and cultural imperialism. *The Lawless Roads* describes the effects of the revolution on religious worship not to decry revolution but to illustrate the losing battle for the Indian's soul.[14]

Greene's comprehension of colonial encounters in *The Lawless Roads* includes the by-products – the flotsam and jetsam – half-English by birth or by association or even assimilation from second-hand imitations. The chief of police tells him when first examining his passport: 'You've come home. Why, everybody in Villahermosa is called Greene – or Graham' and summons a rather scared local Greene to the police station: 'His name was De Witt Greene; he had Dutch, American, English, and pure Indian blood in him . . . His great-grandfather had come from England' (p. 119).

The life histories he collects tell of hazardous journeys in search of a better life; intermarriage; occasionally an Englishman who speaks very little English. The most extraordinary story is that of Mr Fitzpatrick, from Scotland, whose grandson, Dr Robert Fitzpatrick, Greene meets and from whom he pieces together the life of a Victorian adventurer that began when he left London in 1857. What he finds here are relics of deeds of daring and dreams of empire, heroism and disillusion: they are sometimes Spanish, poor, proud, and bitter. Most are absorbed into the local population 'as completely as the Greenes and Grahams, and there was something rather horrifying and foreboding in this – for an unabsorbed Greene' (p. 118).

American tourists arrive with the culture of industrial capitalism: 'They lived in a different world, they lived in a few square inches of American territory; with *Life* and *Time* and coffee at Sanborn's, they were impervious to Mexico' (p. 35). Quite understandably, Greene's comments on the tourist view are scathing. He accentuates the reality of Mexico: the gun-toting pistolero and the faith of the peasants, the plush modernity of Mexico City, 'a city run for Americans', and the crowds of Indians who worship defiantly in churches that are empty or in ruins, and who descend from the mountains to reenact the Passion and death of Christ in a living, noisy communion with the spiritual that Greene comprehends but cannot share.

The Lawless Roads presents what is now known as Liberation Theology in a mixture of faith, indigenous culture, and revolution. The text illustrates the separation of the politician on the balcony from the people, and posits the feudal methods of the rebel General Cedillo as no worse, if not better, than what prevails in the rest of the State:

> The General gave them no pay, but food and clothes and shelter and half of everything the farm produced, and ready cash too if they asked for it and he had it. They even took the fifty chairs he bought for his little private cinema. And they gave him labour and love. It was not a progressive relationship, it was feudal; you may say it was one-sided and he had everything – the New Art furniture, the statuette, the alligator skin, and the coloured picture of Napoleon, but they possessed at any rate more than did their fellow-peasants in other states, living at best on the minimum wage of thirty-five cents a day, with no one caring if they lived or died, with all the responsibility of independence (p. 56).

This may sound like paternalistic benevolence but the novels transmute the idea of a benevolent and caring leader into the theme of responsibility. Greene's memoir *Getting to Know the General* (1984) on General Torrijos of Panama, his despatches on Ho Chi Minh and Fidel Castro also reveal the leader as father figure, albeit a revolutionary one.

As in Liberia, mosquitoes, vultures, heat and flies swamp the landscape of Mexico. Greene's love of Africa as expressed in *Journey*

Without Maps contrasts with his dislike of Mexico which paradoxically makes *The Lawless Roads* the better book; it is less romantic and encompasses battles that range from Monopoly as game and as reality, to the silent, implacable worship of the peasants. The most moving passages in *The Lawless Roads* are those on themes which recur in later fiction: 'revolution in the form of the Sermon on the Mount, treason as a class in domestic economy'; faith in 'the dark-skinned Indian Virgin'. The legend of the Virgin of Guadalupe pervades the text: she appeared first in Amecameca in 1531 but no one paid her any attention; then to an Indian peasant, Diego:

> It is as well to remember how revolutionary this vision must have seemed. It was only ten years since Mexico city had fallen finally to Cortez, the country was not yet subdued, and it is doubtful what kind of greeting the average Spanish adventurer would have given an Indian who claimed to have been addressed as 'my son' by the Mother of God. The legend, one is told by Mexican politicians, was invented by the Church to enslave the Indian mind, but if indeed it had been invented at that period by the Church, it would have been with a very different purpose. This Virgin claimed a church where she might love her Indians and guard them from the Spanish conqueror. The legend gave the Indian self-respect; it gave him a hold over his conqueror; it was a liberating, not an enslaving legend (pp. 86–7).

This discussion of the travelogues suggests the framework of history and faith of Greene's novels. The most distinctive feature of his artistic achievement is the imaginative form given to the life of his times. This is not to say that the work can be categorised as the history and politics of the times but to emphasise the development of a world view based on deep and close knowledge of motives and events, part determined by human beings and part unfolded by the contrivance of an unseen hand. Greene's novels reveal experience that moves from the private to the public sphere of life, from the individual to the social, to encompass global concerns. The travelogues testify to Greene's efforts to learn to see through his cultural inheritance and beyond into a common human basis at a world that is changing.

Unquestionably, it has led him to explore received world views and perceptions and to cross time-honoured boundaries of the Judaeo – Christian tradition to include experience that encompasses all of humanity. His travels which provoked indictments of the British Empire later led him to witness the struggle and birth of new nation states. In subsequent decades the novels have entertained without fudging the issues of injustice and exploitation.

My analysis of the travelogues illustrates the importance of religion in the creative process, and how strongly it underlies the writer's insights. The traveller's religious sensibility is open to other traditions and his own vision of Christianity is evolutionary. Greene acknowledges Cardinal Newman as the most important theological influence, in whose work, he says, the idea of a 'developing' religion is implicit. Questions relating to man and his destiny underlie all Greene's work and are particularly poignant when religious belief generates action.

The artistic validity of Greene's use of Catholicism in his novels can best be appreciated when we come to understand that it functions not in, by and for itself but as a way to exploring reality. The religious structure, when overtly present in his novels, points less to God's transcendence than to His immanence; human relationships define the religious sense; action is made significant within two orders of time, so that the act of the traitor or the sinner introduces human and spiritual ends in relation to an absolute and timeless order. These narrative strategies and the symbolic vocabulary Greene develops, at first overtly and in the later novels as a sort of shorthand for various levels of meaning, constitute the craftsman's art: the novels enthral even as they reveal existential truths and ways of looking at the world. His art illumines the relationship between infinite absolutes and their finite representations, between human values and the mundane routine of life.

Cardinal Newman's notion of Economy, clarified in his essay *The Theory of Developments in Religious Doctrine* contains the most valuable clue to the relation between Greene's vision and artistic skill. It illustrates how ordinary and chaotic feelings and thoughts in human life are artistically ordered for the purposes of argument and discovery into images, figures and fables that economically resemble the complex whole from which they come. The symbols are an approach to reality, not reality itself. Greene's preface to *The Lawless Roads* contains an extract from Cardinal Newman which emphasises the 'terrible aboriginal calamity' in which the human race is implicated. The novels that followed are pessimistic and the tragic sense of the narrative contributed to interpretations of the fiction within a

Jansenist or Manichaen tradition. The following passage, however, is a better clue to the understanding of Greene's technique and vision:

> They [economies] are all developments of one and the same range of ideas; they are all instruments of discovery as to those ideas. They stand for real things, and we can reason with them though they be but symbols, as if they were the things themselves, for which they stand. Yet none of them carries out the lines of truth to their limits; first, one stops in the analysis, then another; like some calculating tables which answer for a thousand times, and miss in the thousand and first. While they answer, we can use them just as if they were the realities; but at length our instrument of discovery issues in some great impossibility of contradiction, or what we call in religion, a mystery. It has run its length; and by its failure shows that all along it has been but an expedient for practical purposes, not a true analysis or adequate image of those recondite laws which are investigated by means of it. It has never fathomed their depths, because it now fails to measure their course. At the same time, no one, because it cannot do everything, would refuse to use it within the range in which it will act; no one would say that it was a system of empty symbols, though it be but a shadow of the unseen. Though we use it with caution, still we use it, as being the nearest approximation to the truth which our condition admits.[15]

Greene reclaims the religious sense by developing the symbolic language of belief to illustrate the mysteries and the vitality, the validity and the futility of life. He sometimes expresses faith as radical doubt. His vision rests less on otherworldly hope than on an expression of humanity through a moral life within the community. In commenting on Greene's novels, therefore, these factors, political and spiritual, are more to the point than details of orthodoxy just as a commentary on Cervantes' work is enriched by cognition of life in sixteenth-century Spain rather than by detailed appreciation of the minutiae of chivalry. The comparison is not misplaced particularly since Greene's work has been brought to a resonant culmination with the publication of *Monsignor Quixote* (1982) which subverts orthodoxy and ideology to understand history and humanity.

The first published novel *The Man Within* (1929) focuses on one dimension of the politics of conscience that underlies all the novels:

the inner life, *It's a Battlefield* (1934) introduces the other dimension – an exploration of life in society which here includes the realities of the Depression, strikes, trade unions, a disintegrating Empire, and the individual's experience of turmoil in day-to-day life. These two novels carry themes that develop later into the main motif: the moral choice implicit in humanity. The fictional exploration is bounded by a consciousness of history liberated by intimations of the eternal.

How could all this be accomplished by a writer who has consistently insisted that his only desire is to entertain his readers, and to tell a story? Greene likes to emphasise his links with Rider Haggard and R. L. Stevenson and is critical of E. M. Forster's relegation of the 'story' to secondary status placing his own emphasis on narrative and action:

> Of course I should be interested to hear that a new novel by E. M. Forster was going to appear this spring but I could never compare that mild expectation of civilised pleasure with the missed heartbeat, the appalled glee I felt when I found on a library shelf a novel by Rider Haggard, Percy Westerman, Captain Brereton, or Stanley Weyman which I had not read before. No, it is in those early years that I would look for the crisis, the moment when life took a new slant in its journey towards death.[16]

Adventure stories that captivated Greene in childhood, as indeed all Englishmen in the heyday of Empire, charged England's will with the energy to go out into the world and explore, conquer and rule. The adventure story seems to have been the counterpart in literature to Empire in politics activating dreams of heroic exploits, of travel, and of dangerous frontiers to be crossed. Martin Green illustrates in his book, *Dreams of Adventure, Deeds of Empire*,[17] the dichotomy in the body of English literature and the two embodiments of imagination – the 'literary' and the popular – to suggest that in turning away from the popular adventure tale the serious writer did in fact turn away from an essential part of modern history. Graham Greene turned away from neither.

Kipling cast an ideological shadow over all the writers of Greene's generation and they found their own resolutions just as an earlier generation had taken a stand against the Empire by turning their back on it. Full appreciation of Greene's contribution reveals a world view that is developed by turning the myth of Empire round on itself. He keeps the ideal of trusteeship and moral integrity, and creates the figure of God as father who is tyrannical and unfathomable as in *The Man Within* and *Doctor Fischer of Geneva*, and in other incarnations appears kind and loving, or working for a just society as in *Our Man in Havana*, *The Honorary Consul* and *The Human Factor*. He borrows the form and the symbols of the adventure story such as the frontier, calls it the border and materialises it in the image of the green baize door which separated the security of home from the brutality of the boarding school.

Martin Green discusses the work of Graham Greene along with that of Evelyn Waugh to suggest links between them not only in their use of the adventure form with variations, but in their Catholicism: 'the mode of the Catholic novel . . . a mode of sensibility characterised by melancholy, disgust with modern society, and a vindictive delight in the failures and poverties of human nature' though offered as a religious conviction can be read equally, he says, as a reaction to England's loss of power: 'It was a reaction against the ideology that had carried England to greatness.'[18]

Martin Green fails to acknowledge that though both novelists were indeed responding to the loss of Empire and to the new realities there are considerable differences in their response. The most clearly articulated perception is that of Evelyn Waugh himself. In his review of Greene's illustrated book *British Dramatists* in 1942 Waugh complains that Greene was excluded from sympathy with the larger part of his subject because of his subscription to 'the popular belief in "the People . . . the new, complicated and stark crazy theory that only the poor are real and important and that the only live art is the art of the People" '.[19] The ideological difference between them is further discussed by Waugh's biographer, Christopher Sykes:

> The friendship of Evelyn and Graham Greene was largely founded on their shared religion, though this did not mean that they were in full agreement on it, Graham Greene was a Socialist and resented the conservatism of Catholic custom and fashion at the time; Evelyn regarded Socialism as the root cause of most modern heresy.[20]

The ideological differences between the two men did not, however, come in the way of their friendship or admiration for each other's work and Waugh's assessment of Graham Greene as being 'equipped to take as his subject the gravest questions that face the destiny of Man'[21] lead one to suspect that he was well aware of the directions of Greene's 'travels' and admired him the more for it although unable and unwilling to make common cause.

Greene's work attempts to link the serious moral imagination with the spirit of adventure and romance and to extend the re-mapping of imaginative geography that was first undertaken by Joseph Conrad. Along with Henry James, Joseph Conrad is his acknowledged master and he has often commented on the fact that he had to stop reading Conrad in order to develop as a writer. Conrad's moral imagination, rooted in a Christian ethos and the white man's ethic of 'one of us' to which he gave expression in varied and subtle questionings influenced Greene in the directions he chose for himself.

Since there is, however, an important difference between the two novelists it is misleading to follow post-colonial discussion of Conrad's work and apply the same perspective to the work of Graham Greene. Conrad's critical reputation has been insepar-able from anti-imperialist ideas general after 1918. He used adventure material but remained resistant to the spirit of the adventure story drawing his material closer to the serious imagin-ation. He continued loyal to England, however, and even glorified the British Empire. Imperialism, within the Conradian oeuvre is to do with King Leopold's infamous world and although he was aware of political and psychological complexities as well as of the sins of imperialism he remained strangely romantic in his attitude to British imperialism. Critical exegesis today is divided between those who are impatient with the limitations of Conrad's percep-tion and those who prefer to discuss and elucidate his technique of constantly calling into question Western perceptions of non-Western reality in order to focus on the issue of race and mperialism.[22]

Greene, working under his influence, absorbed the mood of self-doubt which in Greene's generation was, if anything, more intense. But the moral and political complexities are explored in a discourse that is more open to assumptions of cultures outside his normal experience in an attempt to rethink the entire system of codes. He combines the ideals of his own ethos with a sense of history and of justice inherited from a father with whom he had a relationship that was both distant and ambiguous. The ambiguity is important. If the father's generation idealised the idea of Empire and moral integrity,

Greene set out to undermine and redefine both within a changing world order. These directions are deepened by compassion and a consciousness of eternity. Thus armed he ventures out to explore alternative world views and to create what could be 'the nearest approximation to truth which our condition admits'.

Greene's fiction carries on a critique of Liberalism begun by the Oxford Movement whose hostility to Liberalism cannot be explained as antagonism towards High Church Toryism but as a comprehension of the essential falsity of Liberal and Utilitarian philosophers when brought face to face with the facts of life. His novels are, above all, an expression of the realities of human suffering and of evil though the latter rarely reaches metaphysical depths. It is revealed as perversity and depravity except in the case of Pinkie. The novels are scathing in their indictments of self-satisfied optimism, of Governments, institutions and individuals whose quest for progress, civilisation and fulfilment lack recognition and respect of the human personality.

To live morally in Greene's world view is to live politically. The novels explore ways in which values are destroyed when moral life is interpreted at the level of rituals and legalities. Thus the moral life comes to be defined at the level of responsible conduct and the religious life interpreted through a Church tradition that is not fixed and immutable but a creative spirit manifested through the developing experiences of individuals and communities of which it is composed. Religion and morality thus embrace the idea of social responsibility.

The novels open new ways of seeing reality. The detailed surface of realism combines with depth of feeling to recreate personal life as radically affected by the quality of the general life, and equally the general life is revealed in personal terms. I have drawn here on Raymond Williams's description of the heart of the great tradition of realism although in his analysis of realism in twentieth-century fiction he concludes that Greene's novels lack the necessary balance between the life of society and that of the individuals who compose it.[23] Williams argues that Greene's social settings in Brighton, West Africa, Mexico or Indo-China, are obvious examples of a personalised landscape because they have elements in common that relate 'not to the actual ways of life but to the needs of his characters and of his own emotional pattern. When this is frankly and absolutely done as in Kafka, there is at least no confusion; but ordinarily, with a surface of realism, there is merely the familiar imbalance'[24] and society is presented as an aspect of the character.

Another view might hold this apparent weakness of Greene as a strength. In his approach the individual in a religious sense is supreme and it is in this religious sense that society and the human beings that compose it are absolute and liberated. The common elements in his social settings have less to do with a personal emotional pattern than with the facts of history. Greene's fiction in fact represents a reaction to what Williams calls 'the social exclusiveness and snobbery' of the Bloomsbury group, to their 'failure to realise the nature of the general social element in their own lives'.[25] His novels are apparently light, occasionally schematic and often melodramatic with successful excursions into fantasy so as to probe reality and to apprehend 'people as people and not as social units'. Relationships extend beyond cultural and national boundaries to a human community with a shared moral purpose. The novels attempt a 'vital interpenetration, idea into feeling, person into community, change into settlement, which we need in our divided time'. The themes evolve from the national realities of the 1930s to the global concerns of today but Greene's vision remains unchanged, set as it was, perhaps, when faith came to him in childhood, and knowledge with the betrayals at school. The fiction is discussed as revealing a process of evolution and development in a romantic adventurer's journey through life.

2
The Intimate Enemy

'The political novelist' says Irving Howe in *Politics and the Novel* 'even as he remains fascinated by politics, urges his claim for a moral order beyond ideology . . . the receptive reader, even as he perseveres in his own commitment assents to the novelist's ultimate order.'[1] Graham Greene's early work reveals a search for justice and the moral order in the shifts of political commitments and ideologies. The passions and declamations of political spokesmen like the rites and ritual of religious protagonists are described not for the significance or truth in themselves but to bring out the anguish of the human condition and the permanence of the moral order – inexorable as death. The confrontation between justice and loyalty, cooperation and exploitation, the selfishness that dies and the love that lives – the permanent battlefield between man and his intimate enemy – is described, as it is in every age, in the myths of its time.

It's a Battlefield (1934) for instance, presents a dominant political milieu of workers' socialism and *Stamboul Train* (1932) is fuelled by the passions of a leader who believes in the Revolution that will rid governments of their brutalities. In these, as in other novels, faith – political and religious – reveals the plight of the human condition on both sides of the battlefield. 'At its best,' says Irving Howe 'the political novel generates such intense heat that the ideas it appropriates are melted into its movement and fused with the emotions of its characters.'[2] The early novels are set in a pre-war world, a time of futile hopes and poignant dreams recreated in the way the desire for peace and justice is soon to be trampled by the nemesis of approaching war.

Graham Greene's career as a novelist began at a historical time of crisis and social upheaval when, after the First World War, a whole generation matured with a sense of the loss of an ordered world and faced the realities of the 1930s. The years between 1933 and 1937 were a time when 'private lives disintegrated as the enormous battlefield was prepared'.[3] The struggles of that decade form the matrix of the early novels where without indulging in socialist propaganda and overt political debate the narrative unfolds a world of gangsters and saboteurs and their relationship to business wheeler-dealing, revolution, trade unions, armament sales and international spy rings. It is the underside, as it were, of the myth of Empire – the *Pax Britannica* of progress, development and civilisation – achieved through capitalism and war.

The most important novel of this period is *It's a Battlefield* which Greene calls his most political novel. It was welcomed by *Viewpoint* (later *Left Review*) as a step in the portrayal of revolutionary struggle: 'Graham Greene . . . has some conception of the basis of class struggle which he depicts against a wide and varied social background.'[4] It was on the basis of these early novels that Orwell called Greene 'our first Catholic fellow-traveller'.[5] The shifts in focus between religion and politics and Greene's admirable use of such ambiguities as indeed there are in most men's lives may have baffled his contemporaries and has certainly confounded his critics in any attempt to categorise his fiction in the context of a generation of writers committed to taking sides openly. Greene's commitment is not to an ideology but to a social conscience and accuracy of experience:

> Literature has nothing to do with edification. I am not arguing that literature is amoral but that it presents a personal moral, and the personal morality of an individual is seldom identical with the morality of the group to which he belongs.[6]

He may be said to present an anarchic order of values in order to arrive at accuracy of experience and a world view in which the moral act is revealed through subversion of ideology and orthodoxy. It is therefore not possible to say that Catholicism and Communism presented themselves to Greene as rival doctrines nor did he, like Orwell, regard himself as standing virtually alone 'between the priest and the commissar'.[7] What he does attempt is to combine the faith of the priest and the idealism of the commissar to create a consciousness of realities and a moral view of the world.

In his discussion of the work of novelists of this period Richard Johnstone accentuates the importance of belief in relation to their artistic expression. They sought, he says, not simply 'to subsume their personalities and their art to a cause larger than its components, but rather to reassert the strength and purpose of the individual through the medium of belief.'[8] He puts forward the view that the thirties were a period when Communism and Catholicism were singled out 'as the alternative cures for the sickness of a generation', and that for Graham Greene and Evelyn Waugh 'Catholicism presented itself as the cure for the illness of the times. It became for them not a means of retreat from the modern world, but of ordering, in fiction and in life, a specifically contemporary reality.'[9] Greene's statements do not bear out this claim and his work only partially illustrates it, not least because his novels work best when Catholicism, its rites and its rituals, are not props in the story-line and movement of the plot but are metaphors for human anguish.

Graham Greene has often made it known that his conversion was prompted by a desire to understand and share in his wife's belief and that he had written seven novels before *Brighton Rock* revealed his religious belief to critics and readers. Today he says he finds it increasingly difficult to believe in God. In his introduction to the Collected Edition of *Brighton Rock* he writes:

> Many times since *Brighton Rock* I have been forced to declare myself not a Catholic writer but a writer who happens to be a Catholic. Newman wrote the last word on 'Catholic Literature' in *The Idea of a University*: 'I say, for the nature of the case, if Literature is to be made a study of human nature, you cannot have a Christian Literature. It is a contradiction in terms to attempt a sinless Literature of sinful man. You may gather together something very great and high, something higher than any Literature ever was; and when you have done so, you will find that it is not Literature at all.'[10]

Disloyalty to Catholicism as indeed disloyalty to all isms, has helped him to liberate human experience from confines of ideological or theological moulds: 'Loyalty confines us to accepted opinions: loyalty forbids us to comprehend sympathetically our dissident fellows; but disloyalty encourages us to roam experimentally through any dimension of sympathy.'[11] His art as a novelist rests, one suspects, on his understanding of the subleties of human experience. His appreciation of clear-cut systems like Catholicism, Marxism and the missions that sustained Empire contributes to narrative tension and demystification through characters whose lineaments are derived from the systems they represent. However, the characters transcend the limitations of these systems through a realisation of the facts of existence.

Greene's search for a moral order cannot be understood by merely looking for answers within Catholicism as expressed in his fiction. For one thing there was little of it in evidence in the early years except in the two novels suppressed by Greene – *The Name of Action* (1930) and *Rumour at Nightfall* (1931). Johnstone, in fact, concludes that the Catholicism of these works contains little that could be seen as a solution for the crisis of Greene's generation:

> The gulf separating the modern Englishman from the consolation of faith is emphasized by Greene's placement of his self-questioning heroes in conventional adventure-story settings – the romantic nineteenth-century Spain of *Rumour at Nightfall*, and the equally romanticized Palatine Republic of the twenties in *The Name of Action*. The opposition of scepticism and Catholicism thus corresponds to the opposition of realism and romance, of relevance and irrelevance. Catholicism maintains a shaky presence in the novels by its association with the mysterious and romanticized settings, but by virtue of this association, it also seems to have no connection with the predicament of the modern hero. As Greene began to abandon what may be termed serious romantic fiction, and to concentrate more closely on the reality of the thirties, it became increasingly difficult to maintain even this balance.[12]

The following analysis of the novels of the early period – *The Man Within* (1929); *The Name of Action* (1930); *Rumour at Nightfall* (1931); *Stamboul Train* (1932); *It's a Battlefield* (1934); *A Gun for Sale* (1936) and *Brighton Rock* (1938) – illustrates the points made above. *Brighton Rock* traditionally grouped as a 'Catholic' novel is included here for reasons other than purely chronological. The story of Pinkie and Rose is an intense expression of poverty, squalor and petty crime that grips and destroys many lives. It is held together by these realities rather than by their shared belief. The discussion of good and evil, right and wrong, that so overwhelmed critics at the time of its first publication and has coloured most interpretation of Greene's work ever since, develops in relation to the problem of survival in this world. *The Power and the Glory* on the other hand, could belong here chronologically but has been shifted to a chapter that discusses the religious sense. What must be borne in mind, however, is that Greene explores varieties of human experience of which the religious is one dimension and that his enquiry primarily relates to life in a changing world. The exploration of politics and religion is a continuing process rather than a set of stops pulled out alternately.

*   *   *

Graham Greene was 21 years old when he began *The Man Within* (1929). The story, set in the nineteenth century in a society exposed to smuggling activities off the coast of Sussex, prefigures the tone and mood of the novels of the 1930s. In these Greene subverts the traditional content of adventure stories and inverts the codes of received culture to explore, as here, the ideal of courage. The novel presents traditional virtues extolled in adventure stories that held up the myth of Empire – physical courage, enterprise, moral purpose, romantic idealism – along with a new dimension of experience: the cruelty of the strong towards the weak, physical cowardice balanced by moral strength, the hero as human being with frailties inherent in human nature.

The story of Andrews, who is little more than a boy and – unlike the heroes of adventure stories – a coward, unfolds a set of legal and moral lapses which function as signs in a reinterpretation of heroic action. Such strategies of inversion introduce new codes into the traditional material of the adventure form. Greene has documented his boyhood fascination with the stories of Rider Haggard. His autobiographical writing links his comprehension of social and spiritual power in adult life with his first introduction to representations of good and evil, courage and power in Haggard's stories as well as with experience of it at school.

The Man Within transmutes childhood experience of cruelty, betrayal, terror, beauty, peace and security – though still within a traditional and popular form – to reveal deeper contexts such as Andrews's disloyalty to the ideal jointly pursued by him and his smuggling companion, Carlyon, and his responsibility in the killing of Elizabeth by one of the smugglers. In fact, the very activity of smuggling may be said to be an extension of the traditional activity of the adventure story – scientific exploration, pioneering discovery, heroic enterprise – to illustrate values for the modern world. The confrontation is in representative terms: a group of smugglers, their friends and accomplices pitted against Sir Henry Merriman, the barrister who tries to convict the smugglers on a charge of having murdered one of the gaugers. The search for truth and justice in life, a *leitmotif* in all Greene's fiction, is first revealed here.

Smuggling offers Andrews a chance of escape from realities but he is pursued by these in the attitudes of his comrades who despise his frailty and idealise the valour of his father. The father as valiant leader is a stranger to Andrews who knows only his obverse side through the cruelty meted out to his mother whose sensitivity he has inherited. The adventure develops with Andrews engaged in two battles. The first fought between Andrews and his smuggling companions is extended by drawing him into a world of legal institutions and the police. The second fought within Andrews's mind between his weaker instincts and better self expresses the idea of the intimate enemy that underlies Greene's conception of man and society: Humanity is betrayed by greed and fear; the human being disregards conscience; institutions designed to benefit mankind in society do the reverse – they dehumanise the very societies they are meant to serve; governments betray people and power is sought as an end in itself rather than as means to promote human welfare. The intimate enemy is within and without; it is created by man in his own spirit and likeness and grows as a monster to destroy him.

Andrews's struggle lays bare an internal landscape that develops into conflicts – between an authoritative standard of behaviour and human desires, between what one is and what it is possible for one to become. In Greene's fiction this is the source of action that can properly be called moral and that eventually leads to self-realisation. The framework of this first novel develops later into the most overpowering aspect of Greene's work. The 'man within' of the title represents the voice of conscience, as it were, which reflects on the inner life of the characters and their external roles in society:

> I know I am a coward and altogether despicable, he said to himself with heavy self-depreciation, trying without much hope to under-bid his real character, I know I am embarrassingly made up of two persons, the sentimental, bullying, desiring child and another more stern critic, if someone believed in me – but he did not believe in himself. Always while one part of him spoke, another part stood on one side and wondered, 'Is this I who am speaking? Can I really exist like this?' (p. 24).

The characterisation of Andrews features the theme of disloyalty mythicised from Greene's childhood experience and has a hint of the paradigm of the traitor as hero. It also illustrates the possibilities of romantic illusion in a life of action and the ideal of confrontation. Carlyon's shooting of one of his sailors shatters the 'dear romantic illusion of adventure' in which Carlyon and Andrews take refuge. This first crack is deepened when Andrews betrays the smugglers creating an inevitable confrontation with the law.

The two dreamers and their desire for escape into romantic illusion embodies difference: whereas Carlyon's romantic dream is near perfect, Andrew's dream is not. He has to live with the cruelty of his fellow-smugglers who despise his weak physique and his inability to live up to his father's image of strength and courage. It matters little in the context of the novel that Andrews tells on his comrades in a moment of weakness, in the only way he can show his power over them. The narrative underscores the depth of the betrayal of trust and of the ideal that united the two friends. This is not to say that the two friends are conscious of self in quite the same way. Carlyon is running away from the police, but not from himself and his friends. He escapes 'the dull dirty game' of life in heroic dreams of adventure. There is no sense of shame, much less of wrongdoing except when reality impinges and one of the men is dead.

Andrews, in contrast, is escaping from himself. He has no self-respect and his betrayal is ultimately an act of cowardice, a violent reaction to the constant reminder of his inadequacies. Betrayal, confrontation and the courage to face retribution are the themes of *The Man Within*. The internal landscape is at all times more clearly visualised than the outer world and the novel works really as an extended conversation with the man within: Andrews communing with his conscience through his consciousness of having betrayed trust. Andrews holds within his limited frame a whole range of ideas which Greene was to explore in his later work.

The courage to face life squarely is epitomised by Elizabeth, a highly idealised representation of beauty, goodness and purity. The young novelist is clearly groping for a form that would enable him to return to narrative and to the kind of story-telling that would extend consciousness of the whole texture of life. The main points raised in his first novel suggest the future development of a vision which links the private universe of dreams and conscience to the visible world represented by social forces and conditions of survival. The contrary pulls reach Andrews not merely in terms of his conscience – the man within – but as part of the external world as well and it is in these sections that the novel works best, successfully fusing the two elements of consciousness. For example, Elizabeth and Carlyon both have beautiful voices that entice Andrews:

> He had thought her voice also near to music, and now he sat still, watching with a strange disinterestedness the two musics come in conflict for the mastery of his movements. One was subtle, a thing of suggestions and of memories; the other, plain, clear-cut, ringing. One spoke of a dreamy escape from reality; the other was reality, deliberately sane. If he stayed sooner or later he must face this fear; if he went he left calmness, clarity, instinctive wisdom for a vague uncertain refuge . . . Carlyon was a romantic with his face in the clouds, who hated any one who gave him contact with the grubby earth (pp. 57–8).

Greene has written often and at length about his experience of childhood as idyll marred by the terrors at boarding school where his father was the headmaster.[13] A horror-filled awareness of human cruelties and the pain of growing within an enclosure of divided loyalties separated by the green baize door are now commonplaces of comment on Greene's work. Assessments based on this perspective can sometimes lead to a limited interpretation of the use of disloyalty which in Greene's work has been creative and radical.

John Spurling appreciates the self-examination of Greene's protagonists but suggests that they reflect the feelings of a man who 'could never forgive or forget the process of growing up'. This, as Spurling explains, is one of the central themes of literature, especially English literature, and 'although it may have been handled with broader sympathy and deeper understanding by the greatest writers – including Greene's own first division masters, James and Conrad – it has never been done with more intimate passion than by Greene.[14] The point not made here is that the exploration of the process of growing up, indeed the subversion of the old values – strength, loyalty, self-confidence – reveals the depths of human anguish in a very real sense as part of the very texture of life, and not merely for those in need of spiritual comfort. Frequent returns to the 'lost boyhood of Judas' evoke with compelling power the idea of responsibility allied to conscience.

Contact with the grubby earth described as 'seediness' in later work is the base of Greene's vision. On the one hand the unpurified human condition, notwithstanding the taint of original sin, has the vitality and exuberance of life like the activity of smuggling. On the other hand, the condition of purity represented by Elizabeth who urges him to face the law – does represent justice – even though the law itself in its expression is a degenerate form of legality as far removed from the ideal as the hierarchy is from religion. The working out of the processes of the law occupy only the outer reaches of the novel which only goes to show the intensity of Greene's focus on man's inner life.

The framework of legal and moral offences, social institutions and human values creates a dramatic representation of the most enduring element of the text: the revelation of a religious sense and moral values in the context of political realities. This artistic tension enhances our understanding of issues by blurring and juggling them, even on occasion by distorting them to enhance truth. For instance the transposition of adventure material into a serious framework prompts one to ask why this illegal activity is condoned. The answer would be that an illegality is seen as less heinous than a moral violation of trust. Andrews seeks retribution not merely for his betrayal of Carlyon but more importantly for his moral responsibility in the death of Elizabeth.

Greene's Catholicism enables him in later novels to pull the discourse more fully on to the metaphysical plane which creates space for a totalisation of experience whereby humanism, revolutionary ideologies, *dégagement* and commitment are evaluated against an absolute standard of values provided by the Catholic structure, either overtly or implicitly. This is not to say, however, that the novels should be discussed wholly in a moral and spiritual framework. Such an effort distorts the texts for they offer, above all, life within the limits of specific time and place and are determined by a particular cultural standpoint.

This standpoint is considerably obfuscated in the two novels that followed *A Man Within*. Both these novels, *The Name of Action* (1930) and *Rumour at Nightfall* (1931), have been suppressed by the author because they are 'of a badness beyond the power of criticism properly to evoke'.[15] A review by Frank Swinnerton made him realise where he was going wrong and he stopped reading Conrad altogether until 1959 when he took a copy of *Heart of Darkness* on his journey to the Congo. The novels suggest Greene's deep interest in the world of politics and power although, as he acknowledges, at this stage his understanding of these realities was very limited: in *The Name of Action* 'I was trying to write my first political novel without knowing anything of politics'.[16]

The romantic idealism that permeates these early novels is never quite purged from later work. At this point his extreme youth and perhaps an intense romantic involvement in his personal life may have had something to do with the aspects of this work not least the portrayal of women as disembodied representations of virtue and beauty. This perception is reiterated in the quotation from Donne which Greene used in dedicating *The Name of Action* to his wife: 'Thou art so truth, that thoughts of thee suffice, To make dreams truths, and fables histories.'

There are several touches that appear to be extremely personal. For instance Senorita Monti marries Michael Crane who, unlike Chase, believes in fate and destiny, in 'a shadow land of spiritual belief' – and her faith, Chase believes will create an insurmountable barrier between the two friends. Also to the point here is a description of Caveda in *Rumour at Nightfall*. He is the guerilla described as a man of courage with a sense of humour, whose motives are not clear and could be dubious but who is nevertheless represented in terms that seem archetypal to the politics of Greene's fiction:

> He is a much abused man. He is a Liberal. Oh, yes, he calls himself a Carlist, but what does he care for such politics? The caballero knows what a dirty game they are. Caveda is not a politician. He cares for the great, the fundamental things, Liberalism, the poor, freedom. He does not believe in priests, kings, what are they beside the people? . . . he feels, in his heart, señor, for Liberalism and the people.[17]

The last novel in this first group, *Stamboul Train* (1932), illustrates what Greene refers to as 'a sense of movement in prose'.[8] It is almost wholly located in a moving train and as a literary device this is effective in revealing character, mood and incident in glimpses and flashes. As the train speeds on to its destination and the narrative to its close, one has a sense of human lives being borne along to an inexorable destiny. The technique is also influenced by the grammar of film: tracking of characters on to close-ups, the panning, as it were, of the landscape of life. The narrative takes the shape of frames edited most naturally along the geography of the train: its corridors, sleepers and the stations along the way create a dramatic juxtaposition of character and event. Greene himself prefers to see the technique in this novel as influenced by his enduring interest in theatre:

There are, I think, a few points of academic interest in *Stamboul Train* . . . I can detect . . . the influence of my early passion for playwriting which had never quite died. In those days I thought in terms of a key scene – I would even chart its position on a sheet of paper before I began to write. 'Chapter 3. So-and-so comes alive.' Often these scenes consisted of isolating two characters – hiding in a railway shed in *Stamboul Train*, in an empty house in *A Gun for Sale*. It was as though I wanted to escape from the vast liquidity of the novel and to play out the most important situation on a narrow stage where I could direct every movement of my characters. A scene like that halts the progress of the novel with dramatic emphasis, just as in a film a close-up makes the picture momentarily pause.[19]

Dramatic emphasis and narrative speed are characteristic of Greene's fiction and are particularly evident in *Stamboul Train* which projects a group of people casually brought together on a short journey, then explores interpersonal relations and relates them to economic, political and racial questions. Although Carleton Myatt, the young Jewish businessman who is travelling with his mind burdened with figures and strategies to outwit the associates he is going to meet, is revealed with characteristics which may be called stereotyped, he is simultaneously endowed with sensitivity and feelings of concern for Coral Musker, the young chorus girl he befriends on the journey. The flashes that illuminate his character suggest insights that Myatt has into his own person, and his awareness of how others perceive him.

Myatt is conscious of his otherness as imposed on him by 'a hostile world' which if anything, suggests a lack of prejudice in the novelist. He is described, for instance, as 'bolstered by the knowledge of his fur coat, of his suit from Savile Row, his money or his position in the firm to hearten him', as aware of there being 'no permanent settlement to one of his race' (p. 19). He shrugs his shoulders deprecatingly and 'might have been a pawnbroker undervaluing a watch or a vase' when Coral thanks him for his magnanimous gesture: he had allowed her to use his first-class sleeper for the night when she fainted from exhaustion, and slept himself in the cold corridor. Thus the narrative juxtaposes typical gestures and characteristics sometimes actually described as 'a trick of his race' with actions that are generous, warm-hearted and sensitive in order to subvert the stereotype and to present the individual. A fine example of this is Myatt's regret at the end when he foresees a safe future with beautiful Janet, niece of Mr Stein – his business partner – a future he might have been prepared to give up if Coral had been found.

The embodiment of pernicious capitalism as a Jew (Sir Marcus in *A Gun for Sale* and Colleoni in *Brighton Rock*) has made Greene open to the charge of purveying twentieth-century propaganda of the Jew as Devil. Harold Fisch in his book, *The Dual Image*, which discusses the image of the Jew in English Literature argues that 'the real Devil–Jew still functions in the collective unconscious' and that the figure comes back to the surface 'in an actively religious sensibility such as that of Graham Greene'.

Fisch's thesis is that whether he appears as Saint or Devil, or both simultaneously, the Jew functions as literary archetype. In his brief illustration from Greene's novels he writes:

> *Brighton Rock* is a novel conducted at the level of theological symbolism or allegory. Pinkie is the villain, but he lives within the world of spiritual realities (i.e. Catholic spirituality). He knows Heaven and Hell, Sin and Grace. On the other hand, the Jew, Colleoni, knows only the *World*. His self-possession is the sign of his utterly negative and corrupt function . . . Colleoni is not a Jew just by chance; he is rather *the Jew*. As he passes Pinkie in the car, he appears to symbolise the eternal Jew.[20]

Fisch argues that *A Gun for Sale* presents the same Jew–Devil archetype in the person of Sir Marcus who through murder and conspiracy manipulates the fate of nations and threatens the world with war. Fisch concludes that Greene's fiction combines 'maximum of realism with the maximum of fantasy' but subverts realism so that 'one finds oneself suddenly in a looking glass world of medieval monsters and monks tales. [This is the subject of medieval Mysteries but these authors] did not claim as he does that he holds the mirror up to contemporary life'.[21]

Greene was apparently sensitive to such charges. In the revised editions of *Brighton Rock*, for instance, the word 'Jew' has been sometimes replaced by 'tycoon'. A careful reading of the texts reveals that Greene was at pains to distinguish between the Jew as the embodiment of capitalism and the Jew as a human being with a particular cultural identity. This is an important theme in *Stamboul Train* but Fisch ignores this novel altogether presumably because it

runs counter to his theory. Here the main character of Carleton
Myatt, a Jew, stands out as the most warm-hearted and generous.
To the very end of the novel the narrative weaves the political and
the personal strands to create a poignant texture not merely in
relation to the struggle in the Balkans. With remarkable prescience
the novel bears within the lively pace of its thriller form intimations
of Jewish experience that compel a moral awareness. Nowhere is
this reality more anguishing than in the final sections when Myatt
searches in the darkness and the storm for Coral. He finds himself
with no recourse at all and becomes aware of danger when alone
with her guards:

> in the small hungry eyes shone hatred and a desire to kill; it was as
> if all the oppressions, the pogroms, the chains, and the envy and
> superstition which caused them, had been herded into a dark cup
> of the earth and now he stared down at them from the rim (p. 172).

> [He] was frightened; he had seen in the soldier's attitude the spirit
> which made pogroms possible (p. 182).

Myatt emerges neither as Saint nor Devil but as an ordinary
human being in a portrayal where his Jewishness, in fact, dominates
his perception of himself and the relations of his fellow-passengers
with him, far more than it does in the case of Colleoni and Sir Marcus
who are revealed as exploiters and as representatives of the Big
Battalions – forces that oppose social justice. They embody the
theme first expressed in *Stamboul Train*: 'You put the small thief in
prison but the big thief lives in a palace' (p. 165). Through them
Greene appears to be conveying the ethos of a period when the Jews
did indeed control much of big business so that the argument is
really against industrial capitalism and against those who manipulate
human lives under the cover of market forces. The intention is not to
present the Devil–Jew.[22] In fact, Graham Greene has recorded that
A Gun for Sale was written at a time when he had attended a trial
inquiring into the private manufacture and sale of armaments:

> Did I attend one of the hearings because I was already writing *A
> Gun for Sale* or did the idea come to me after attending the trial? My
> chief memory of the hearings was one of the politeness and
> feebleness of the cross-examination. Some great firms were con-
> cerned and over and over again counsel found that essential

papers were missing or had not been brought to court . . . About the same time somebody had written the life of Sir Basil Zaharoff, a more plausible villain for those days than the man in Buchan's *The Thirty Nine Steps* . . . Sir Marcus in *A Gun for Sale* is, of course, not Sir Basil, but the family resemblance is plain.[23]

Greene is particularly good at suggesting human vulnerability as in the characterisation of Coral Musker in *Stamboul Train* though the attempt to probe class-consciousness and working-class goals through her is only partially successfully. Exhausted by her precarious livelihood as a chorus girl she yearns for economic and emotional security but confuses both with ambitions to be mistaken for a lady. The text reveals her class-consciousness in relation to the *petit bourgeois* – Mr and Mrs Peters – projected as selfish and lacking in feeling, and in relation to Dr Czinner the revolutionary, who disguised as Richard John – a school teacher – is returning from exile in England to lead an uprising at home in Belgrade. Czinner's analysis of class is no better than Coral's. He posits the values of the gentleman as professional alongside the avarice of the business classes and the labour of the working class:

the proletariat have their virtues, and the gentleman is often good, just and brave. He is paid for something useful, for governing or teaching, or healing, or his money is his father's. He does not deserve it perhaps but he has done no one harm to get it. But the bourgeois – he buys cheap and sells dear. He buys from the worker and sells back to the worker. He is useless (p. 110).

Coral is bewildered by his explanation and in the end becomes the victim of his plan without understanding either the plan or the ideals for which he is working. Czinner rationalises the scruple he feels in implicating the blameless Coral – 'only a party in power could possess scruple' – and does not seem to be altogether convinced of the values he proclaims. His political work is an expression of compassion and not ideology which is why he finds himself wishing for a world shaped to the pattern he loved and longed for, a world of 'generosity, charity and meticulous codes of honour'.

Such idealism reveals a vision that is not ideological or political but human. Czinner's plans mess up Coral's life though she is a member of the class Czinner would like to protect. This little twist illustrates that romantic sloganising and revolutionary fervour count for very little since human welfare cannot be worked out in terms of general prescription, nor through social institutions and an ideology that denies personal identities.

The passengers in the train represent a cross-section of urban society which includes a thief and murderer who, in the kind of narrative favoured by Greene, manages to escape to freedom with facilities organised by Myatt to look for and help the innocent Coral. The relationships established by the passengers either by choice or by circumstance parallel the pressures and cynicism of ideological choice. Even in these early novels the rigours of orthodoxy are tempered to focus on private anguish; the bizarre comedy of life, the suspense of the adventure story and the cinematic detail that enriches the texture of the novels combine to depict the inadequacies of human justice and the contradictions of creeds to be explored in the later fiction.

*   *   *

In the novels of this period Greene intensifies his search for a new paradigm. Though the narrative retains the traditional adventure form of concepts of war, nation and frontier, it encodes perceptions of values, forces and moral choices within two orders of time, the eternal always present within the visible landscape. The text does not withdraw from the process of history but strives to create a myth for our time within the new framework of a changing world order.

The changed frame of reference is first suggested in *Stamboul Train* when Dr Czinner says in the course of his address to the police who are on the point of convicting him: 'How old-fashioned you are with your frontiers and your patriotism; even your financiers don't recognise frontiers' (p. 165). In his introduction to the Collected edition of *A Gun for Sale* Greene recognised that the old adventure tale was dead:

> Patriotism had lost its appeal, and for a schoolboy, at Passchen-daele, talk of the Empire brought forth to mind the Beaverbrook Crusader, while it was difficult during the years of the Depression to believe in the high purposes of the city of London or of the British Constitution. The hunger marchers seemed more real than the politicians. It was no longer a Buchan world. The hunted man was Raven not Hannay: a man out to revenge himself for all the dirty tricks of life; not to save his country.[24]

The novels of this period evoke the culture of the time and present insights into the forces of Capitalism, Socialism, Communism and Fascism. The scene of these novels is the city as centre of human life and the focus is clearly on political, economic and moral issues, on aspirations that would liberate the poor and exploited from the enemies within of greed and selfishness. The dynamics of plot are provided by the working of the Law, the Police Force, Government, trade unions, and industry, in particular the armament industry. Characters are members of the proletariat and white-collar workers as well as members of the establishment and misfits still clinging to the old order.

It's a Battlefield (1934) which Greene considers his most political novel introduces a framework often used in the fiction to illustrate consciousness of the old order in conflict with contemporary culture. Its theme, says Greene, is the injustice of man's justice. The values and creeds that sustained the Empire are brought into play indirectly and the idea of justice, duty and responsibility is given meaning within the widest possible framework: that of human life in the world. The character of the Assistant Commissioner of Police, the persona representing these confrontations, is a development of the institutional policeman as reference point in explorations of justice. The Assistant Commissioner brings to his job in London a whole tradition of values and experience which belong to a power structure that is changing. One of the most incisive elements of this novel is that the plot is built around a sifting of codes and an examination of new forces that are measured and evaluated within the context of immediate realities.

Greene has said that the character of the Assistant Commissioner owes something of his 'stiff, inhibited, bachelor integrity' to his uncle Graham Greene, Secretary to the Admiralty under Churchill during the First World War, and one of the founders of Naval Intelligence. Greene himself had no experience of the outposts of the British Empire at the time of writing but he endows his character with such experience. This narrative strategy gains in objectivity because of the manner in which Greene confronts the British Empire in his fiction: he dissociates the instruments of the Empire from the structure and morality of imperialism; he upholds aspects of social institutions and exposes the manner in which they contribute to social upheaval.

The text evokes inadequacies of human justice through the consciousness of the Assistant Commissioner who is mainly concerned with his duty; the experience of workers elaborates this theme. The Assistant Commissioner's perception of justice is at all times related to duties in the outposts of the Empire when he walked not in the city of London but on 'damp paths steaming in the heat under leaves like hairy hands' (p. 7).[25] Here the guilty man was pursued

> by this path and that, and only as a last resort, when there was no other means of ensuring a murderer's punishment, did one burn his village. Justice had nothing to do with the matter. One left justice to Magistrates, to judges and juries, to members of Parliament, to the Home Secretary' (p. 7).

Flashes of personal history that make up his character suggest the past:

> pursed lips which frequent fevers had drained of colour and left dry and pale . . . He had only his pay on which to live: it had been hard to save in the East; he had preserved nothing but the gourds, the native weapons, the sentimental debris of a hard career' (p. 8).

An effective strategy develops the contrast by presenting him in relation to a representative of the new order, the private secretary to the Home minister. He is tall, with 'round, smooth features and ashen hair, he shone with publicity; he had the glamour and consciousness of innumerable photographs' (p. 9). The Assistant Commissioner is greeted with amusement and patronage, when he goes to meet him and feels 'suddenly old and dusty: as if he had just returned from one of his horrid tedious marches with a man left dangling in the jungle for the birds to peck, to find at headquarters a young cool messenger from the Governor' (p. 9).

The novel works on two main juxtapositions and parallelisms: the contrasting relationships between the Assistant Commissioner who has returned from a spell of arduous service in one of the outposts of Empire and the smooth-faced, urbane secretary to the Minister in London; the troubles of an industrial worker who attends a meeting of the Communist Party and is involved in the accidental killing of the policeman, his experiences of those who are supposed to protect him and those who are the guardians of the law. The background of Empire is suggested not only by the Assistant Commissioner's recall of his work but also by a contrast between the practice of justice at the centre and at the periphery. The implications stand revealed in sharp inversions: justice in the outposts was simple and effective and contributed to human welfare though it was subordinate to the preservation of Empire whereas justice at the very centre of Empire which proclaims democracy and equity is a travesty perpetrated both by the guardians of law and order and by political parties. Another inversion which also, like the city of London, unites the complex themes of the novel is that the instrument or the functionary in the novel, the Assistant Commissioner, mitigates the hypocrisies of ideological claims like Empire and worker's welfare by conscientious protests, futile though they may be in preventing injustice.

The novel sets out to explore parallel injustices in human existence within a framework of social institutions and individual responsibility and the text illustrates the constraining influence of dominant culture and ideology that blunts the edge of Greene's highly developed social consciousness. The resultant discontinuity subverts reality and creates the illusion that the enforcement of law and order in the outposts of Empire was a simpler matter and involved less moral confusion than the exercise of similar duties in London. Here the lack of justice is felt more keenly because in the Assistant Commissioner's old job, human justice was meted out within a framework of morals and ethics though the State itself – the structure of imperialism – was a tyrant. In London the State is democratic and committed to human rights and welfare but in actual fact its legal institutions are ineffective and its instruments powerless.

In this sense the lack of justice is felt more intensely by the professional in London functioning inside what is a democratic set-up. Such a version of imperialist activity, however humane the professional individual, is less radical than is conveyed by a text that bristles with contemporary realities, because it clouds the issue of the experience of 'natives' for whom what is seen by the Assistant Commissioner as 'duty' or by the State as 'justice', is in their experience a denial of sovereignty and human rights. Greene's political insights in fiction, as opposed to travelogues and journalism, proceed from a consciousness that accepts the idealism and values of individuals employed by an exploitative power and only remotely implies a denunciation of imperialist activity as far as the British Empire is concerned. His discussion of American hegemony has greater power and is analysed in a later section of this book. Thus, though Greene's novels reveal levels of questioning of the ethic of moral superiority that are courageous and honest there is no condemnation of British imperialism. The moral values of those who served, suffered and died in the service of the Empire are exalted and though he does not express any clear endorsement of the Empire as such, there is a lingering feeling that the ideals of the old structures of imperialism – France in Indo-China for instance – were somehow more benevolent than modern superpowers.[26]

This is less an evasion than a pragmatic way of exploring the pressures of life and however unsatisfactory the resolution of this artistic tension, it is unfair to say that the text amounts to an endorsement of the Empire itself. What does emerge from the Assistant Commissioner's constant recall of the old way of life in preference to present realities is the enduring trap of paternalist benevolence. In fact, in *The Human Factor* (1978) nostalgia for the Empire is an important element in the characterisation of Sir John Hargreaves, the head of MI5 of the British Secret Service. When he discusses 'Uncle Remus', a plan for the defence of apartheid in South Africa in which the USA, West Germany and England are involved, his loyalties and idealism surface:

I don't like the idea of Uncle Remus any more than you do. It's what the politicians call a realistic policy, and realism never got very far in the kind of Africa I used to know. My Africa was a sentimental Africa. I really loved Africa, Castle. The Chinese don't, nor do the Russians, nor the Americans – but we have to go with the White House . . . How easy it was in the old days when we dealt with chiefs and witch doctors and bush schools and devils and rain queens. My Africa was still a little like the Africa of Rider Haggard . . . The Emperor Chaka was a lot better than Field Marshall Amin Dada (p. 55).

It is important, however, not to confuse the loyalties of these characters with Greene's understanding of realities, which is always honest and clear. A pessimistic view of social reform deepens the structure of the narrative at the expense of clarities in the expression of political ideology. This is, in a sense, a strength: Greene illustrates that no political ideology can by itself promote social justice. The distinction between those who wield power and those who discharge duties to preserve an existing order is expressed in the opening chapter of *It's a Battlefield*, in the words of the Assistant Commissioner:

I wish I had asked him how he came to be unemployed; it might have been possible to find him work; but what good after all would that have been? he is only one; it is impossible for me to help these men, only the State can do that, the State which employs me to keep order, to see that the unemployed beg and do not demand (p. 163).

Power and responsibility in Greene's fiction are rarely seen to coexist for the promotion of equity and justice.

The Assistant Commissioner's conflict with the Deputy Inspector in London, though minor, represents a fundamental conflict between the exercise of power and responsibility for the preservation of Empire and for delivering justice to the people entrusted to his care. Greene, however, makes the conflict subordinate to a more serious conflict where at the hub of Empire even elementary justice which gets meted out in the colonies is denied to the poor: 'He may know how to hang a few natives in the jungle, but he's no good for London' (p. 52). The old wars had rules he could grasp more easily; he could salvage his conscience privately for atrocities committed in the line of duty. The present war in London

> was a civil war. His enemies were not only the brutal and the depraved but the very men he pitied, the men he wanted to help; if he had done his duty the unemployed man would have been arrested for begging. The buildings seemed to him then to lose a little of their dignity; the peace of Sunday in Pall Mall was like the peace which follows a massacre, a war of elimination; poverty here had been successfully contested, driven back on the one side towards Notting Hill, on the other towards Vauxhall (pp. 165–6).

These insights are only partially substantiated so that the text appears to endorse a preference for the old codes with a suggestion that 'a native hanged' or a village burnt was somehow less important, perhaps because less immediate, than the unemployed in jail or begging in London. A little elaboration could have diminished this uneasy juxtaposition which seems to suggest not merely the Assistant Commissioner's point of view which is realistic and true to character but also implies the novelist's endorsement of the Commissioner's view of his duties. This amounts to a reiteration of old assumptions that the Empire through its professionals contributed to the welfare of the people and that absolute authority was only a necessary rule, with exploitation as by-product.

The other part of the battlefield of the novel is where authority contends with emerging forces of industrial action. These are represented in the life of Jim Drover, a quiet and gentle factory worker who accidentally kills a policeman in the confusion following a party meeting and is arrested for murder. The fact that he is a Communist works against him and a witch-hunt follows: every worker is indiscriminately branded a Communist. An extraordinary conversation between the Private Secretary to the Minister and the Assistant Commissioner reveals the main protagonists and the issues that need to be resolved to illustrate that political expediency and private gain will determine the issue of Jim Drover's reprieve.

The idea of social injustice prevails not merely in the main story-line – workers' demands, union and party meetings, an establishment that seeks to preserve itself, accidental death of a policeman, resultant individual struggles – but is woven into the intricate mechanics of the plot which follows parallel journeys and pursuits across the city of London. The first journey is that of the Assistant Commissioner to meet the Private Secretary and illustrates the first class of interests and codes. Jim's wife goes in search of the policeman's widow to enlist her support for the petition on Jim's behalf, and the Assistant Commissioner goes on another journey in pursuit of the trunk murderer, a pursuit that has no relation to the main plot but heightens the sense of violence and confusion.

The voices of the city make themselves heard through the consciousness of the Assistant Commissioner who in yet another journey with the Secretary goes to visit Jim in prison. The geography of the city along the route he takes sharpens the class-divide far better than mere discussion or dialogue could do. The longest journey and the one most closely woven into the narrative is Conrad's pursuit of the Assistant Commissioner. He is Jim's brother and seeks a violent solution to the problem that is destroying his family. By investing him with a feeling of inadequacy, which he tries to sublimate through his quest for a solution, Greene creates a link between the individual and the social situation. At no point in the novel are the two – the individual and the social – not connected. The theme of individual struggle acquires a mythic quality with the clever juxtaposition of individuals as members of society, of organised groups, and professions, and in relation to family.

The city of London ingeniously used to define the Assistant Commissioner's identity and to relate the struggles in London to distant ones, stretches across Candahar Road, Khyber Terrace,

Kabul Street towards imperial boundaries echoing imperial wars. They afford insights into the question of justice as fundamental to life, into the human being inside his professional mask grappling with conflicting demands of office and ideals of justice that are often irreconcilable with professional duty.

The only life-enhancing journey is that of Kay Rimmer, who with her boyfriend Jules, drives out into the country. In her determination not to be weighed down with factory work, unemployment and the general atmosphere of confusion and upheaval the narrative suggests a wholeness of experience. Through her involvement with Surrogate, an author who professes sympathy for the workers, it suggests hypocrisies that often underlie talk of Capitalism, ideology and Proletariat.

The pressures of survival and conflicts between the working class and the white-collar worker are introduced through Kay who feels sympathy for her sister's tragedy but is helpless because she fears that demanding support from the workforce at the factory could mean the loss of her own job. In her eyes Conrad's education gave him the greater freedom:

> She explained: 'But I couldn't ask people at the works. I couldn't let them know it was Milly's husband.' With pale asperity he prepared a dagger thrust: 'You won't do a little thing', but her appearance daunted him. Behind her were all the machines of the factory. With orange lips and waved hair she fought their uniformity and grey steel but she was as one with them as a frivolous dash of bright paint on a shafting. 'The manager wouldn't like it. He'd sack me when he got a chance.'
> It was not cowardice but realism that spoke, 'What's the use of a dozen names? One must live. It's different wth you' . . . 'Anyone can do my job. But you . . . (p. 32).

'You' is the accusation levelled at Conrad, a white-collar worker, and so separated by what seems like a chasm in Kay's eyes. It reveals the lonely struggle of individuals against various sets of hostile elements, poignantly, through Kay's conduct: she is willing to attend party meetings, to submit to Surrogate's amorous attentions if it will help Jim, but not to jeopardise her own position by organising her mates.

The education that Kay envies Conrad is felt by him as a burden and since he lacks the vitality of Kay which is really the vitality of the worker, he emerges as less resilient, less gifted with the capacity to live. Though the novel bristles with contemporary political issues it is the human connection that is explored as influenced by the State, authority, duty and class differences in an industrial capitalist setting. The predominant mood is one of unease and constraint and there is no attempt at political resolutions. Socialist ideals pervade the text but the struggle is individual, and the metaphor of the title suggests social upheaval with separate battles being waged, each of varying intensity but interconnected although following its single course. The idea is suggested in the epigraph to the novel taken from Kinglake's description of the Crimean War:

> In so far as the battlefield presented itself to the bare eyesight of men, it had no entirety, no length, no breadth, no depth, no size, no shape, and was made up of nothing except small numberless circlets commensurate with such ranges of vision as the mist might allow at each spot . . . In such conditions, each separate gathering of English soldiery went on fighting its own little battle in happy and advantageous ignorance of the general state of the action; nay, even very often in ignorance of the fact that any great conflict was raging.

In *A Gun for Sale* (1936) Raven unwittingly triggers off a war by killing, for purely mercenary reasons, the pacifist Minister of War of an unnamed European country. He discovers the duplicity of his employers when he realises that he has been paid in stolen notes and that the police are now firmly on his track. His determination to revenge himself constitutes the action of the novel. The two pursuits, that by Raven of the lawless moneyed and that by the police of Raven, heightens the contrasts between justice and legality.

The novel accentuates in tones more startling than the earlier work the aggression of the powerful against the weak. The structure of the text establishes interconnections between capitalism, the armaments industry, the poor, the underfed and the unemployed. The threat of war is suffocating. The momentum of events as they overtake Yugoslavia, Italy and France parallels the pace of the police as they pursue Raven across London into Nottwich to the headquarters of Midland Steel where the chief protagonists in the two wars confront each other. The novel raises fundamental questions on the attainability of social justice, peace and freedom, and exposes the working of establishments whose ostensible purpose is the protection of a peaceful society. Raven's purely individual struggle is fought with no sense of self-preservation – as he is a penniless orphan and a social outcast he has nothing to lose and he blazes a trail that unwittingly exposes the malpractices of those in power.

The connections between capitalism and war with poverty as a seed-bed for both and war itself as a symptom of diseases of the body politic are expressed through a kind of parable art with caricatured representations of vices and virtues: Acky the obscene defrocked priest, Cholmondley the glutton, Sir Marcus the predatory industrial baron who is powerful enough to trigger off a war to save his empire at Midland Steel by boosting the sales of armament shares. Crooked with age, dehumanised by avarice and senility, his mind is still sharp enough to plot strategies of survival that involve attempts to corrupt the Police Chief. In this world of the Big Battalions of finance what hope is there for the lone struggle of Raven, the son of a hanged criminal and a suicide, a reject of society who has escaped from an orphanage? From the depths of his own bloody battle he cries out: 'All this talk of war. It doesn't mean a thing to me. Why should I care if there's war. There's always been a war for me.'[27]

Sir Marcus manipulates capital and human beings; the death of a nameless cypher, as far as he is concerned, is the last step for the successful completion of a neat operation:

> Armament shares continued to rise, and with them steel. It made no difference at all that the British Government had stopped all export licences; the country itself was now absorbing more armaments than it had ever done since the peak year of Haig's assaults on the Hindenburg Line. Sir Marcus had many friends, in many countries; he wintered with them regularly . . . he was the intimate friend of Mrs Cranbeim. It was impossible now to export arms, but it was still possible to export nickel and most of the other metals which were necessary to the arming of nations. Even when war was declared, Mrs Cranbeim had been able to say quite definitely . . . the British Government would not forbid the export of nickel to Switzerland or other neutral countries so long as the British requirements were first met. The future was very rosy indeed, for you could trust Mrs Cranbeim's word. She spoke directly from the horse's mouth, if you could so describe the elder statesman whose confidence she shared (p. 115).

The text redefines words such as 'crime' and 'murderer'; the deprivation experienced by Raven defines 'evil' and 'good' in terms of human relationships so that Anne's warmth and generosity even in the midst of her terror emerges as the most powerful representation of what Greene means by the religious sense. She is the first person to seem quite oblivious of Raven's ugly, deformed face, and to break his guard by treating him naturally. Her joy and relief at the end when she is reunited with her fiancé – the policeman Mather, in charge of Raven's case – are clouded by a sense of failure:

> a shade of disquiet remained, a fading spectre of Raven . . . it seemed to Anne for a few moments that this sense of failure would never die from her brain, that it would cloud a little every happiness; it was something she could never explain' (pp. 184–5).

And although she moves on into her future with a 'sigh of unshadowed happiness' the last sentence she utters – 'we're home' – carries the echo of homelessness through her earlier empathy with Raven. Such brief juxtapositions, barely glimpsed, define reality and moral values. Mather, the policeman, though humane and inspired by idealism, becomes the unwilling tool of institutionalised 'crime' whose members engage in a battle for survival against the petty villain, Raven. The last lingering perception of Raven relates class exploitation with the human condition: 'If his immortality was to be on the lips of living men, he was fighting now his last losing fight against extinction' (p. 184).

The two protagonists and the two wars come together in the novel's clearly visualised finale where social and class issues merge with individual situations. An ironical reversal presents Sir Marcus, the manipulator of lives, as 'a very old, sick man with a little wisp of white beard on his chin resembling chicken fluff':

> He gave the effect of having withered inside his clothes like a kernel in a nut. He spoke with the faintest foreign accent and it was difficult to determine whether he was Jewish or of an ancient English family. He gave the impression that very many cities had rubbed him smooth. If there was a touch of Jerusalem there was also a touch of St James's, if of some Central European capital, there were also marks of the most exclusive clubs in Cannes (p. 107).

The text presents the exploiter as both individual and representative of a social class. When Raven enters the office of Midland Steel concealed in a gas mask it is left to him to expose Sir Marcus to an ultimately uncaring Establishment. His fury at being cheated of his legitimate 'fee', and at being framed turns to outrage when he realises the innocence of his victims and the extent of the corruption into which he has been implicated:

'I wouldn't have done it . . . if I'd known the old man was like he was. I smashed his skull for him. And the old woman, a bullet in both eyes.' He shouted at Sir Marcus, 'That was your doing. How do you like that?' but the old man sat there apparently unmoved; old age had killed the imagination. The deaths he had ordered were no more than the deaths he read about in the newspapers (p. 165).

The subversion of the content of the traditional adventure form reaches its apotheosis in *A Gun for Sale* with the themes of heroic action, violence, the exploiter and the exploited, courage and hope explored at various levels. The empire of capitalism is exposed with a hero who is ugly and deformed. His only sense of purpose is provoked by a deep and sullen rage rather than by heroism; his courage is despair. The description of Sir Marcus lifts him out of nationality and race to make him the embodiment of the forces of exploitation that are a continuing element of contemporary life. The trade in armaments by vested interests – individuals at the time, individual Governments today – was as real at the time as it is today with the threat of war that pervades society.

* * *

If war and disorder without are the manifestations of the fight with the intimate enemy within, the tragedy is essentially one of the human condition, a theme that is worked out fully and poignantly in *Brighton Rock* (1938). The clearly visualised detail of this novel evokes more than any other the constraints of existence as well as the transient pleasures of urban masses, their wistful attempts at fun and the whole phenomenon of the need for escape. Varieties of escape deepen the poignancy of the story of Pinkie and Rose. Bank holiday crowds, innocent and bewildered, rush determinedly to have a good day as they step into 'the fresh and glittering air' and jostle against gangsters and small-time fall guys. A generalised picture of fun and pleasure that illustrates escape from routine is paralleled by escape via murder and retribution, to underscore the horror of life, the duplicity of the law, and the need to escape from it all. Greene has conceded that he has chosen to accentuate only one face of Brighton in order to achieve full thematic power, in a narrative that recreates escape from routine, from boredom and from institutionalised hypocrisy.

For the holidaying crowds Brighton is new, shiny, and bright with surface joy; the band playing, flower gardens neatly laid out, vanishing clouds. It is relief from routine, escape from care into the 'early morning sun', into 'the cool Whitsun wind off the sea', with the slow delicious lick of sticks of Brighton rock as they extricate 'with immense labour and immense patience from the long day the grain of pleasure'. That the escape is limited and time-bound is suggested by sentences such as this: 'this sun, this music, the rattle of the miniature cars, the ghost train diving between the grinning skeletons under the aquarium promenade, the sticks of Brighton rock, the paper sailor caps . . . '.[28] Soon the party must end.

That *Brighton Rock* was a seminal influence is too well known to need elaboration. In her discussion of the novel in 1966 for the series 'How Well Have they Worn?' in *The Times* Marghanita Laski stresses the contemporaneity of the environment: 'If that was what our world was like in 1938, few of us saw it so then. Rather we recognise it as the way we see much of our world today.' She comments on the environmental horror of *1984*, on Orwell's role in swinging intellectual interest in the 'pastimes of the people from the wheelwright's shop to the culture of the seaside postcard', and concludes that already, in 1938, Greene had assimilated these new angles of vision into the art of *Brighton Rock*.[29]

Many of Greene's characters live in surroundings that are squalid and shabby in conditions of gross underprivilege that range from the flapping gutters of Paradise Piece (*Brighton Rock*) to the mosquito-infested shacks in Mexico (*The Power and the Glory*). In fact, the fiction viewed as a whole can be said to project the experience of poverty and deprivation, injustice and cruelty, and the devastations effected by temporal power, in a set of parallel patterns that encompass the world. Jim Drover and his family in London, Raven in London, Pinkie in Brighton, Coral Musker looking for a job from London to Istanbul are as much victims as the homeless in Mexico, the destitute in Haiti, and the hungry in Paraguay. The fiction is a consistent exposure of the capitalist system to suggest that exploitation is more subtle and sophisticated, and its influence more extensive. That the situation remains unchanged is suggested in Greene's comments with reference to his non-fiction book, *J'Accuse* (1982) which exposes corruption in high places: ' I cannot write a novel about this situation. I have already written it in 1938: *Brighton Rock*'.

Much of this thought is projected by way of a visible landscape, often a repetitive picture in that Greene's selection of detail is conditioned by his world view. This is not to say that these realities should be dismissed as the obsessions of a 'Catholic' novelist with a pessimistic view of the world. Man is bounded by a merciless sky, by soulless masses of concrete construction, and is a component of the push-button civilisation. The novels focus insistently on urban life as affected by consumerism, multinational systems and business empires that create a climate for 'meanness, malice and snobbery' that dispels the dream of England. Such a framework places in a cosmic perspective the demands of the working class for greater control over their lives without trivialising their rights or obfuscating them in a high-minded contemplation of eternal truths and verities.

Rose finds escape from her loveless home in her first job; she is 'running away from things, running towards things' (p. 49). Will she ever escape the slum altogether? This theme runs through the novel and is accentuated by the innocent fun of crowds, the gaiety of Ida, and by Rose's experience which she shares with Pinkie, the teenage criminal who struggles to fight the world that exploits him. The novel contains very little detail of Pinkie's underprivileged childhood except his disgust with parental activity in 'the room at the bend of the stairs where Saturday night exercises had taken place' (p. 90).

Despite this lack of detail, Pinkie's situation comes alive with the cry of pain and despair, anger and violent revolt. The focus on Rose's ramshackle home, on Pinkie striving to preserve the purity of his territory inside Frank's corner house with the crumb-strewn bed, the dirt and the smells, illuminates layers of reality to explore ultimately man's capacity for cruelty. It is not Pinkie's Catholicism that gives him his sure knowledge of hell; it is his experience of it in his life. This parallel construction lends depth and tension to what is perhaps Greene's best novel. Pinkie's unshakeable belief in hell contributes to the exposure of a social milieu where Colleoni, the Mafia boss, enjoys police protection, where the small crook goes hungry and is chased and destroyed while the establishments connive to cover up bigger crimes.

The whole weight of an inescapable menace is contained in the opening line of the novel: 'Hale knew before he had been in Brighton three hours, that they meant to murder him'. The sentence has a ring of doom, of suspense and terror. These elements are juxtaposed alongside the happy crowd among whom he moves. The private hell of Pinkie's life is suggested by the glossy world that shuts him out: a parade of posh hotels, acres of deep carpet, the American Bar, the Louis Seize waiting room, the Pompadour Boudoir, Mr Colleoni in double-breasted waistcoat, gold cigarette lighter in hand, talking to Pinkie in threadbare coat. Chasms divide them. Heat, dust, the smell of bottled beer, cheap one-night stands, grubby hand with slashing razor confronts expansive good humour, grapes, flowers, and the total impregnability of the man who appears to 'own the whole world, Parliament and the Law' (p. 65). It may seem like a juxtaposition of extremes, and a generalising overview yet such symbolic representation brings home the truth of these realities.

Power, exploitation, excess on the one hand confront underprivilege, despair, sincerity and vulnerability on the other. As in *The Man Within* the legal and the moral underscore the cruelty of Pinkie, the legal offender when the novel opens, in relation to the moral offences of an establishment that threatens to wipe him out and is justified in doing so because of his legal offences. His killing of Hale which is a moral offence, and his meanness and cruelty to Rose, in particular, are part of a design intended to create a character that is worthy of damnation. But the text betrays the author's purpose and Pinkie's stifled cry of pain redeems him. The boy-hero trapped by poverty, and sucked into a criminal world mediates the idea of social injustice far more clearly than the idea of sin.

Greene is less interested in the development of character than in determining in all their complexity the forces that shape life and motivate action. The social sin of injustice and exploitation underlie the 'evil' actions of Pinkie. Nowhere does the power of these forces, both socioeconomic and spiritual, come alive more vividly than in *Brighton Rock*. The world from which Pinkie would like to escape is cold and insensitive, hollow and selfish. Its landscape is visualised in brief phrases that encapsulate material values: women with 'bright brassy hair', 'painted polished nails', who cackle 'metallic confidences'; young men 'in huge motoring coats' accompany 'small tinted creatures who rang like expensive glass when they were touched but who conveyed the impression of being as sharp and tough as tin' (p. 69). The choice of words suggest the brittle, hard and unfeeling nature and the ephemeral gloss of materialism. Such passages echo a cry for a pristine world, a world of innocence, which pervades all Greene's work.

Brighton Rock was the first of Greene's novels to be spotted as 'Catholic'. It took him ten years, he once said, after his conversion to Catholicism, to understand enough about Catholics to be able to write about them. Even so, Catholic dogma exists in the novel as part of the motivating machinery of a political novel. Its discussion of good and evil dramatises the struggle of Pinkie in this world and hell exists in relation to the social condition of his life. Orwell did not comment favourably on this aspect of the novel:

> In Brighton Rock . . . the central situation is incredible since it presupposes that the most brutishly stupid person can, merely by having been brought up a Catholic, be capable of greater intellectual subtlety. Pinkie the racecourse gangster, is a species of satanist, while his still more limited girlfriend understands and even states the difference between the categories 'right and wrong' and 'good and evil'.[30]

Yet, Brighton Rock is not a theological discussion nor an intellectual positing of these ideas but a living representation of the way society functions and human action is evaluated. Legal offences – Pinkie is a 'race-course gangster' – are set alongside moral offences: exploitation by Colleoni and the responsibility of social institutions that protect him. Pinkie's legal offence leads to the killing which is both a legal and a moral offence. His death at the end of the novel is thus retribution which, as the priest suggests, a merciful God may view in a different light. Ida is concerned with Pinkie as a legal offender, and hence the emphasis on right and wrong. She understands the law and Pinkie has broken the law. The morality of action does not affect her and this is illustrated with considerable irony in her enjoyment of the thrill of the chase that leads to Pinkie's death. She seeks 'enjoyment' – the Ouida board, sex, the bar, betting on a winning horse, hunting Pinkie down – yet these pursuits suggest limitations far greater then Pinkie's brutishness and Rose's simplicity. Angus Wilson commenting on the novel shows himself to be the more perceptive interpreter of what the text reveals:

It was 1938. A time when we all needed painful truths that would stick. Did not want easy answers that would fade after they had jogged us along a little. We all needed a confirmation of the civil forces that were manifesting themselves. Needed to realise, and more important to feel, something deeper than just right and wrong, good guys and rotten eggs. The world of that big – both hearted and breasted – decent, sensible, no-nonsense woman, Ida Arnold, was not going to be enough. Ida it was, I think, that first gave me the sense that Graham Greene's novels had a depth that was unknown to the novel of that day which was also a good story.

Rose, it is true, was a moving martyr; Pinkie, irredeemably evil. But the insufficiency of Ida's no-nonsense good sense, her certainty of right and wrong as the limit of the depths of the human spirit, was, as I remember it, hard to take in a world clinging to optimism; yet the final conviction was total.

The realisation that jog-along decency, human justice, right or wrong as being enough, just couldn't satisfy was, as I have found discussing the novel with many many people, a moment of truth all the stronger because Ida was so real.

Added to this, of course, was Mr Greene's extraordinary power of plot-making, of suspense and of narration that moves continuously both in time and space and in emotion. In *Brighton Rock*, I found for the first time that I could obtain from the same modern novel the simple pleasures of a good read and the exciting demand of a novel of great depth.

It did not mean that the excitement of the experimental novels of our century were not as important as they seemed, but it did mean that so much that had been vital to my enjoyment in boyhood was now open to me again in young manhood, and, not as I had thought, to be found only by a return to the masters of the last century.[31]

The inner life of Pinkie and Rose illustrates the dimension that Ida lacks, and Catholicism enables Greene to mediate these truths. The narrative explores the working of social institutions and the importance of the religious sense in the context of social relations. It is their religious sense that gives Pinkie and Rose the courage to face life even if the confrontation is presented as an escape. For in escaping from life's realities Greene's youthful pair are, indeed, facing them at the deepest level.

Rose hoped to escape the drudgeries of her life through her marriage to Pinkie. Her trust is complete and does not waver when she comes to realise that he is a fugitive from justice. All earthly logic and human philosophy should have prompted her to leave him but there is a deeper call that binds her to him: a loyalty and compassion, and a sense that even though he is apparently depraved there is a spirit in him to which she responds and which transcends the commonsense, material world whose safety Ida offers her. For Greene evil is a summation of social wrong and institutional injustice which deprives people like Pinkie of human sensibilities. Although the narrative loads the character of Pinkie to make him worthy of damnation, the world of various levels of power and insensitivity around Pinkie redeems him, so that the reader is inclined to agree that 'between the stirrup and the ground' Pinkie's humanity is restored. These elements impart a strong religious sense and the externals which Greene imposes of sin, damnation, right and wrong, good and evil, may be taken only as pointers and can be discarded once the deeper implications of the novel are comprehended in its exploration of despair and want, the yearnings for love and compassion.

The novel unfolds problems relating to society but resolves them in terms of the eternal dimension. To be diverted by the dramatic intensity of the theological overlay contributed by the theme of good and evil is to sidestep the main issue: Pinkie's cruelty even if satanic and Rose's limited perception are to be evaluated in relation to Colleoni's less visible cruelty and Ida's motherly, ethical concern which lacks compassion.

Though the characterisation of Rose does not develop she springs to life within the context of the narrative as representing a life of total risk, of the courage to live precariously and to reject the safety that Ida offers her. To choose that safety entails her betrayal of Pinkie which, in Greene's view, would be the greater offence. Later she breaks religious codes and the sum of all these actions illustrates the meaning of freedom and self-realisation in the context of the pressures of social injustice, and repression.

The theme of good and evil has distracted critical discussion from the main issues. As in *The Man Within* the novel reveals that the enforcement of the law, and human beings abiding by the law do not in themselves constitute a just society, or a moral life. Catholic belief mediates these truths and is intended as in all Greene's fiction where it is introduced overtly to dramatise and elucidate a discourse on political realities and moral values.

3
The Religious Sense

The Power and the Glory (1940) marks a development in Greene's writing: it explores moral values beyond frontiers previously perceived. The shift to the symbolic language of Catholic orthodoxy, the change of scene from England and Europe to Mexico, the return to Sierra Leone during the war, and the new contexts of the postwar world lead Greene's artistic imagination to realities outside England and in modern Europe eventually resting the scene within the framework of world politics. Experience of political and spiritual realities in Mexico resulted in keener understanding of the meaning of faith. He writes:

> I read and listened to stories of corruption which were said to have justified the persecution of the Church under Calles and Cardenas, but I also observed for myself how courage and the sense of responsibility had revived with persecution – I had seen the devotion of peasants praying in the priestless churches and I had attended Masses in upper rooms where the sanctus bell could not sound for fear of the police.[1]

Kingsley Martin's review of *The Lawless Roads* noted Greene's ability to communicate the essential spirit of Catholicism, a 'living Church'.[2] These aspects of the church and religion in lived experience, are discussed here.

The Power and the Glory (1940), *The Heart of the Matter*(1948), *The End of the Affair* (1955) and *A Burnt-Out Case* (1961) have been grouped together because they represent an evocation of the religious sense. Greene regrets its loss in the English novel in his essay on François Mauriac:

> with the death of Henry James the religious sense was lost to the English novel, and with the religious sense went the sense of the importance of the human act. It was as if the world of fiction had lost a dimension: the characters of such distinguished writers as Mrs Virginia Woolf and Mr E. M. Forster wandered like cardboard

symbols through a world that was paper-thin. Even in one of the most materialistic of our great novelists – Trollope – we are aware of another world against which the actions of the characters are thrown into relief. . . The novelist, perhaps unconsciously aware of his predicament, took refuge in the subjective novel. It was as if he thought that by mining into layers of personality hitherto untouched he could unearth the secret of 'importance', but in these mining operations he lost yet another dimension. The visible world for him ceased to exist as completely as the spiritual.[3]

The Power and the Glory (1940) has a Catholic priest as protagonist in confrontation with a representative of the State whose official ideology has no place for religion. Belief then is part of the structure of the text. Scobie in *The Heart of the Matter* (1948) is a convert to Catholicism; Sarah in *The End of the Affair* (1955) has been baptised but is not aware of the fact and does not practise her religion until quite late in the novel when she renounces the world, as it were, to return to her God. Querry in *A Burnt-Out Case* (1961) says he has 'retired from Catholicism' but the novel itself is described by Greene as 'an attempt to give dramatic expression to various types of belief, half-belief, and non-belief'.[4] Except for *The Burnt-Out Case* the novels are structured within religious belief, and all four reveal faith as expressed within social relations. The protagonists share a set of *a priori* values in various degrees with the difference that their awareness of orthodoxy burdens the Priest and Scobie. Their acceptance of received wisdom, however, acquires meaning only when it is tested in individual experience.

The novels grouped here are primarily concerned with man's inner life and its expression in the routine of living. In *The Power and the Glory* political revolution with the Church under threat intensifies the discourse begun in the early novels in a more specific confrontation; it introduces the dialectic between socialist ideals and a spiritual dimension to life which underlies much of Greene's work. *A Burnt-Out Case* set in a leproserie attempts the reverse. Greene here places his characters quite deliberately in a setting 'removed from world-politics and household preoccupations'.[5] The most significant departure occurs in *The Heart of the Matter* which is set in Africa but apparently ignores the colonial situation in order to focus on an internalised conflict. The scene for *The End of the Affair* is what Anthony Burgess calls 'the jungle of the Blitz',[6] but the war provides only the central incident for a moving and true expression of feeling.

The artistic merit of these novels, often discussed in terms of the intensity of spiritual anguish portrayed, lies in the subtlety with which the story-line coheres with the exploration of moral values expressed in a movement from belief to faith and accomplished through exposure of the protagonist to life's constraints. The experience creates questioning, self-consciousness, and a search. Though the expression of religious feeling is confined to a Catholic structure of belief the novels encompass values held commonly by any spiritual vision of life. In the spirit of Cardinal Newman's discourse on the 'Bearing of Theology on Other Knowledge' Graham Greene, though writing as a Catholic, does not presume Catholicism is true but uses Catholic language to comprehend man and society. Indeed the novels reveal what Cardinal Newman calls 'the Science of God' by eschewing polemics of any kind:

> for instance, what are called 'the Evidences of Religion', or 'the Christian Evidences'; for, though these constitute a science supplemental to Theology and are necessary in their place, they are not Theology itself, unless an army is synonymous with the body politic. Nor . . . that vague thing called 'Christianity' or 'our common Christianity', or 'Christianity, the law of the land', if there is any man alive who can tell what it is . . . I simply mean the Science of God.[7]

Ideals of justice, freedom and responsibility as essential elements relate the spiritual quest to the tensions of modern living. The narrative construct reveals a world in which 'behind the veil of the visible universe there is an invisible intelligible Being, acting on and through it, as and when He will'.[8] A life of action, or a choice imposed as much by the pressure of events as by the values underlying individual belief illumine religious truth as belief in a God who is infinite yet personal, eternal yet immanent in space and time. Evil is not from Him because 'evil has no substance of its own, but is only the defect, excess, perversion, or corruption of that which has substance'.[9]

The novels are deep and poignant precisely because they evoke the religious sense as defined above within intellectual, moral, social and political life in the world today. Each of the novels explores the man/God relationship in here-and-now confrontations with social, political and religious institutions. These cover interpersonal, professional and political relationships thereby accentuating the links in the human chain and the fact that modern man lives in an interdependent world. Preoccupation with religious belief thus adds a dimension to the novels of the middle years, a dimension first seen in *Brighton Rock*. The spiritual journey of the protagonist becomes a major theme, not the variety of orthodoxy. When externalised such experience enlarges the scope of fiction from concerns that are immediate, social and transient to those that are permanent, universal and transcendent and thereby define the religious sense.

The God of Greene's religion is a merciful God, the source of all love; a Being who is 'the Supreme Good, or has all the attributes of Good in infinite intenseness'.[10] As a convert to Catholicism, he is not burdened by the traditions of theology, the weight of dogma which is why sin is so effortlessly and artfully externalised. François Mauriac sums up Greene's belief and art:

What I find most authentic in Greene's novels is Grace . . . [it is the] Truth that man does not know. With his English education and Protestant tradition he sees this truth in a light altogether different from the one we, French Catholics, are familiar with, coming as we do from a Jansenist tradition. He enables us to rediscover Christian faith; his solutions to the problems posed by Grace and salvation are free from the rigid categories of our theologians and our casuists. The liberty he grants to God over mankind is at once terrifying and reassuring because, at the final count, God is love and if nothing is possible to man, everything is possible to Eternal love.[11]

This sense of freedom with which Greene approaches Catholicism paradoxically makes his evocation of the spiritual more real. The novels attempt an expression of faith and the moral imperatives implicit in humanity through the use of confession, sacrilegious communion, and what one may be permitted to call the 'externals' or the 'apparatus' of belief.[12] Through dogma, orthodoxy and their subversion the narrative symbolically expresses what Cardinal Newman calls 'the nearest approximation of truth which our condition admits'. Sin and guilt are recreated in order to emphasise the moral order, the religious sense, and self-realisation.

It is tempting but misleading to discuss the novels as representing a 'neo-Manichean heresy'. Anthony Burgess suggests that the implied doctrines of the novels approach Jansenism, which has been repeatedly condemned by Rome:

In Jansen, original sin was not mere 'imputation': it expressed itself in the depravation of nature (whose order was, contrary to official teaching, distinct from the supernatural order), in appetite and in concupiscence. The horror of the natural world is one of the most fascinating aspects of Greene's fiction. Sin is not cool and intellectual matter for theological dissertations: sin is expressed in the joyless sex of *Brighton Rock*, with its broken toenails in the bed; the curious landscape of *The Power and the Glory*; the hell of Haiti in *The Comedians*.[13]

Such discussion is helpful but, if pursued, the interpretation muddies Greene's radical comprehension of religion in life. He has little patience for discussion of orthodoxies and says those that call him a Jansenist 'have not read theology. Mauriac is closer to Jansenism'.[14] Greene's vision of fallen man is not pessimistic – faith is made to transcend despair in a complex and ambiguous way and his novels offer something better than symbol or allegory. They offer life itself where the transgressions of the protagonists bring them face to face with God. Of the real presence of God, says George D. Painter in his review of *The Heart of the Matter* 'there has been no more authoritative statement in the modern novel'.[15]

The power of this evocation has not a little to do with the landscape inhabited by the characters. In trying to suggest mankind's fallen condition the experience transmuted in the novels is overshadowed by the appalling vision of mankind living on an 'abandoned star'. His characters live 'in a vast abandonment' under 'a merciless sky' that does not protect them from the intimate enemy. Such separation between a merciful God and fallen man is not merely stated. The narrative exploits life's choices to suggest the working of fate which nullifies human propositions and extends the discourse to human experience which reaches beyond time into eternity. When this happens, as it often does, it is easy to confuse the real for an externalisation of the metaphysical, which indeed it also is. Landscape, thus, is often made to function as metaphor for theme and has no doubt contributed to the term 'Greeneland'. In externalising the concept of original sin Greene creates a world that is dark and despairing, from whose depths emerges the redemptive power of love.

The shifts of reality to areas of economic deprivation, social upheaval and political strife reinforces the fallen spiritual condition of man and simultaneously accentuates man-made evil. Is this purely a device to dramatise spiritual struggle? Can one argue with Anthony Burgess that the 'Jansenist in him is led to the places where the squalor of sin is exposed in its rawest forms' and that Greene moves away from parochial England in search of a suitable stage for the enactment of spiritual drama?[16] I would prefer to concur with George Woodcock who discusses Greene's portrayal of spiritual struggle along with his concern with the actual violence of human life. The struggle is a moral conflict, even more than the conflict of a soul and is 'centred in the relationships of men'.[17]

Hell lies about man in his infancy as in the case of Andrews, Raven, Pinkie, Rose – the protagonists of the early novels. The fruit of knowledge is 'the ugly cry of birth' and betrayal is exposure to human relationships. Associational patterns link the Fall with the trap of existence. Man is condemned to existence:

> by a judge just as [men] are condemned to prison. They have no choice, no escape. They have been put behind bars for life . . . So [Leon Rivas] sits on the floor of his cell and [tries] to make some sense of things . . . [He is] no theologian (p. 221).

This quotation from *The Honorary Consul* (1973) is apposite because it emphasises the direction of the artistic vision in a search for being within the constraints of routine existence without separating experience as religious, social and political. Greene's work integrates these elements to create a composite view of life in the world in which freedom, justice and a spiritual dimension to life are imperatives. The first expression of this view of identity is the juxtaposition of the lieutenant and the priest in *The Power and the Glory*; the priest's gradual self-realisation in the cell amid criminality, sexual promiscuity and complacent piety gives him a perception of faith he lacked when free and secure. The conversations between Leon Rivas and Eduardo Plarr in *The Honorary Consul* similarly isolated from 'respectable' society in a little hut develops the idea of faith and political consciousness. Greene writes in his introduction to the Collected edition of *Brighton Rock* (1970) that his work since those years reflects his concern with the meaning of faith in relation to action. The discussion finally comes to rest in the more comradely dialectic of *Monsignor Quixote* where humanity is defined by subverting ideology and orthodoxy.

The protagonist of *The Honorary Consul* epitomises ideas as embodied in a Greene hero whose evolution began with the social outcast of the early fiction. The development of intellectual convictions, of 'the will to believe' draws the fiction into orthodoxy but its rigours are interpreted: the lawbreaker becomes the sinner to illustrate human values and the true meaning of social justice. Religious law in the context of life generates an awareness and it is in their consciousness of transgression that the protagonists realise their humanity. Terry Eagleton argues that the result of this tension is a striking paradox:

> Greene's protagonists turn, at the risk of damnation, from a soul-saving theology to the insidious pressures of humanity, but only in the context of a continually undermining disbelief in the final validity of such claims. Orthodox Catholicism is denied in the name of 'humanism'; yet that humanism is itself critically qualified by traditionally Catholic ways of feeling. The upshot of this is a kind of deadlock: the human value of men like Scobie or the whisky priest lies in their readiness to reject an orthodoxy in which they nevertheless continue to believe; yet to acknowledge the superior truth of that orthodoxy, in the act of refusing it, is to confront the inadequacy of the sheerly human commitments they embrace.[18]

My interpretation of the novels suggests that Greene uses orthodoxy to develop a symbolic language which deepens the texture of the narrative and arrives at the truth of human experience, at the realities of politics and faith. The novels consistently relate orthodoxy and ideology to experience in order to reinforce a commitment to the ideals underlying them. Eagleton reveals the paradox at the heart of Greene's work; it is a paradox which underpins the human condition – the constraints, legalities and rituals which often make a mockery of ideals they are meant to preserve. Greene's novels subvert orthodox Catholicism not to deny it but to emphasise humanism. Both the code and the truth encoded are thus revealed and the revelation takes place when the code is broken but this does not invalidate or deny the code. The novels appeal because such a recreation of the religious sense in fact transcends any particular religion.

Life acquires meaning with recognition of a spiritual dimension. The structure of Catholicism does not uphold its theology but helps to signify what it means to be human and to express faith in man's capacity to realise himself. Transgressions which are both religious and moral – the priest's responsibility for his illegitimate daughter, Scobie's responsibility for the murder of Ali – attract retribution and the moral life is defined in various ways including the illustration of it in Querry's rejection of material success, and in Sarah's sacrifice. Her self-denial leads her into realisation of self. In this sense *The End of the Affair* is Greene's most religious novel for it depends less on orthodoxy than on the intensity of Sarah's inner life.

* * *

Belief is inseparable from characterisation in the four novels discussed here. They are peopled by believers and non-believers. *The Power and the Glory* (1940), where the human aspect of priesthood is an important theme, illustrates individual struggle with two sets of apparently contradictory beliefs juxtaposed and realises the conflict through protagonists who are nameless. They are known only by their roles – the priest and the lieutenant – and are presented with the integrity characteristic of Greene's fiction which is fair to both sides. Parallel construction enhances the irony of a situation where the lieutenant is endowed with a moral character and sense of purpose traditionally associated with priesthood, Greene writes:

> As for the idealism of my lieutenant it was sadly lacking among these shabby revolutionaries . . . I had not found the integrity of the lieutenant among the police and *pistoleros* I had encountered – I had to invent him as a counter to the failed priest: the idealistic police officer who stifled life from the best possible motives; the drunken priest who continued to pass life on.[19]

An important feature of *The Power and the Glory* is that it expresses a confrontation between the themes of social justice and faith. Greene's later novels attempt to resolve these tensions by integrating the theme of personal faith with political struggle. But here religion and politics, the Church and the State, are in opposite camps. The priest is a member of the establishment to be wiped out so that social justice can prevail; the lieutenant, member of another establishment, leads the crusade.

Their awareness of the unfair demands of their professional duties balances the contrast between the priest and the lieutenant. Both hate the role and feel enslaved by the demands of office: The priest is 'shaken by a tiny rage' and feels 'a monstrous bitterness' at being denied the chance to escape to freedom when a child requests that he attend his sick mother. The pressures of existence stretch the demands of duty to limits neither anticipated. The narrative elaborates qualities which differentiate the hunter from the hunted – pride and humility, confidence and fear – until in the final chapters the two antagonists face each other as human beings, and shed briefly the trappings of the role each has endured.

The priest first appears as he

> sat there like a question mark, ready to go, ready to stay, poised on the chair. He looked disreputable in his grey three-days beard, and weak . . . [he had] an air in his hollowness and neglect, of somebody of no account who had been beaten up incidentally, by ill-health and restlessness – dark suit, sloping shoulders, serious mouth.[20]

Later he is 'in torn peasant clothes', 'a man in a shabby drill suit' with his 'eyes to the ground and the shoulders hunched as though he felt exposed' (p. 20). In contrast the lieutenant walks proud; a dapper figure

> whose gaiters were polished and his pistol holster; his buttons were all sewn on. He had a sharp crooked nose jutting out of a lean dancer's face; his neatness gave an effect of inordinate ambition in the shabby city (p. 20).

The purity of their ideal and the questionable conduct with which they pursue it – the lieutenant through violence and repression, the priest through dissolution – heightens the parallel characterisation. Human inadequacy and the claims of duty are vividly juxtaposed when the priest is on the run with the lieutenant in pursuit. He emerges famished and exhausted by sleeplessness at a little village where his arrival is greeted with a mixture of fear and relief by the villagers; they fear the reprisals should the presence of the priest in their midst be betrayed but are glad of the opportunity to participate in ritual that the law has denied them. Dazed with fatigue, hunger and lack of sleep, in fact in a state of semi-consciousness he finds himself compelled to hear the confession of a whole village whose members have sheltered him for the night. Even though some of these details exaggerate the practice of believers to incredible limits, the irony in these sections contributes to the power of the narrative.

It links idea and action: the priest as human being and in his role as the last priest in the region; as the last hope amid the hopeless who, paradoxically, do not give up hope; the intangibles of faith that compel the villagers to risk the lives of able-bodied men to protect the priest; the realities of survival that involve both parties to this relationship in a surreal haggling over 'fees' to be paid by the impoverished 'congregation' to the equally deprived priest.

The demands of his profession burden the lieutenant equally. As he walks in front of his men he appears 'chained to them unwillingly – perhaps the scar on his jaw was the relic of an escape' (p. 20). His superior, like that of the priest, fails in his role: the Bishop escapes to safety; the Chief of Police takes his duties lightly, concerning himself with toothache rather than with the struggle for a just society, and reveals himself as the best customer for illicit liquor. *The Honorary Consul* extends these themes – the Bishop and the Dictator dine together and the two establishments, it is suggested, work in collusion.

Greene calls *The Power and the Glory* a pilgrimage and there are flashbacks along the journey to a time when the priest acted out his role in a state of freedom as a respected member of society. He was then

> a youngish man in Roman collar . . . You could imagine him petted with small delicacies . . . He sat there, plump, with pro-tuberant eyes, bubbling with harmless feminine jokes . . . a well-shaved, well-powdered jowl much too developed for his age. The good things of life had come to him too early (pp. 21–2).

Pursued by his conscience, by fear of God and of the law, the priest descends to abysmal depths. He becomes not merely a whisky priest but a cowering animal who simultaneously attains a comprehension of his humanity with a relentless consciousness of his own actions.

Contrasts other than the major one with the lieutenant accentuate his predicament. The first of these, the idealised portrait of a martyred priest whose story is carefully integrated into the main story-line, is recounted by a pious mother to her children. The narrative tone emphasises the unreality of this tale with its emphasis on saintliness and superhuman sacrifice rather than human inadequacy and courage. The young son rejects so hallowed a vision of heroism; his little sisters lap it up as they would a fairy tale; life, says the narrative voice, is not like that. Spiritual values must be grounded in life and action and not in remote visions of martyrdom and eternal glory. The life of Padre José, who satisfies the demands of the State by getting married, provides the second contrast. The narrative does not deride the frailty of the whisky priest and of Padre José but presents their experience as means for human qualities to surface. It helps them to transcend roles, to grow into self-knowledge, and to proceed from belief to faith. The extent of the moral decline of the priest opens the way to self-realisation and enables him to perceive his own earlier complacency when he was free to practise his religion in security and comfort. When he is cast into prison he finds a sense of companionship which he had never experienced in the old days when pious people came kissing his black cotton glove. Later, when he finds a safe place to stay he catches himself slipping into the old habits where values are often platitudes and belief a habit of piety:

> He could hear authority, the old parish intonation coming back into his voice, as if the last years had been a dream and he had never really been away from the Guilds, the Children of Mary, and the daily Mass (p. 167).

The narrative in *The Power and the Glory* follows the descent of the priest into a life of humiliation and degradation when he is pursued both by his own weakness and by the power of the Socialist Republic that has declared a war on religion. It is less important to ask why he has chosen to stay behind and face persecution when he could so easily have escaped than to understand that Greene does not intend his character to die a martyr in the idealised and ritualised sense: such heroic action is not the stuff of common experience. The disintegration of the priest when the supportive structures are destroyed leads to the question of faith and to the revelation that it is not the structure that gives meaning to the role but faith. Paradoxically, only the denial of both structure and role creates a self-awareness in the individual. The death of the priest at the end is not intended as martyrdom but as retribution for moral lapses, a fact of which the priest is well aware.

The lieutenant, in contrast, is left unsullied to the last. His spartan nature, single-minded vision of socialism, and high level of personal integrity does not seem to conflict with the violent course of his actions. When he faces the priest as human being without his

Roman collar, the characters spring to life with all the complexities of human response. For example, the lieutenant breaks his official code when he gives the priest, whom he has not recognised, some money for food and shelter when he leaves the prison for the first time. More poignantly, the second encounter reveals the lieutenant offering to fetch Padre José, should he agree, to hear the priest's last confession. He also smuggles some brandy into the cell so as to make the priest's last night before his execution comfortable. In breaking professional codes the actions emphasise human values of the two protagonists.

The lieutenant's passion for justice and a better society for the children he encounters on the streets is as deep as the priest's terrified acceptance of faith. But the triumphs of his role give him neither joy nor peace. To him belongs the honour of seeing the 'last' priest in the State put to death, yet his success leaves him feeling empty. His struggle for justice in society awakens him to a different perspective of justice and human ties in the relationship he establishes with the priest, his prisoner. The patterns of thought and the movement of the narrative cohere with powerful intensity which makes this Greene's most effective evocation of some of the themes that permeate his work.

Greene uses the techniques of dream narration to fill in gaps. Two dreams at the end of *The Power and the Glory* deepen the main thematic concerns of social justice. The structure of text and idea jointly suggest the meaning of faith in life and of religion in the context of human relationships. Physically and morally exhausted by his pursuit of the priest, subconsciously undermined by his role as purger of human beings supposedly inimical to the State, the lieutenant falls asleep and dreams. All he can recall of the dream is 'nothing but laughter, laughter all the time, and a long passage in which he could find no door' (p. 207). The dream is nihilistic and our view of the lieutenant that of a man with a final sensation of void. After purifying the State for socialism 'the dynamic love which used to move his trigger finger felt flat and dead' – Greene's final answer to ideologies devoid of spiritual dimensions.

It would be wrong to conclude, however, that the narrative accepts the premises of the Catholic Church and its authority on human conduct as final. The priest's dream is equally radical in its impact precisely because it subverts accepted codes. In his dream Coral Fellows, the child who once sheltered him, appears to help him in the same responsible and wise manner as she had once protected him from the lieutenant. Her efforts this time fulfil his most basic needs: food and drink. They talk in their private language – the Morse Code – which Coral tries to teach him. The message encoded is love and trust among men. There is a Mass in progress but the whisky priest is oblivious of the priest at the altar. All he can see clearly is the child who feeds him and teaches him Morse. Her taps are echoed by an invisible congregation and the message of this private language is decoded by Coral. The narrative line here authenticates the importance of human connections without which neither belief nor ideology have any meaning. Greene considers *The Power and the Glory* his most successful attempt at myth-making. The reason is clear: the plot is subsidiary, at all times, to the central idea of belief and struggle; the one flows from the other and it is the passionate illustration of the idea as expressed in life that gives the novel its legend.

*   *   *

The Heart of the Matter[21] and *The End of the Affair* extend the scope of belief by expressing it in social and personal relations. In *The Heart of the Matter* Scobie, the Assistant Commissioner of Police in Freetown, Sierra Leone, commits a series of transgressions for reasons that are more complex than can be explained away by the given fact that he is easily moved to pity. The novel does not explore the unnatural condition of his work, his awareness of the contradictions which he embodies in his professional life as arbiter of law and order when his very presence in Sierra Leone rests on an unjust premise and hence 'the futility of all effort'. The text in fact is stripped of all ideologies and the character of Scobie examined both in terms of his professional role and as human being inexorably divesting himself of the diktats of religion and society to live, as he thinks, a moral life by discharging his responsibilities.

Greene's grasp of life in society contributes to action that weaves personal life with the colonial situation and the larger international framework of the war. Scobie's actions are impelled as much by the pressure of events as by his character. The result is a complex portrayal of a weak but heroic man who betrays shades of moral superiority and allows himself to be overwhelmed by the demands of human relationships. This leads to transgressions of professional, moral and religious codes. What is worse is that all who come in close contact with him are more or less tainted by his perception of them as objects of pity or scorn. The only exceptions are Ali, the black boy who has served him loyally for fifteen years and whom he loves, and Yusef, the trader and diamond smuggler, whose oily self-assurance elicits no pity.

The novel introduces Scobie after fifteen years of colonial service, a man broken by the circumstances of his life – the death of an only child, and the lack of communication with his wife. The fact that he is just and has proved incorruptible is represented as just another burden of 'reputation'; his daughter's death is revealed gradually, with understatement, although its inexorable consequences provide much of the psychological motivation in the narrative. Scobie's first transgression – he destroys the letter he confiscates from the Portuguese ship instead of handing it in, and begins a whole chain of lies to cover up the transgression – takes place because he is disorientated as a result of a conversation that takes place in the Captain's cabin. When appealing to Scobie for help the Captain discloses that the letter is addressed to his daughter and is therefore a harmless piece of writing: ' "If you had a daughter you'd understand. You haven't got one" ' he accused, as though there were a crime in sterility' (p. 50). Scobie appears to lose control, in fact, to lose faith in the whole 'act' demanded of him by his profession, and he destroys the letter less to help the Captain than as an expression of exhaustion. This first subtle indication of Scobie's emotional and psychological state takes place when the reader knows nothing of his child and at this stage Scobie's action seems incomprehensible given his reputation for good work and integrity. Only much later does the narrative disclose the bare fact recorded in his diary – C died.

Actions such as this reveal his inner life. Much of the depth of this life rests on the pain of death – the trauma of loss never quite confronted by a weak and good man – which in turn draws him into traps laid by life's coincidences. The fact that his subsequent transgressions are also provoked by the memory of death and vulnerability – a suffering child, a defenceless and childlike widow – merges with the idea of responsibility to be discharged. This sense of responsibility makes up, perhaps subliminally, for the void in his own life. Greene creatively inhabits this consciousness and communicates the intensity of feeling even when objectively attacking the morality of Scobie's actions.

Death can develop a bond among those left behind but in the case of Scobie and his wife, Louise, it deepens the chasm. His relationship with the 19-year-old Helen Rolt widowed after one month of

marriage, a child in relation to his own age, begins with their joint
sense of tragedy. They are surrounded by death from their very first
meeting at the makeshift hospital where the survivors from the
accident are sheltered, and later by her isolation which reaches out
to his: 'They came together over two deaths without reserve' and it
is to her that he confides an anguish he had not been able to share
with his wife (p. 156). Scobie's actions are explored as expressive of
the truth of feeling and it is in his breaking official and religious codes
that the deeper meaning of life in society is illustrated.

Scobie's burning of the letter initiates a whole process of disintegration. From this point his transgressions are rapid and integrated
into the structure of the novel which revolves round Scobie as
keeper of the law, and his personal life as husband and lover.
Greene's ability to blend the various strains, pulls and duties in the
life of the Assistant Commissioner is the secret of the novel's
narrative power. It is easy to understand the weakness which led
him to borrow money from the smuggler Yusef so as to pay for his
wife's holiday. The politico-economic machinations of modern
society as well as the strains of colonial life are interwoven to create
the need for this further transgression. Had the sympathetic bank
manager, for instance, given Scobie the loan he needs so desperately
Yusef would have been out of the picture altogether.

Corruption sets in; the diamond-smuggler is invested with power
and his demands implicate Scobie in a plot to frame his business
rival, Tallit. Yet, the relationship between Scobie and Yusef has a
warmth and a dimension that stretch beyond these sordid transactions. Greene's skills humanise the 'villain' who is presented as an
affectionate scoundrel. Although Scobie's character is overburdened
as repository of the novel's argument he comes alive as a human
being, and particularly so in his dealings with Yusef who instinctively
understands the man's weakness and integrity. Because Yusef
needs no pity, Scobie is most himself in Yusef's company where the
paradoxes and hypocrisies of his professional life do not have to be
disguised. Both men stand unmasked: the lawbreaker and the
upholder of the law. With his 'unashamed villainy, his sophistry,
his crooked arguments, and his genuine need for love and company,
and his respect'[22] Yusef is a perfect example of Greene's ability to
understand human relationships.

Scobie's love affair with Helen, doomed as much by his own
furtive guilt as by the attitudes of the colonial group to which they
belong, furthers the complications. Professional spies, informers,

and gossips together conspire to destroy individual peace. Scobie's poignant awareness of the consequences of his actions illustrates the religious sense with greater conviction than the academic elaboration of Scobie's guilt in relation to the sacraments of confession and communion and the matter of his suicide. Father Rank's statement at the end suggests the movement from belief to faith, and the fact that such matters are beyond human judgement:

> For goodness sake, Mrs Scobie, don't imagine you – or I – know a thing about God's mercy . . . I know the Church says. The Church knows all the rules. But it doesn't know what goes on in a single human heart' (p. 272).

Despite the power of the narrative the web of lies and deception in which Scobie finds himself enmeshed exhausts not merely Scobie but our own willingness to accept some of the contradictions of his character: he is both selfless and self-absorbed. Haunted by his inadequacy he nonetheless feels sufficiently superior to think he can take on responsibility for all the 'objects' of his pity. Pity is thus rendered as the destructive element, the obverse side of pride, the negative side of compassion. Too deeply wounded to care about anything until he meets Helen Rolt he seems capable only of pity and his feeling for Helen is clouded by this.

When pity is extended to the black population under his jurisdiction, it communicates itself as thinly-veiled paternalism. And when at the end of the novel Scobie plays into the hands of Yusef to become an accomplice in the death of Ali, the boy who had served him with loyalty and affection, little can be said to extenuate his conduct. There is some presumption in the narrative tone in descriptions of the rulers and the subject race. Scobie sees himself as morally superior to both, hating the one and sorry for the other, unable to escape from either. In fact he is unwilling to escape because Freetown with its familiar shapes has become home. Yet it is an uneasy home; he can do little to improve his situation or that of the poor and the destitute, nor does he try. He moves, instead, in a state of moral exhaustion from one problem worthy of his pity to the other. At one level the narrative suggests that personal responsibility to his wife and mistress overwhelm him and ultimately destroy him.

A disjunction in the narrative arises from the two contrary strands: one that links the human motives to a subconscious but plausible reaction to life's traumas, such as the death of the child, which provokes the first transgression; the other that describes the action as motivated by pity and is the novelist's actual intent:

> I had meant the story of Scobie to enlarge a theme which I had touched on in *The Ministry of Fear*, the disastrous effect on human beings of pity as distinct from compassion . . . The character of Scobie was intended to show that pity can be the expression of an almost monstrous pride.[23]

What comes through is the portrait of a man growing into deepening self-knowledge: the spiritual journey of a weak and good man who is not destroyed by pity but led into selfhood by his humanity.

Apart from Yusef, the characters surrounding Scobie are insufficiently realised. The Scobies rarely function in normal human terms since there is always a feeling of condescension and continual judgement which both share – they judge each other and the colonial society in which they live. Subconsciously they despise each other and the company they keep. Everything is tainted by this and the tension introduced after Scobie's involvement with Helen is an artificial one revolving round adultery as sin, the need to go to confession, the consequences of sacrilegious communion, all of which are part of the apparatus of belief, not the expression of it. More realistic is the concern Scobie feels for the shipwrecked Helen and the child who dies as he is reading a story to him – a tender passage with Scobie as father-figure and the child bringing back memories of his own dead.

Except in one scene omitted in the earlier editions Louise's point of view is rarely given a chance. She is not allowed to emerge beyond her role as the Assistant Commissioner's wife, afraid of rats, anxious for promotions, self-conscious at the Club, or scrupulous about observing the rules of her religion without much evidence of its spirit in her relations with people. She is described as smug and self-absorbed by those with whom she comes in contact and the immature Wilson's devotion to her is not particularly flattering. Her lack of feeling is suggested by making her seem apparently untouched by the death of an only child, a tragedy that has scarred Scobie for life. Yet it was she who kept watch at the child's dying. In the scene that has been restored in the Collected edition (Chapter II, Part II, Book I) her spirit and moral sense penetrate to the surface.

Greene often comments on the importance of the craft of fiction, of the effects achieved with a skilful use of point of view. In restoring the scene he corrects as he says 'a technical fault rather than a psychological one' and gives Louise a chance to establish her perspective even if briefly:

> In the original draft of the novel a scene was played between Mrs Scobie and Wilson, the MI5 agent who is in love with her, on their evening walk along the abandoned railway track below Hill Station. This put Mrs Scobie's character in a more favourable light, for the scene had to be represented through the eyes of Wilson, but this scene – so I thought when I was preparing the novel for publication – broke Scobie's point of view prematurely; the drive of the narrative appeared to slacken. By eliminating it I thought I gained intensity and impetus, but I had sacrificed tone. In later editions I reinserted the passage.[24]

Scobie's identity is realised almost wholly in terms of his role which he detests and finds ineffective. A later section of this book discusses his role in the political sense with reference to the colonial set-up. Although he works with conscientiousness he has no belief in human justice:

> Round the corner, in front of the old cotton tree, where the earliest settlers had gathered their first day on the unfriendly shore, stood the law courts and police station, a great stone building like the grandiloquent boast of weak men. Inside that massive frame the human being rattled in the corridors like a kernel. No one could have been adequate to so rhetorical a conception. But the idea in any case was only one room deep. In the dark narrow passage behind, in the charge-room and the cells, Scobie could always detect the odour of human meanness and injustice – it was the smell of a zoo, of sawdust, excrement, ammonia, and lack of liberty. The place was scrubbed daily, but you could never eliminate the smell. Prisoners and policemen carried it in their clothing like cigarette smoke (p. 15).

This view of justice and the ineffectiveness of his role is paradoxical since Scobie's refuge is his office. It is there that he finds the peace and security that eludes him at home. This is quintessential Greene weaving contrary strands of story-line and narrative tone so as to accentuate the ambiguities of life and the fact that 'home' and identity' are indeed a complex matter particularly in a war-torn world. The idea extends to the destruction of Helen Rolt's 'home' and her new identity as a married woman before it could even be constructed.

Scobie stands revealed as a man overwhelmingly conscious of his office in the sense of responsibility. The novel does not explore the ineffectiveness of his role as arbiter of justice but develops the theme of the disintegration of a marital relationship and of the man himself due to the constraints of exile and weakness of character. The validity of this completely plausible situation is undermined by Scobie's flawed perception of his wife. Even at home the professional life is in control: impending promotions, claims for holidays which his salary can ill afford, the constraints of having to socialise with colleagues and their wives with whom he has little in common, are the details that colour our perception of social relations in the novel. Pity, his only link with Louise, is complemented by an alarming sense of responsibility for her happiness and well-being. Greene's immersion in Scobie's emotional conflicts is so intense, that the narrative communicates a real residue of feeling between husband and wife, even if it is only the comfort that comes from habit. These contradictions and complexities where the artistic imagination transforms the writer's intention make *The Heart of the Matter* a powerful novel.

The novel's achievement is the recreation of a spiritual journey through indirection which was not the novelist's obvious intent or why else should the paraphernalia of religion have been given so insistent an elaboration? What the narrative finally reveals is that Ali's murder is the major crime and Scobie's awareness of these depths is, in a sense, his redemption. In the eyes of the world his suicide, and his friendship with Yusef are unpardonable transgressions but the religious sense points elsewhere. These subtleties, suggested but not sufficiently defined, underlie the skilfully controlled ambiguity which heightens narrative tension and deepens existential truth but has led to misinterpretation of the text. Greene has commented on his sense of shock at the public response to the novel and its protagonist. What he clearly intended as exposure of pride founded on pity was received as the sad portrayal of a sympathetic figure involved in a human dilemma brought on by a hard and insensitive wife. The emphasis on pity and the fact that the novel was indeed written at a time of great personal anguish to Greene when his own personal problems had rough parallels with Scobie's is undoubtedly responsible for the novel's weakness – an excessive focus on religious scruple.

The society in which Greene places his characters is alive in detail of scene, sight and smell but does not accentuate the real tensions which underlie colonial society. Since the protagonist is represented facing personal and professional issues with ineffective humanitarian concern rather than with realism, it is easy to find fault and interpret it as an evasion of reality. This aspect of the novel is discussed in a later section of the book. Can one indict a novelist who has such a clear awareness of political realities for not having explored the personal or the professional situation but taken refuge, as it were, in his own dilemma, and created a novel that forever set him in the 'Catholic' mould?

Since Greene dislikes the novel and judges it harshly one ought, perhaps, to look at its good points. The thematic argument – the necessity of taking on responsibility – is here set down as dogma in Greene's view of the world. That the power of this argument is somewhat distorted by the weakness of the protagonist and by Greene's own preoccupation with religious scruple, belief, and faith, is indeed a pity: it obscures the real point of the novel which suggests that Scobie's implication in the murder of Ali is the most grievous of his transgressions. When the novel abandons the perspective of the religious sense to sentimentalise over the idea of sin, and to examine religious 'regulations', it fails to enthuse despite the intensity with which subjective experience is rendered.

The End of the Affair (1955) is much more than a love story in which the eternal triangle is given an interesting twist with God as one of the protagonists. Its powerful representation of a journey into a new awareness, a spiritual journey, in fact, which connects love of man with love of God works best in the early sections of the novel and in Sarah's diary when the accoutrements of faith do not hinder the flow of experience. After her death the conversations about baptism, conversion, miracles, and the relative merits of burial and cremation, destroy the poignant truth of the story.

The movement from human love to love of God is made explicit in the structure whose formal brilliance – use of time-shifts, alternate points of view, the first-person narrative – manipulates the plot so that belief and faith are revealed in a realistic framework of lived experience. Its passionate evocation transforms what could have been on the surface of it a trivial love story into an experience that is deep, resonant, and altogether human. Sarah, the beautiful wife of Henry, a stolid but well-meaning bureaucrat, abandons herself in an affair with Bendrix, a writer who is tormented by vindictive jealousy.

A shell bursting in war-torn London drives Sarah to make a desperate bargain with a God in whom she only vaguely believes. She prays for the safety of her lover. If Bendrix has not been killed in the explosion, she promises she will never see him again. The inexorability of her vow hits her when she sees her lover emerge from the debris.

The structural device of keeping Bendrix unaware of the motive for Sarah's withdrawal gives the novel its sense of controlled passion and intense despair. Shifts in time flash back to days of joy and abandonment in a moving expression of sexuality rare in a Greene novel – and of tenderness. Skilful use of point of view ensures the reader's complete involvement in Sarah's commitment and conveys the power of the lovers feelings when together, as well as when apart but living parallel inner lives. The resultant tensions create a moving dialectic between despair and peace so that her self-denial is revealed as an expression of faith. The rational Bendrix's brooding narration, ironic, disbelieving in tone and yet deeply felt gives the novel its overpowering intensity.

'Abandonment' is a key word. It suggests the fullness of the joy of the lovers' meeting as well as the quality of Sarah's eventual leap into faith. The text is rich in parallel journeys and pursuits. Sarah flees from Bendrix, is pursued by her memory of him, by her desire to believe in God, and by a detective engaged by the jealous Bendrix to shadow her. The generosity of her actions, her emotionally exhausting ordeals, and her truly selfless love illustrate faith and humanity when juxtaposed against Bendrix's jealousy, his petty egoistic possessiveness, his incomprehension. Her diary which contains Greene's most powerful writing, introduces a sympathetic side of Bendrix, an element also revealed in aspects of his narrative that communicate an urgent sense of time running short, of human beings alive to each other – precious moments clouded by a sense of impermanence.

In his anguished expression of such experience Bendrix, the rational writer, comes near to jealous 'hate'; fury at his inability to solve the riddle of Sarah's withdrawal springs to life with a complexity that elicits the reader's sympathy and understanding. He questions every motive, and imagines infidelities where there are none; Sarah is quite the reverse which is why her 'abandonment' is so convincing. It is represented through her agonised expression of it in her diary, in her recollection of each meeting with Bendrix, in her tenderness for Henry. She is a 'natural', generous and unstudied in her responses and motives which are never self-absorbed.

The intensity of Sarah's love and her passionate struggle to protect Bendrix by depriving herself of the comfort of his love evoke the religious sense. It is irrelevant to ask why Sarah should take her vow so seriously when she is not a specifically religious person. The narrative suggests the nature of Sarah's commitment: another's life hangs by her word. She is neither a rationalist like her lover nor a believer like Richard Smythe but realises herself through an expression of feeling. Her vow is one such expression and her tenacious struggle validates her love. So is her change of mind when having decided to break her vow and live with Bendrix she abandons the idea because she comes upon Henry in tears. Although she is unaware of their cause she senses his need and decides to stay. Sarah's ability to live deeply a rich emotional life destroys her even as it ultimately saves her.

All this is convincing because it is worked into the narrative as experience and not presented overtly as linked with religious belief. The opening paragraph conveys the power of the supernatural as a sense of destiny prompting action. The narrative works at two levels: it illustrates action as directed invisibly by God, and as proceeding from the conscious motives of characters. Everything that happens appears to emanate from an incomprehensible force and from contingencies such as the air raids which were the most immediate reality of the time.

Sarah's renunciation of Bendrix is an expression of her love for him rather than of belief in God. And yet the novel is deeply religious. In renouncing Bendrix, Sarah expresses a deeper love and the *noche escura* created by the renunciation heightens her inner life. Her diary expresses her love and questions God in terms that apply simultaneously to both human and spiritual love. It is here that the text reveals the religious sense in the most poignant terms:

Did I ever love Maurice as much before I loved You? Or was it really You I loved all the time? Did I touch You when I touched him?

Could I have touched You if I hadn't touched him first? . . . But was it me he loved or You? For he hated in me the things you hate. He was on Your side all the time without knowing it. You willed our separation but he willed it too. He worked for it with his anger and his jealousy and he worked for it with his love. For he gave me so much love, and I gave him so much love that soon there wasn't anything left when we'd finished but You.[25]

The complexity of experience and the intensity of the writing make *The End of the Affair* extraordinarily moving despite the uncharacteristic clumsiness of the final chapters where the 'subjective beauty of the story is caricatured by the objective action'.[26] This comment is in fact Greene's objection to passages in Henry James's *Altar of the Dead*, and describes the kind of flawed religious sense that sometimes mars his own best work. At its best the writing reveals the human as the spiritual experience and Greene consciously uses the same language to describe both:

The words of human love have been used by the saints to describe their vision of God: and so, I suppose, we might use the terms of prayer, meditation, contemplation to explain the intensity of the love we feel for a woman. We too surrender memory, intellect, intelligence, and we too experience the deprivation, the *noche escura*, and sometimes as a reward a kind of peace (p. 46).

There are two realities in Sarah's life, her love for Bendrix and the war – the German flares in the darkness, the relentless dropping of robots, the suspense before the devastation. The fact that the interruption in the relationship is altogether linked with the destruction around emphasises the reality of both experiences even though most of the novel concentrates on Sarah's inner life, her spiritual journey, Bendrix's disbelieving pursuit and the doubt which finally humanises him.

*   *   *

A significant change of tone follows *The Power and the Glory, The Heart of the Matter* and *The End of the Affair* which introduces the themes and structures of religious belief quite overtly. Personal anxieties about religious belief now appear in muted form in a sort of resolution. Anguish about sin and damnation is replaced by deep faith as expressed in action which is sometimes political struggle. The perspective of experience widens to reveal how much the novelist has drawn on his experience of war as a correspondent in Saigon, and on his travels in Kenya, Liberia, Haiti and Central America.

The religious sense, however, is not wholly abandoned, not even in what have been called his secular novels. His insight into political process makes him take into account structures and categories of a changing sociopolitical scene even when he wants to be merely light, lucid and witty as in *Our Man in Havana* (1958). The preoccupation now is less with religion than with the religious sense as fundamental to the private vision, less with politics as ideology than with the fact that in a world of cold-war confrontations, the demands of individual freedom and human needs require constant definition.

The novels beginning with *The Quiet American* (1955) often contain overtly political themes and the religious sense is given a universal significance. That belief is still a major concern is suggested by the fact that a novel dealing quite directly with American involvement in Vietnam is followed by *A Burnt-Out Case* (1961) which sets out to examine 'stages of belief, half belief and non-belief, in the kind of setting removed from world politics and household preoccupations, where such differences are felt acutely and find expression'.[27] My reading of the novels disturbs chronology to discuss *A Burnt-Out Case* here. The three novels that precede it follow in discussions in a later section where they belong thematically.

In *A Burnt-Out Case* Greene seizes on a searing metaphor to explore fundamental realisation of humanity. The novel has two epigraphs and the first, taken from Dante, effectively describes Querry's psychological state: 'I did not die, yet nothing of life remained.' The second epigraph taken from a pamphlet on leprosy specifically connects the diseased psyche with physical deformities brought on by disease:

Within limits of normality, every individual loves himself. In cases where he has a deformity or abnormality, or develops it later, his own aesthetic sense revolts and he develops a sort of disquiet towards himself. Though with time he becomes reconciled to his deformities, it is only at the conscious level. His subconscious mind, which continues to bear the mark of injury, brings about certain changes in his whole personality, making him suspicious of society.

In his notes in *The Portable Graham Greene* Philip Stratford suggests that Querry, the internationally successful architect who escapes from the world and from success to the furthest point he can reach which is a leproserie in the Congo, is a hunted character born out of the persecution following the publication of *The Heart of the Matter*. The novel was Greene's first popular success and created 'a great deal of faulty identification between and author and his hero. He found himself in the centre of a sometimes passionate, often silly public debate. He was pursued by all manner of cranks and unhappy people'.[28] Be that as it may, in *A Burnt-Out Case* Greene abandons the habitual structures of religion to seek its essence in relation to the active life. The setting of the novel in a leproserie achieves two effects. The first is the juxtaposition of the characters of Querry and Deo Gratias. Querry, once an internationally renowned architect, fêted by success, pursued by women and the press, finds himself dead to feeling and sapped of creativity. Deo Gratias, the boy assigned to look after him in the leproserie, medically a burnt-out case, has stumps for hands which are dead to feeling. Success has caused the mutilation of Querry; disease has eaten away Deo Gratias's limbs.

Further juxtapositions reveal the inner life of the man. Dr Colin, the rationalist with a pragmatic commitment to eradicate the disease and to alleviate pain; the Superior of the Mission and the priests who illustrate aspects of the religious life; Rycker, the factory manager, as pharisee; Parkinson, the journalist, who represents the 'world' in pursuit of 'success' and of cult-heroes made by headlines that subvert truth. The Congo of the novel is indeed a 'region of the mind'.

The second effect achieved is that by setting the novel in a community set apart by disease and incapable of normal social relations in society the text arrives at the more fundamental meaning of social relations. Cut off from the normal world, the inmates of the leproserie, both the diseased and the healthy, find meaning in relationships and activities that depend on and arise from the most fundamental needs. Deprived of conventional external forms, both physical and social, the members of the community have to draw on inner resources and basic needs to continue to survive.

This context serves admirably for a discourse on worldly advancement and self-realisation. The yearnings for absolute reality which finds expression in Querry's self-disgust are finally explained and 'cured' in human terms. To say that Greene sets the rationalist Dr Colin and the pragmatic Superior on a plane slightly less elevated than that finally achieved by Querry is to miss the point of the novel. *A Burnt-Out Case* is really about the self-regarding artist whose sexual excesses and material successes lead to an undermining of his humanity. The movement of the narrative is a journey from this dead point of civilisation towards the vital, primitive, point of humanity.

The Superior's sermon to the congregation subverts the edifice of social and religious moralities to define truth and justice. Although couched in language that exasperates the intellectual Querry with its simplifications, the sermon illustrates human connections and spiritual ends in the deepest context:

> Now I tell you when a man loves, he must be Klistian. When a man is merciful he must be Klistian. In this village do you think you are the only Klistians – you who come to Church? There is a doctor who lives near the well beyond Maria Akimbu's house and he prays to Nzambe and he makes bad medicine. He worships a false God, but once when a piccin was ill and his father and mother were in hospital he took no money; he gave bad medicine but he took no money: he made a big God palaver with Nzambe for the piccin but took no money. I tell you then he was a Klistian, a better Klistian than the man who broke Henry Okapa's bicycle, he did not believe in Yezu but he was a Klistian. Yezu made love, he made mercy. Everybody in the world has something that Yezu made. Everybody in the world is that much a Klistian. There is no man so wicked he never once in his life show in his heart something that God made (p. 81).

To argue as Ogude does that the oversimplification of Christian ideas is intended to suggest merely 'the assumptions of Christian missionaries when confronted with a congregation of simple barbarous natives' is to be deliberately blind to much that the novel tries to say.[29] Analysis of the fiction in rigid categories of economic materialism and post-colonial discourse distorts the insights and leads to entirely unacceptable conclusions such as that arrived at by Eagleton:

> while [Querry's] concern for Deo Gratias is at one level an intellectual interest which is not allowed to count in his favour, the African's curious disappearance stirs in him, at a deeper level, that yearning for an absolute reality which renders him in some sense morally superior to those more committed rationalists or pragmatists who discount such strivings – Dr Colin, or Father Superior.[30]

Such views distort the perspective sought by Greene who assumes an innocence and uses 'simplification' precisely to undermine the logic of economic determinism and to suggest the distance Christianity itself has travelled from the purity of its original character. Greene's manipulation of ambiguities should not obscure our view of the realities. Eagleton, however, does finally concede in his conclusion that Greene:

> the metaphysical novelist is more deeply influenced by the pressures and limits of a particular social world than the novels would have us believe; in feeling and attitude, he is closer to Orwell, and to a specific strain in the English novel, than to the more overtly theological writers with whom he is often compared.[31]

When the Father Superior expounds Christianity to his black congregation and talks to his colleague Father Thomas about the culture of Africa he attempts deeper meanings than mere emphasis on the European missionary's lack of understanding of the people he seeks to convert. The text suggests cultural and spiritual values within African society that the Christian missionary must needs respect and it is Greene's sensitivity to cultures other than his own that led him to comment that it is 'not the European who has brought God to Africa; too often he has driven Him out'.[32]

Father Thomas illustrates another dimension of self-deception. His scrupulous, egoistic concern with his religious duties as soul-saving diminishes the true meaning of the religious sense as revealed in the characterisation of the Father Superior who plots and plans for the leproserie, and the priests who function as electricians and as plumbers or as Captain of the boat when not teaching moral theology and canon law, adapting theology and intellect to human needs. It is indeed a limited reading of the text that seeks to interpret such activity as aspects of the materialistic tendencies of the Christian religion. Aware of these tendencies Greene's work goes beyond cultures in so far as it is possible to arrive at the human and universal. A life of action directed outside the self defines the spiritual life and gives Querry insights into other meanings of success and achievement.

In Rycker who ill-treats his youthful wife Maria, in *A Burnt-Out Case* Greene achieves a scathing characterisation of pharisaism: the habit of piety, self-righteous complacency, the sense of so-called duty being done, and a complete lack of human feeling. His hollow phrases about grace, the sacrament, duty and love are glib; his idea that sex is a religious duty deserves the derisory comment that for him religion is no more than 'the open doorway in a red-lamp district [leading] inevitably to sex' (p. 65). Swift and deft strokes in which Greene specialises reveal the truth of experience in the most moving terms. These describe what would be 'sins' and 'irregularities' in conventional society functioning as norms in this community so deprived. The breaking of conventional norms is shown to harm no one and to enrich an impoverished life. Truth of feeling, the gift of life itself, and the fulfilment of basic physical needs make Father Thomas's questions of moral theology irrelevant.

The juxtaposition of Querry and Dr Colin in *A Burnt-Out Case* emphasises the value of suffering as a means of developing an awareness of others. Querry's self-regarding past life – only suggested by his own self-disgust and the extravagant descriptions of it by those who wish to make him a saint or a hero – extends the discourse into dimensions of the public life which destroys the private self, and urban culture that deifies the successful man even as it connives at his disintegration. In choosing the profession of architecture for his hero, Greene develops the theme of egotism:

I don't deny it once meant a lot to me. So have women. But the use of what I made was never important to me. I wasn't a builder of council houses or factories. When I made something I made it for my own pleasure . . . Your vocation is quite a different one, doctor. You are concerned with people. I wasn't concerned with the people who occupied my space – only with the space (p. 44).

Dr Colin, in contrast, has suffered the death of a beloved wife. His work is altogether connected with suffering and with human life. He reflects that the search for suffering and the remembrance of suffering 'are the only means we have to get ourselves in touch with the whole human condition. With suffering we become part of the Christian myth.' Through his scientific and humane perspective the text expresses an evolutionary concept of Christianity. The narrative reveals Querry as lacking self-realisation, Dr Colin and the Superior as expressing themselves in an active life engaged in relieving human suffering. Their work illustrates the religious sense in life and the fact that Dr Colin is a non-believer is irrelevant. Querry begins to realise these truths so that the novel is as much a comment on his individual character as on the society from which he seeks to escape.

Querry's relationship with Deo Gratias begins in purely utilitarian, non-personal terms. Deo Gratias is more object than human being in Querry's perception of him until he disappears, after which Querry sets off in search of him out of curiosity rather than concern. The change in Querry's attitude occurs only when he reaches the depth of the forest and discovers Deo Gratias's plight. His panic at being left alone again while Querry attempts to go back to fetch help establishes the human connection. Deo Gratias's disappearance from a community that feeds, clothes and cures him in a way parallels Querry's own flight from society, and his physical closeness to the moaning, vulnerable Deo Gratias impels an involvement. He touches the boy to comfort him. His return to human connections continues through his involvement with designs for the leproserie which needs him for his skills rather than his renown. He becomes a builder, gets down to basic work, and thus begins a process of recovery of the self.

Although Greene warns in his introduction to the novel that it is not a *roman à clef* there is much that appears to be personal and is transmuted in very thinly veiled references to the architect-writer as creative artist, as human being in society, and to craftsmanship which has its own structure of meaning and value. In the fable which Querry relates to Marie Rycker and in countless references in the text the narrative explores realities that unite the truth of the Crucifixion and the Resurrection with what endures in life and art.

The novels examined above illustrate the religious sense defined in terms of social relevance. Action is conceived within two orders of time in order to emphasise that moral life and individual choice are facts of contemporary existence. The sinner's self-consciousness is interpreted in relation to the lack of awareness of the decent man. The idea of human destiny in the fiction can be frightening and burdensome because the narrative posits the ultimates and the dire consequences of individual actions.

The structure of Catholicism helps to externalise the spiritual quest, and the human act is conceived as a sign whereby the individual communicates a subjective meaning. It is therefore essential to appreciate the complexity of the narrative technique which illustrates values in the context of ordinary human intercourse and the need of our cognition of death which alone can help to make some sense of life. That the structure is that of Catholicism does not diminish the discourse to belief but extends it to define the religious sense in truly human and universal terms.

4

England, My England

A dream of England, precious and fleeting haunts all Greene's work and is overpowering in its presence in the novels discussed here – *England Made Me* (1935), *The Confidential Agent* (1939), and *The Ministry of Fear* (1943). It is expressed at several levels: the changes that came after the devastations of the First World War – a psychological and political loss of confidence and power among the élite; the slow decline of belief in ideals once cherished and the questioning of an education and a moral system which was inextricably linked with the idea of Empire; a lost innocence recalled to extend perception of political and existential realities. George Woodcock whose book *The Writer and Politics* was published at a time when Greene was in fact being hailed as a 'Catholic' novelist, comments on this aspect of Greene's work and on the understanding and engagement with political process as illustrated in the novels:

> Greene's novels form . . . one of the most comprehensive surveys of modern social violence that has yet been made in European fiction. They show clearly the nature of the class struggle in modern society, and also go beyond the Marxists to a realisation of that even more fundamental struggle, in progress throughout the world today, between the individual and the collective, the common man and the State.[1]

The idea of internationalism as a political and economic concept underlies the narrative – it includes a Fifth Column based in London helping the Fascist cause as well as an economic empire that is as unscrupulous even though no Fascist is involved. Words are seen to acquire a new meaning; events such as a fun-fair, once innocent, now cover up enemy activity. It is a world of distrust and betrayal which requires a redefinition of terms.

For Greene's generation 'abroad' and 'frontier' were code-words from a received tradition to be recoded for a changing cultural and political scene. When Auden first conjured the journey across the frontier it was a journey 'out of the familiar and secure into the unknown and frightening which had to be taken if one was to reach the new life'.[2] Greene recreates the journey to extend and sharpen the connotations of threat and reality. The novels evoke a changing world order that cuts across national frontiers to reveal a world of international collusion in war, finance and business. The later fiction explores the polarisation of power and hegemonic confrontation that is the reality of our lives; satellite nations and individuals are seen as trapped on either side of the frontier.

Greene's vision unites an awareness of these realities with a constant adumbration of lost innocence, an authentic world forever destroyed. Man's capacity for cruelty is a running theme but so is his capacity for compassion. The characterisation of Kate and Anthony Farrant (*England Made Me*) and Arthur Rowe (*The Ministry of Fear*) in particular, attempts a poignant illustration of the situation in England when, after the First World War, words such as patriotism and nationalism had lost their heroic and romantic connotations and were soon to be used to justify Fascism and Racism. Greene has suggested that the portrait of Anthony Farrant is a highly idealised portrait of his eldest brother, Herbert. The novel illustrates a last, long, lingering look at the virtues that went into the making of the old nation-states and the values and education of Greene's own social class who had to find the inner resources and the professional skills to cope with a changing world.

Martin Green suggests some of the directions travelled by the writers of Greene's generation in their rebellion against the world of their fathers which had let them down. For them 'treachery was not a category of greatest evil, nor patriotism of greatest good' and the only way to rebel fully against England, he says, was the path that led Philby to Russia and Auden to become an American citizen. He develops this argument by taking the First World War as a watershed and Kipling's *Kim* and Greene's *Our Man in Havana* as examples to point out the differences between England and English manhood before 1914 and after 1918. In *Kim*, as Martin Green points out:

the secret service men believe in what they are doing and derive moral health from doing it. After 1918 the services gradually became – in literal image but also apparently in literal fact – a grotesque and preposterous fantasy that bred cynicism and unhealth.

For these writers the First World War meant:

not so much the great mistake as the great failure – it meant the political diminishment of England and the moral enfeeblement of the new post-war Englishman. But both interpretations aroused the same horror of war and of the official patriotism that had energised it. The men of letters remembered that, and since the nation as a whole was not going to change, they in some sense withdrew from the nation.[3]

Graham Greene does not withdraw from the nation. My interpretation of the novels emphasises a persistent confrontation of issues affecting England and the world, albeit a confrontation tinged with nostalgia for a lost world which is composed of the ordered certainties of prewar England, and the innocence of the 'cloudless world of unknowing'. These themes are juxtaposed in various ways. The values and education of Kate and Anthony Farrant, who along with the journalist Minty evoke a public school ethos, and structures of discipline which are balanced against new power structures in the professional world. D, the confidential agent of the title, is a foreigner who through substantial sections of the novel recalls his past visit to London to contrast the peace of 'then' with the chaos of 'now'. The brilliant structure of *The Ministry of Fear* where guilt, self-absorption and amnesia occasioned by a bomb attack during the Second World War contribute to an ingenious and breathless plotting of experience which captures the worlds of innocence and knowledge, a pastoral vision of England which was being clouded by premonitions of the abuses of science and technology and destroyed by war in the service of ideology. In positing this new world the novels examine the nature of power as wielded by political and industrial establishments.

England Made Me (1935) published just before The Second World War defines values underlying traditional morality by exposing the forms and conventions of middle-class education, its ethos constructed from and for imperial achievement and grand dreams, now devitalised and producing charming but shiftless and seedy adventurers like Anthony Farrant who live on their wits, and embittered exiles like the journalist Minty. They are the first of Greene's Englishmen abroad through whom he scrutinises the world order. Kate Farrant's candour, her ability to face the strengths and weaknesses of her upbringing, and her cold-blooded attempt to find a place in the new world reveals prophetically that England at the time was unprepared for the ruthless pragmatism of postwar global change.

Though set in Stockholm the novel is really about England in relation to the new world: Dickens, Scott, Shakespeare, a stiff upper lip, and implicit faith in human nature as insufficient defences with which to face a postwar world:

> Good looks and Conscience . . . the fine flowers of our class. We're done, we're broke, we belong to the past, we haven't the energy to do more than hang on to something new for what we can make out of it . . . We're national . . . from the soles of our feet. But nationality's finished' (p. 135).

Kate Farrant plots and plans; she even disregards her conscience to safeguard the interests of her brother whom she loves. She deliberately steels herself to be ruthless and unscrupulous and blots out the values instilled by her father. Yet, she finds it impossible, in the final resort, to be completely heartless – a theme which Greene later was to develop as a parallel to suggest the differences between the paternalistic benevolence of the British Empire and the machinations of new empires. In her single-minded attempts to succeed in the new world Kate deliberately turns away from

> the thought that there had been a straightness about the poor national past which the international present did without. It hadn't been very grand, but in their class at any rate, there had been gentleness and kindness once (p. 136).

This perception works best through the characterisation of Minty, a drop-out from the public-school system, who captures and transmits through his person the whole spirit of the discourse. His hatred for the impersonal disciplines of Harrow and his nostalgia for secretly nurtured friendships while he was there are the furies and passions that sustain him.

The juxtaposition of the two worlds – England and the new frontiers – is achieved through Kate's relationship with the two men in her life: Anthony her brother and Krogh, the industrialist, who is her employer and her lover. Kate, determined to succeed in the new world and to find a place for Anthony in it, drives herself with eyes wide open into compromise. She is prepared to sacrifice principles to any limit, so it seems, as long as she can have her brother with her. Anthony is portrayed as lacking in ambition but lovable. He still retains some of the values of conventional morality and is not unscrupulous enough to be successful in the world of Krogh who fixes deals in a frontierless empire of international capitalism that stretches from Sweden to America: 'They call it fraud, this clarity, this long intricate equation of which at last he can see the solution.' A small man once, he now feels an inhuman joy thanks to the 'intricate network of subsidiary companies . . . knitted together by his personal credit'. No Depression can touch Krogh's world. It has no place for 'old honesties, old dusty poverties.' Though once a worker himself, he now has a hatchet man and a new ethic to deal with strikers who believe in Socialism.

The business conglomerates of today are prefigured in the description of Krogh's business premises. It is not dusty and informal like a London city office but clinical and impersonal: glassy cleanliness, the latest fashionable sculpture, sound-proof floors, dictaphones, and Mr Krogh sitting in 'Arctic isolation'. This description and the loneliness of the man who controls the business empire comes full circle forty years later in the conception of Doctor Fischer in *Doctor Fischer of Geneva or The Bomb Party* (1980) whose wealth and financial manipulations isolate him physically and spiritually. His millions create a world within which he is effectively snowbound from human contact. The character of Dr Fischer though conceived, in a sense, as a point making evocation rather than with the complexities of flesh and blood, is better developed than that of Krogh, not least because Greene wrote the earlier novel before multinationalism became a commonplace of the modern world. Greene muses in his introduction: 'Would I have written the book any better now when I can easily find in my memories a model for Krogh, the industrialist, who so obstinately at that time refused to come alive? I doubt it.'[4]

The 'me' of the title of *England Made Me* has many nuances; it encloses the world of the fathers whose ideals are neither betrayed nor abandoned even when they are most earnestly being questioned through the course of the novel. It includes Minty, who, unlike Anthony, actually went to Harrow, and now lives in the shadow of public-school myth and hides his failure behind a sure sense of a lost hope. His self-awareness balances the self-deception of Anthony and Kate's more poignant evasions. Her devotion to her brother and their memory of shared ideals are partially professed through love which itself is expressed through stealth and guilt. Their incestuous love gives the necessary twist in the narrative to suggest guilt-ridden and no-longer-legitimate claims of Greene's class, the ruling class, and carries with it intimations of disaster.

Greene's own idea of the novel is more modest than what is actually achieved by his art: 'The subject – apart from the economic background of the Thirties and that sense of capitalism staggering from crisis to crisis – was simple and unpolitical, a brother and sister in the confusion of incestuous love.'[5] Through Kate and Anthony Farrant Greene offers an intimate appraisal of his own background and that of bourgeois England – the assurance of knowledge is evident in the handling of gestures, attitudes and conversation. But Minty, conceived as a minor figure, 'some fellow-outsider who would recognise – as only a countryman can – the fraudulent element in Anthony, who could detect the old Harrovian tie and know at once that it did not belong', steals the plot as it were and deepens the discourse with a poignant recall of an England that taught its young to dare and dream.

The argument implicit in the narrative that old forms of exploitation as practised in the old imperialisms of France and Britain were tempered and mitigated by a sense of justice, chivalry, culture and respect for human rights and were therefore superior and preferable to the soulless and single-minded speculations of Krogh wears thin when seen from the point of view of the exploited. To strengthen the argument Greene makes the exploiter of the old variety an innocent and feckless wanderer who has stumbled into his role with no plan or purpose but is an unwitting result of an education designed for empire-builders. Kate's remark at the end – 'We're all thieves . . . Stealing a livelihood here and there and everywhere, giving nothing back' – does not have the required force to balance the affection for the irresponsible Anthony established as innocent and even heroic in relation to Krogh's world. However weak Greene's approach is to the problem of contrasting forms of exploitation it is to the credit of Greene that he does not fudge the basic issue of exploitation itself.

England Made Me is yet another example of Greene's ability to turn a truism on its head as it were in order to bare the truth. Though he is introduced as an impostor at several levels and rarely seen as speaking the truth, Anthony emerges as humane and generous, incapable of being a party to Krogh's wheeler-dealing. His cultural integrity is hence applauded, even if in a left-handed way. The assumption underlying the novel is that ideals of patriotism, nation and the old world of which Anthony and Kate are both products and inheritors are no longer valid. Nevertheless Anthony rejects the change so assiduously sought by Kate and spurns the job she procures for him. The motives are complex but the deepest meaning of his act of rejection is the hope of saving his sister from the evil world of Krogh. Such considerations, though human, rest on logic that is faulty and on solutions that are far-fetched and unrealistic. Another weakness in Greene's approach – and from another point of view it might even be a strength – is that Greene cannot unreservedly condemn his ethos and his class which on all counts has lost the right to rule. His questioning and rejection of assumptions is not a conscious act as in the case of Orwell. Hence the novels communicate a lingering feeling of affection for a culture whose confidence and security rested in large measure on assumptions of the imperial idea, which Greene indicts in sections of *Journey Without Maps*.

An important point to be borne in mind is that Greene's journalism and travel writing is scrupulously critical of what Claud Cockburn calls 'the personalities and forces – political, financial, commercial – which motivated and directed the imperial machine';[6] in the fiction, even though he does not deal directly with the Empire as here, the ideals and morality of the past consistently underlie the text in relation to present realities and at the final count the old world, which doubles as the lost innocence of childhood, is always recalled as more humane. Despite his liberal-Left political vision Greene's fiction remains a prisoner of received ideologies of culture which undermine the radicalism of his political positions. In a later section of this book the novels are discussed as a sensitive expression of the reality of post-colonial societies. Yet, validation of the British Empire as more humane than what has followed it prevails in the entire oeuvre.

The action in *The Confidential Agent* (1939) and *The Ministry of Fear* (1943) proceeds from a war that is in progress. Although Greene does not localise the conflict it is the Spanish Civil War, he says, which furnished the background of *The Confidential Agent* and 'it was the Munich Agreement which created the urgency'. The city of London, threatened and then devastated by war, illustrates the contrast between the bliss of a prewar world and the disasters of the present. D, the confidential agent of the title – a professor of Romance literature with romantic and passionate attitudes – is characteristic of Greene's gallery of middle-aged and middle-class rebels from Dr Czinner in *Stamboul Train*, to Castle in *The Human Factor*. Some of them become revolutionaries but most end as outsiders and exiles, their idealism acquiring overtones of irony, cynicism and detachment, and descending into despair. But the romance and chivalry that goes with lost causes remain and are summoned, as ever, to sustain them.

In his introduction to *The Confidential Agent* Greene writes:

> I had a vague ambition to create something legendary out of a contemporary thriller: the hunted man who becomes in turn the hunter, the peaceful man who turns at bay, the man who has learnt to love justice by suffering injustice. A legend for modern times.[7]

Greene's oeuvre, in fact, is a legend for modern times worked out through his method of producing 'a central figure who represents some idea of reasonable simplicity.' The plot, he says, is useful only in so far as it allows the novelist 'to ascend into myth'. Myth and not plot, then, is of the essence: the representation of reality, of the real truth about the world, in a novel is primarily the function of what Greene calls myth.[8]

D, the confidential agent of the title, travels from his own war-torn country to London to negotiate a coal deal that would help his side with the war against the Fascists who appear to have the help of powerful international establishments. His moves are checkmated at every stage by L, the agent representing the Fascists. The opening sections of the novel when D lands at Dover evoke the mood and images of death, mourning and disaster in the description of landscape and set it against the vitality of a boisterous football team. With a few strokes of a technique which Anthony Burgess aptly describes as 'no fat, no self-indulgence, no pyrotechnics and no cadenzas, in which everything fits into everything else'[9] – Greene plots his myth amid the mourning of gulls, the cold foggy deck, a 'deck like a map marked with trenches, impossible positions, salients, deaths' (p. 10).

The war, the coal deal, the two parties that stand to benefit, England as holding the power that could exercise influence on the course of the war – these are the bare bones of a story written in six weeks so as to provide for his family before war broke out and he was called up. The plot spirals with pursuits and reversals which are a necessary aspect of the adventure story as thriller. The political dimension rests on the inseparables of economic power and war, a theme repeated more emphatically from the earlier novel, *A Gun for Sale*, where the theme of the sale of armaments supported by political power is linked with the more fundamental issue of exploitation and cruelty. War and struggle, the interests of industrial capitalism and justice are woven together more closely and realism considerably enhanced through the characterisation of D. He is not a rebel against society like Raven, but a political worker fighting for a cause. He is not maladjusted but wholly aware and in Greene's terms, this wholeness of life is realised not as a bystander but as an active combatant in war as struggle and in his willingness to face the consequences.

In *The Confidential Agent* Greene deliberately did not name the two agents, D and L, so as not to localise the conflict; the absence of proper names and the conflict focused in professional designations – the priest, the lieutenant, the Assistant Commissioner of Police – is a technique often used in allegory to mythicise struggle and ideals. D and L walk the deck separated by distrust and disquiet and the facts that the ship is English and that they are both heading for Dover and England, create the tension implicit in the narrative: a tension between illusion and reality, between the dream of England, its peace and justice, and the plots and plans of which the English people are still unaware:

> D thought: he will probably try to rob me, perhaps he will try to have me killed. He would certainly have more helpers and more money and more friends. He would bear letters of introduction to peers and ministers – he had once had some kind of title himself, years ago, before the republic . . . count, marquis . . . D had forgotten exactly what (p. 11).

D carries the war with him. From his individual national involvement the myth rises to larger international issues across the frontier, and also confronts the basics of the human condition: public causes and private grief, the tragic loss of his wife, the death of Rose's mother, the cruel death of Else, and human suffering that is, in a sense, the condition of life. The two agents carry the war into England, a country seen as unprepared, indeed unaware of impending disaster.

Life in a peaceful city is blissfully protected from undercurrents of violence felt and experienced by D alone. Its point of contact is in pure fantasy-land – the Entrenatiano Language Centre whose director, Dr Bellows, shares the simple idealism of 'love of all the world . . . desire to be able to exchange – ideas – with – everybody' with a later creation, Mr Smith in *The Comedians* (1966). D carries a dire reality within his very person and moves through a deceptively peaceful landscape that does not reflect the dangers threatening society. Since he has memories of a more innocent time when he had walked the streets of London as a carefree student devoted to his young wife, to his scholarship and to the ideals these enshrined, every movement he makes is heightened by awareness at every turn, of then and now.

The characterisation of D as a professor of Romance literature opens up the past at several levels. Memories of prewar England, of his wife, of research in the British Library jostle in his mind with consciousness of his war-torn country and of the realities of the present London scene – a scene where external peace conceals secret meetings in fantastic surroundings, counter-espionage, and innocents such as Else enmeshed in a world where the establishments of power are prepared to perpetrate the greatest betrayals.

The threat of war in the apparent peace of London is reinforced by a juxtaposition of illusion and reality, a confrontation so developed that it is difficult to say which is which. D meets violence in a peaceful square and loses faith in what are ostensibly civilised business deals. Sadly reflecting on the state of the nation, the nature of society and exploitation, D remembers the past so that, as in *It's a Battlefield*, the present is defined in relation to the past. Constant use of phrases such as 'the England of books and learning', 'this is London', 'a city of peace', 'the best policed city in the world', emphasise the unreality of a precarious peace and the brutal realities that often underlie talk of civilisation. The fact that the operation of the coal-mines crucial to D's side winning the war is controlled by Lord Benditch, whose daughter Rose Cullen falls in love with D may seem like an excess of coincidence but the weakness inherent in such a device, is balanced by the humaneness of Rose's choice: she abandons her wealth and social position for a human commitment and in a sense returns to ideals across the frontier crossed by her father when he travelled from small beginnings as a miner to his present position of power.

As is frequent in Greene's novels, there is an intentional romanticisation of the past in *The Confidential Agent*, a perspective which blurs the otherwise sharp focus:

Fighting was better in the old days. Roland had companions at Roncesvalles – Oliver and Turpin: the whole chivalry of Europe was riding to help him. Men were united by a common belief. Even a heretic would be on the side of Christendom against the

Moors; they might differ about the persons of the Trinity, but on the main issue they were like rock. Now there were so many varieties of economic materialism, so many initial letters (p. 21).

The plot of *The Confidential Agent* is developed like a game of chess and a military manoeuvre all at once. When D loses the game but not the war to his enemy as a last recourse he addresses the miners, who, he hopes, would understand the republican cause. Bates, the union leader, has qualities suggested in the workers' meeting in *It's a Battlefield* which underscores the idea that the worker as individual, or even as member of a group is manipulated by both the union leader and the sympathetic intellectual: Bates does not have the courage of his convictions, 'his weak mouth carried his shock of hair like a disguise, suggesting a violence, a radicalism which wasn't his at all' (p. 169). D's desperate bid is thwarted by Bates. He prefers to believe Lord Benditch and his Board who decide to bluff their way and evade the law to sell the coal to L:

> I think the best we can do . . . is to ask a definite assurance from Lord Benditch's agent that the coal is going to Holland – and only to Holland . . . If he gives that, why, we can go to work tomorrow with a clear conscience (p. 170).

That Holland is only a cover-up does not concern Bates and the fact that the miners need the wages and that the opening of the mines will provide the jobs that are needed introduces the complex layers of the politics of survival.

The power of the novel lies as much in its exposure of the collusions and betrayals of war as in establishing the bond between D and Rose Cullen, and gains much in the fact that the wheeler-dealing that frustrates D's hopes takes place in England with the establishment of the country involved in helping the Fascist side. To look in Greene's fiction for direct indictments of Hitler or Fascism and for clear ideological directions that could be related to political parties or to an expression of polemical points is futile for the artist is, as ever, engaged in primarily creating a legend. As always with Greene, D's ideals suggest a generalised revulsion of materialism as represented by popular culture. The frail figure of Else, a helpless, exploited waif makes D realise that he prefers the bombed streets and food queues from which a new world can be constructed to what parades as civilisation – 'the crowded prosperous streets, the women trooping in for coffee at Buzzards, the lady-in-waiting at King Edward's Court, and the sinking, drowning child' (p. 51).

The Confidential Agent is important not least because it contains the lines quoted by Philby to explain his attitude to Stalinism.[10] The issue discussed here is loyalty and it seems apt to comment here on Greene's own loyalty to his friend Philby. His open expression of admiration for a man who risked all for his ideals appears tinged with a schoolboy yearning for 'daring', for the sheer enormity of Philby's powers in playing the dangerous game. The two friends have maintained contact over the years. Personal friendship for Greene, and for Greene's England, is the supreme ethic. Le Carré observes that for Greene individual loyalties matter more than 'social or human loyalties, even philosophic loyalties'.[11] I would qualify this by adding that for Greene individual loyalties matter, and particularly so when he can imaginatively sympathise with the idealism that prompts a certain course of action. That Greene's individual loyalties are also intimately bound up with his social, human and philosophic loyalties is adequately borne out by the idealism of his work. The lines quoted by Philby are:

> He said 'You've got to choose some line of action and live by it. Otherwise nothing matters at all. You probably end with a gas-oven. I've chosen certain people who've had the lean portion for some centuries now.'
> 'But your people are betrayed all the time.'
> 'It doesn't matter. You might say it's the only job left for anyone – sticking to a job. It's no good taking a moral line. My people commit atrocities like others. I suppose if I believed in a god it would be simpler.'
> 'Do you believe' she said, 'that *your* leaders are any better than L's?' She swallowed her brandy and began to tap the counter nervously with the little metal bullet.
> 'No. Of course not. But I still prefer the people they lead – even if they lead them all wrong.'
> 'The poor, right or wrong', she scoffed.
> 'It's no worse – is it? – than my country, right or wrong. You choose your side once and for all. Of course, it may be the wrong side. Only history can tell that' (p. 60).

Greene has not moved from this position despite the realities of repression in Communist societies. Philby, he says, was behaving well from his point of view. He was taking great risks for a cause he believed in and Greene admires the courage which he says he lacks himself. He hastens to add that he does not agree that ends justify means and has frequently spoken out in defence of writers imprisoned in Russia.

Greene's comments on *The Confidential Agent* suggest the many strands that make up the novel:

There are certain things I like in this book: for example the predicament of the agent with scruples, who is not trusted by his own party and who realises that his party is right not to trust him. In this case it was the predicament of a Communist (although D did not in fact possess a Party card). A writer who is a Catholic cannot help having a sympathy for any faith which is sincerely held and I was glad when Philby quoted this novel explaining his attitude to Stalinism. It seemed to indicate that I had not been far wrong, although at the period I wrote I knew nothing of Intelligence work.[12]

The fact that he kept aloof and did not join the Left Crusade of his contemporaries during the Spanish Civil War in an idealistic support of the Loyalist cause did not cloud issues in the novel. Greene's sympathies 'were more engaged by the Catholic struggle against Franco than with the competing sectarians in Madrid'. On being further pressed on the issue he clarified his point: the anti-Catholic Loyalist Movement was guilty as well – 'their hands were not clean'.[13] His present enthusiastic support for the Sandinista Government in Nicaragua suggests the ideals of religion and politics that underlie his life and work. Although his concern with developments in Central America is a continuation of insights that began with an understanding of issues in the 1930s it is a limited interpretation of Greene's work to infer, as John Le Carré has, that Greene's perception of events is frozen within polemics of the 1930s:

It makes a lot of sense to me to call Greene 'a man of the Thirties', and I sometimes feel, when reading *The Human Factor*, for example, the later Greene, that he has almost deliberately frozen his experience of England in that formative period, when there was a clear choice between communism and capitalism, in order, one might almost say, to exploit that artistically. I don't think very many people these days seriously choose between communism and capitalism, communism and Catholicism. I believe that those choices really have become for him artistic metaphors of doubt, and artistic metaphors of human anguish. But they remain cloaked in the wardrobe of the Thirties.[14]

Le Carré admires Greene but feels that there are parts of his political career

which have been marked by great simplicity not to say naivety. He has, at times, given vent to very strange utterances. And I think anyway that Greene the writer, whom I know and enormously love, is really much more at home with the unresolved story, and the unresolved relationship. I don't really believe that he was ever equipped to venture into the field of polemics and politics.[15]

Greene's political insights convince precisely because he keeps away from polemics and illustrates the ambiguities of experience in a world of ideologies and orthodoxies. He can be accused of romantic idealism, and of trying to merge irreconcilable elements in the interest of his art, but he cannot be said to simplify issues. These are sifted and exposed in a variety of ways, in relation to individuals, to social groups, to national demands and to international developments. The fact that *The Confidential Agent* has an unresolved political solution and a happy romantic ending, for instance, does not diminish its grasp of struggle that is political and economic. Greene's statements have always been made in relation to policies and positions adopted by Western governments and economic establishments that compromise conscience and morality. In this sense *The Confidential Agent* though set in a nameless country reflects directly on Chamberlain's policies of appeasement. In its choice of presenting the issue of freedom as within the control of industrial establishments Greene's novel validates comments made polemically by George Orwell in his essay, *England, Your England*, in 1941:

The mishandling of England's domestic problems during the nineteen-twenties had been bad enough, but British foreign policy between 1931 and 1939 is one of the wonders of the world. Why? . . . The underlying fact was that the whole position of the moneyed class had long ceased to be justifiable. There they sat, at the centre of a vast empire and a world-wide financial network, drawing interest and profits . . . Only half a million people, the people in the country houses, definitely benefited from the existing system.[16]

Greene has always attacked the stranglehold of capitalism and has said that America represents capitalism 'in its most Stalinist form'. He also disclosed that he has no fixed attitude towards Communism but hopes that in the next 100 years of struggles and upheavals 'something will emerge from Communism which will be preferable to the brutalising affluence of America'.[17]

An intricate narrative strategy gives *The Ministry of Fear* (1943) its distinctive structure of shifting images: a city under siege, the vain search for lost innocence, an irrecoverable life of trust and peace, danger lurking in pastoral surroundings. Nothing is what it seems. Its most dramatic aspect is the setting of the London blitz during the Second World War. Equally important is the chief characteristic of the protagonist Arthur Rowe whose sense of guilt gives the novel its psychological and moral power. Greene here returns to a juxtaposition of legality and morality. Although the court has acquitted him of murder Rowe's guilt haunts him as does his motive for the crime: pity for another's suffering.

The Ministry of Fear has been hailed as a masterpiece of the thriller form but its artistry lies in breaking the mould of the thriller to integrate concerns that are tragic and spiritual. The novel thus has the spellbinding excitements of the thriller and the moral questionings of tragic form accomplished through an evenly paced interweaving of public and private experience – the inner life of Arthur Rowe in wartime London which leads him, unsuspecting, into the manipulations of a Fifth Column. The plot merges these twin concerns in a realism that combines the meticulous detail of surface life with actions that spring from Rowe's conflicts and impulses. Through this structure Greene presents a longing for the past amid the incoherence and chaos of the present; man as self-absorbed, and the need for self-knowledge which entails awareness of the world; the loss of self – rendered through the story-line as amnesia occasioned by a bomb attack – and the recovery of self. The two levels evoke the nightmare of war, the idealisms that sometimes underlie it, and the psychological state of Arthur Rowe. The condition of England suggested in *England Made Me* is carried into deeper dimensions where the analysis of an ethos moves beyond class to include man in the world.

Written in Freetown, Sierra Leone, during the war, the novel draws much of its power from minute details recorded by Greene when working as an air raid warden in London. As V. S. Pritchett notes, *The Ministry of Fear* is studiously unmelodramatic, continuously realistic and minutely observed:

> one could not find a better picture of the blitz than this novel gives . . . an experience taken in its off moments . . . small details for authenticity – the illusion of the sideways movement of the floor when the bomb falls, the warden lighting 'the yellows up', the grey emptiness'.[18]

The city of London is heartland of war; innocent public functions and England's green and pleasant countryside camouflage the work of a Fascist idealist. The choice of innocuous professions for the spies – a doctor, a pastor, a master-tailor, a society hostess, the headquarters for the whole operation in the office of what seems a harmless group of social workers that brings to mind benign old ladies – a charity called: 'The Mothers of Free Nations' – all add up to a succession of dramatic incidents, and comic situations with dire consequences. Here is fantasy in the service of truth. Here too is Greene's ambition to create a legend realised with consummate flair. Arthur Rowe becomes, through his inner conflicts and physical experiences, a mythical figure and the city of London a mythical centre of reality.

The fair to which Arthur Rowe is drawn calls him 'like innocence' but carries intimations of disaster:

> There was something threatening, it seemed to him, in the very perfection of the day. Between the plane trees which shaded the treasure-ground he could see the ruined section of the square; it was as if Providence had led him to exactly this point to indicate the difference between then and now' (pp. 14–15).[19]

These are code-signs to suggest personal and public disaster, private tragedy and the anguish of a society devastated by war, the guilt of knowledge and the realisation of truth. 'Knowledge' is revealed in Greene's novels at various levels as experience of human cruelty, poverty, exploitation, as well as the reality of war. When Arthur Rowe speaks of a world of peace that he once knew all these levels are sounded – a wife much-loved, his implication in her death, his guilt, a world of trust forever lost:

Now in the strange torn landscape where London shops were reduced to a stone ground-plan like those of Pompeii he moved with familiarity; he was part of the destruction as he was no longer part of the past – the long weekends in the country, the laughter up lanes in the evening, the swallows gathering on telegraph wires, peace (p. 40).

The structure of the novel relates the form and the content of the adventure story to invert it and suggest that the idealism and heroism of boyhood, and its romance is hideously transformed. Crouching in an air-raid shelter he dreams and talks to his mother explaining to her that thrillers are like life

> more like life than you are, this lawn, your sandwiches, that pine. You used to laugh at the books Miss Savage read – about spies, and murders, and violence, and wild motor-car chases, but dear, that's real life: it's what we've all made of the world since you died. I'm your little Arthur who wouldn't hurt a beetle and I'm a murderer too. The world has been remade by William Le Queux' (p. 65).

Although the world of romance and reality are enmeshed in his consciousness and he is living the adventure stories as nightmare he no longer has codes that could help: 'I'm a learner, I'm right at the beginning trying to find my way about. I thought life was much simpler and grander . . . It's as if one had been sent on a journey with the wrong map' (p. 65). More than any other novel *The Ministry of Fear* evokes lost innocence in Rowe's constant recall of a nostalgic past – in the frequent imagery of loss of direction, of enemy territory within secure and familiar surroundings, of treachery. These images extend the inner quest within an atmosphere of doubt, change and distrust that infects the world of the novel. The green baize door appears in its most deadly form to reveal inhuman cruelty, and ultimately the intense pain of self-knowledge.

Rowe's blind search for release from guilt leads him unsuspecting into an espionage ring among whom, though innocent, he is judged guilty enough to be eliminated. The unravelling of this mystery in a dizzying spiral of events and clearly visualised imagery reveal Greene's ability to suggest desolation. The gritty horrors of underground shelters, a boarded-up London whose familiar streets have lost their shape amid rubble and destruction, lead to the starkly composed picture of the isolation of city life in the image of a modern hotel where Anna Hilfe and Arthur Rowe are trapped while Hilfe waits for the bomb to explode and destroy them. The reader shares in Rowe's desolation:

> He followed at the page's heels down interminable corridors lit by concealed lighting . . . the back, the tight little blue trousers and the bum-freezer jacket, just went on ahead. It seemed to Rowe that one could be lost here for a lifetime: only the clerk at the desk would have a clue to one's whereabouts, and it was doubtful whether he ever penetrated very far in person into the enormous wilderness . . . A door in the passage was ajar and odd sounds came through it as though someone were alternately whistling and sighing, but nothing to the page seemed strange. He just went on: he was a child of this building. People of every kind came in for a night with or without luggage and then went away again; a few died here and the bodies were removed unobtrusively by the service lift . . . The page took everything for granted (p. 96).

The sense of a rich and close community life replaced by an urban desert is very strong in all Greene's fiction and an important element of the dream England that died with 'growing up'. His sense of justice doubtless sees the merits of the postwar Welfare State but the fiction is underpinned by disgust with the endless gratification of consumer tastes, of a civilisation that panders to human acquisitiveness. The wistful longing for simple pleasures, for humdrum domesticity where feelings are shared is compellingly evoked in the sequence where Rowe emerges from his 'happy', ignorant and innocent state in a sanatorium for the shellshocked to discover the underside of this idyllic retreat – a cover for Nazi activity. Dr Forester's cures, in fact, prefigure the politically motivated diagnoses of madness that are the reality of so many lives today.

Rowe escapes from the sanatorium and brings back, from London, an investigating officer from the Special Branch, to break the Fifth Column that has infected both city and countryside with treachery, injustice and cruelty. His awareness of this taint and corruption is set against a world of simple joys which are beyond his grasp. He feels removed from the 'profound common experiences of men. Rowe felt a longing to get back into that world: into the world of homes and children and quiet love and the ordinary unspecified fears and anxieties the neighbour shared' (p. 178).

An important element of Greene's fiction is his ability to create an atmosphere of 'them' and 'us', of villains and victims within the grey areas of human experience, so that when the chase is completed and the good deed done there is no feeling of victory, nor indeed justice. Hilfe and Forrester are seen as human, motivated by ideals however misguided. Through Rowe's guilt – the idea with which the novel begins – the narrative unfolds a world at war as well as man who is as 'a creature at war with himself. Further he is a self-deceptive creature who thinks he is feeling one thing or acting from one motive when his actual feelings and motives are quite different'. This is the process that leads Rowe to self-awareness and he realises that he has killed his wife 'to escape his own pain, not hers'. Hilfe, the 'villain' who suffers no pain for anyone and is capable of complete inhumanity in pursuing his ideal which is beyond humanity, an abstraction, is finally revealed – a pathetic creature retching in an urinal after a vain attempt to complete his mission.

The novel's most evocative inversion is that of the title which is first used to suggest control through fear for political ends and later transformed to a call for protection of human connections. The political and the human move together all through the course of the novel, merging in the human factor. The Ministry of Fear that once spread an atmosphere of distrust so that you could not depend on a soul is inverted. At the close, Rowe feels he has joined the permanent staff of the Ministry:

> But it wasn't the small Ministry to which Johns had referred, with limited aims like winning a war or changing a constitution. It was a Ministry as large as life to which all who loved belonged. If one loved one feared (p. 229).

It is in this sense too, that Greene has often said that his interest is in politics where the issue is life and death.

The three novels discussed illustrate the dream, the values and the love of a traditional Englishness that has never left Greene's fiction. Although he is the first English writer to recognise the validity of alternative world views – a perspective discussed in a later section of this book – these novels subliminally recall England as once the intellectual and moral centre for a large part of the world and in that sense Greene's value-system is inextricably linked with the idea of Empire although the Empire is never defended. The important point is that it is from the standpoint of this definition of what England once stood for, and still idealistically stands for in Greene's imagination, that Greene confronts the world and the new empires. Le Carré points out quite rightly that Greene has accomplished something amazing 'in making his form of Englishness a universality for artistic purposes'.[20]

5

Colons, Intermediaries and Exiles

Of the twenty-five novels written by Graham Greene seventeen are set outside England,[1] a fact that has led to criticism that the settings of his fiction are exotic, unreal, a country of the mind called 'Greeneland'. In all such discussions an important factor is often overlooked and this is his perception of the realities of societies which in modern political vocabulary would be called Third World, a term Greene neither uses nor wishes to validate. It is true that he does treat these societies as a collective identity, as victims of imperialism, of the West, and of superpower hegemonies. But he breaks ranks with the usual run of writers from the West to explore these societies as culturally autonomous. Greene responds to mental and spiritual worlds unfamiliar to the Judaeo-Christian tradition and recognises aspirations of societies who do have an existence – albeit rarely recognised outside their own frontiers – deeper than categories that feature in the vocabulary of development economics.

Journey Without Maps (1936) and *The Lawless Roads* (1939) illustrate Greene's openness and sensitivity to societies other than his own, and the candour with which he recognises and respects the original cultures of Africa and Mexico. His understanding of economic and cultural exploitation contains indictments of what is called coastal culture, the Coast being the West Coast of Africa. Cultural influence here is described as an unholy assimilation of the externals of both civilisations: the grafting of a bit of Europe on a substratum of Africa. It is a process that helped imperial advancement and was economically advantageous to some of the subject-race. Greene's work argues that such a process of half-education undermines the original culture. Bereft of the fundamental values of either civilisation the result is gross materialism, dehumanisation unchecked.

To create a character whose culture is completely alien to one's own involves difficulties that can be daunting and Greene has confessed his initial hesitation, for instance, in making the Priest in *The Power and the Glory* a Mexican. In subsequent novels, existential problems and political realities are approached through an English-man's point of view which gives him a reference point for his characters in terms he can communicate more fully; occasionally there is a departure, as in *The Honorary Consul* (1983) where Dr Plarr, though not an Englishman, has a link with England by birth. Although the narrative then reaches out into the experience of the other, Greene has sometimes been accused of using these societies as material for an exploration of the modern experience of exile and alienation, of the white liberal's guilt or, as some would prefer to have it, of his obsession with conscience and damnation.

The novels examined here have been divided into two sections with a preliminary section that introduces the context of ideas. The first group of novels consists of the two set in Africa – *The Heart of the Matter* (1948) and *A Burnt-Out Case* (1961), and includes *Travels with my Aunt* (1969). Though it is not set in Africa *Travels with my Aunt* portrays an African as a central character in marked difference to the first two novels where African characters have relatively minor roles. The novel also brings together concerns and a theme from *The Heart of the Matter* that connect the Anglo-Saxon, the Mediterranean and the African worlds in a close relationship.

The second group of novels evokes the theme of exile and reveals a grasp and comprehension of the complexities of the sociopolitical scene. The power of this reality makes up for what the novels lack: detail of individual and community life which could only come from close contact with societies in Vietnam, Haiti, Cuba and Paraguay where the novels are set. Greene's insights are valued because he remains the sympathetic outsider with a deeper awareness of political means and ends than he is sometimes given credit for, and indeed would care to exhibit.

*   *   *

Few writers have explored the possibilities of the novel as the literary form of 'transcendental homelessness' with more diverse a range of experience than Graham Greene. As with Joseph Conrad, exile is the aesthetic principle that underpins his work. Insights proceed from a sense of isolation and separation from the past towards a courageous confrontation of a changing world order. The sense of exile first emanates from experience of dislocation between the ordered and stable world of home and the unsettling betrayals of boarding-school where, with his father as headmaster, he felt 'the

son of a quisling in a country under occupation'. Such early experience was deepened with instabilities of the 1930s, the Second World
War and with the awareness that values and discipline enshrined in
received codes of conduct no longer made sense. These perceptions,
first revealed in novels of the 1930s, have been enriched by travel
into new dimensions of experience motivated, one suspects, by a
sense of physical and intellectual exile as well as by curiosity and
concern.

In his reflections on exile as an aesthetic principle Edward Said
has suggested that the exile knows that in a secular and contingent
world, homes are provisional.[2] Borders and barriers which enclose
us within the safety of familiar territory can also become prisons;
they are often defended beyond reason and necessity. Exiles cross
borders, break barriers of thought and experience. They do more.
They look at home with an exile's detachment. Graham Greene's
England is hence an exile's view of his homeland, and this is not
because he does not live there. Ever since the early years of his
career as a novelist Graham Greene has practised in his art the
morality of 'not to be at home in one's home' so as to question dogma
and orthodoxy as well as received views of culture, history and
assumptions that govern human relationships in situations of global
relevance.

At home nowhere and everywhere, Greene transmutes experience through English characters separated from their heritage and
through them transcends his tradition to encode a whole range of
meanings. In so doing he breaks the hegemony of the 'Natopolitan
world'[3] to include new cultures, new societies, and emerging visions
of social, political, aesthetic and spiritual order. Greene sets about
this exploration with characters whom I have grouped in the
categories of exiles, *colons* and intermediaries. Together they form a
microcosm: people who belong to two or more cultures and are
thrown together apparently for professional reasons. Their relationships are developed in the text to deepen political and spiritual
realities. The condition of physical exile extends into a search for
recovery of self but it is also poignantly historical. Greene's understated evocation of the horror of modern warfare and totalitarianism
and of the sunset of imperialism is shot through with spirituality
which gives a definite character to the concept of exile.

As for Conrad, Africa has been an important continent for Greene.
Both used Africa as background for testing European concerns of a
dying imperial ethic and a disintegrating moral order. To analyse

Greene's novels of Africa, it is helpful to work with the categories of *colon* and intermediary. Equally important is the category of 'the foreign novel of Africa' some of whose characteristics – paternalism, enchantment with pristine beauty, affection for the simple, unsophisticated, childlike African and scorn for the educated counterpart – are occasionally shared by *The Heart of the Matter* and *A Burnt-Out Case*. The foreign novel of Africa may be said to be a record, an evocation and an interpretation of the life and situation of a foreign people for the education and entertainment of the author's native readers. Michael Echeruo defines it:

> the author uses the distanced peoples and lands of his narrative to make assertions of a large and general kind about human life and human values. The argument of such novels derives cogency almost entirely from the character and meaning which the author ascribes to the foreign lands and foreign peoples about whom he writes . . . the valuation of its episodes and of its characters is determined by an imposed moral code specifically defined for it by the novelist and his cultural assumptions. In such circumstances the fidelity of rapportage becomes of secondary importance to the novelist's overall conception of his foreign context. The foreign novel of Africa is particularly liable to this tendency because it falls so insistently on a long standing, highly developed, and culturally validated notion of the African scene itself.[4]

Greene has more than one novel set in Africa and continues with his concerns with the African people even in a novel set in London: *The Human Factor* (1978). He travelled along directions set out by Conrad and beyond. Since he approaches the reality of African experience in its human dimensions his strategy is considerably different from that of E. M. Forster,[5] Joyce Cary,[6] and George Orwell,[7] who plunge headlong into imperial and cultural confrontations. It is important, however, to remember that 'the human' as defined by the outsider is not always imaginatively or emotionally in keeping with the point of view of the inhabitants of the region of Africa where the novels are set. It is this last point that determines the degree to which Greene struggles successfully to extend his awareness beyond his own cultural assumptions in order to understand the scene about which he writes.

Greene first travelled to Liberia when he was 30 years old and seems to have undertaken this journey as much under the influence of his boyhood fascination for the novels of Rider Haggard as to follow the lure of the times for writers to take themselves off to the outposts of Empire to seek perilous encounters, less dangerous but no less exhilarating than the missed experiences of the battlefields of the First World War. Samuel Hynes discusses the phenomenon in *The Auden Generation*:

> One clear feature of the 'thirties is that as the decade passed, Englishmen became increasingly aware of the presence and importance of the world-out-there: as the Abroad became a threat, it became a reality. In the case of young writers this meant shift of attention away from English subjects, toward foreign scenes and problems. This had happened quite clearly in the decade in some cases: Isherwood had gone to Berlin, Lehmann and Spender had gone to Vienna, Orwell had gone down and out in Paris, and all of them had written parables of the realities they had found. The travel books of the end of the decade simply extended the limits of out-there, as the perimeter of awareness and the community of disaster expanded – to Africa, to Mexico, to China, to the whole troubled world.[8]

Among those who went beyond Europe like Greene were Peter Fleming and Evelyn Waugh. Greene's account of the trip in *Journey Without Maps* alternates between a learning process and blind acceptance of the assumptions current in the tradition of 'the foreign novel of Africa' not least its search for a different, less guilt-ridden sexuality:

> It isn't that one wants to stay in Africa: I have no yearning for a mindless sensuality, even if it were to be found there: It is only that when one has appreciated such a beginning, its terrors as well as its placidity, the power as well as the gentleness, the pity for what we have done with ourselves is driven more forcibly home (p. 249).

Joyce Cary who wrote several novels set in Africa is in a different category altogether. He knew the scene far better than Greene and, like Kipling in India, had lived and worked in Africa for a considerable time. He had therefore greater knowledge of African culture and of the effects of the confrontation with Western Christian traditions. His novels are set amid direct interactions: colonial encounters with the indigenous population based on six years of experience in Africa. Even so Echeruo concludes that Cary

> would have had to re-live his African experience in the light of a new metaphysics, learn to separate his former attitudes from his accounts of episodes and depend entirely on his critical intelligence for the reappraisal of the message of his six years experience in Africa.[9]

In the many novels Greene has set outside England the inter-action between characters has, in a general sense, been very wisely created as an interaction between *colons* and intermediaries without any suggestion of direct knowledge of indigenous culture, or indeed of intimate experience with the colonised. As used here these terms require little explanation except to say that they describe Europeans who make a living in non-European societies and individuals from the local population who have acquired skills to mediate between the cultures so that the *colon* can carry on making his living and the intermediary may derive what benefit he can from the situation. These relationships, always exploitative, are approached from the human standpoint, with the economic situation merely suggested but never entirely absent. The narrative is placed, in an important sense, outside indigenous experience. The writer explores imagin-atively and through subtle indirection areas to which he has no access. There is some development, however, in the characterisation of the intermediary so that in the later novels they are transformed into articulate representatives of the oppressed with moorings in an educated class, but with the suggestion that the intermediary can also be the new oppressor in post-colonial societies.

Colons refers usually to planters, settlers, colonists; it is in this sense of bourgeois occupations that Greene uses the word in *A Burnt-Out Case* and then turns it over to suggest that there are individual *colons* who have courage, tenacity and discipline and are free from the hypocrisy as well as insensitivity of many who despise the *colon*. He once said in an interview that were he to write a novel about the Mau Mau period in Africa despite his sympathy for the Mau Mau he would probably write about the settler to see the situation from his perspective as he did in despatches from Malaya where the plight of the planter and his family is described.

The African as member of the urban middle class makes no appearance in Greene's novels, much less the African who speaks no English. Though the novels in the main deal with intermediaries, exiles, *colons*/colonial officers, the narrative attempts a grasp of political realities from the African point of view. The minor African characters in *The Heart of the Matter* and *A Burnt-Out Case* need therefore to be seen in relation to Wordsworth in *Travels with my Aunt* who is derived from the tradition of the noble savage but illustrates Greene's pained perceptions of the truths of the colonial encounter. It is in this context that the novels are examined to determine the extent to which Greene inherits and subscribes to European notions of scenes in foreign climes and the development of his work in exploring the assumptions of imperialism, not far removed from the élitism that has replaced imperialism today.

Both E. M. Forster and Graham Greene travelled less in the heyday of Empire than at a time when colonial assumptions were being dumped. Forster's novel precedes Greene's *The Heart of the Matter* by a couple of decades and he places the colonials and intermediaries within a political framework as did Orwell in *Burmese Days*. Greene refrains from such a strategy and yet arrives at the realities of colonialism which elude Forster whose obsessions led him into other dimensions of experience. The cultural encounter in *A Passage to India* and *Burmese Days* is ultimately rendered from within the perspective of the ruling race. This structure is never really abandoned even when it is being most earnestly questioned and exposed which results in cultural stereotypes being forced into characters of the rulers and the subject race. Yusef as intermediary in Greene's novel is a far more successful creation than Forster's Aziz or Orwell's Veeraswami and U Po Kyin both as human being and as participant in colonial enterprise.

Less ambitious in design than *A Passage to India* Greene's novel uncovers depths both political and cultural because he structures the whole within the human context. From a writer with so clear a perception of the political dimensions of life it is indeed a surprise that there should be no direct confrontation with the British Empire in his fiction, as there has been, for instance, of American imperialism. 'It was over', he says, 'and there was nothing to write about.' Nevertheless, statements in *Journey Without Maps*, the central metaphor in *A Burnt-Out Case* as well as the relationship between Aunt Augusta, Wordsworth and Visconti in *Travels with my Aunt* come closer than any English novelist this century has cared to come to the truths of the colonial encounter.

Greene's novels occasionally exasperate with unrestricted

idealisation of lost innocence, of an irrecoverable, non-technological, less urban landscape, a strategy he adopts as dramatic counterpoint to the oppressions of the present. His view of the African with whom Marie Rycker, for instance, cannot communicate because she is limited by her culture has to be examined within this context. Such Africans people his travelogues and *Journey Without Maps* reveals the traveller's reliance on his interpreter Amedoo. The intermediaries of fiction share elements of language and skills of communication with the *colon*.

If Greene's Africa is often unbearably romantic so is one aspect of his England. The vision of these two unspoilt civilisations accentuates contemporary experience although Greene cannot be entirely absolved of being free from imperialist attitudes. Just as Forster sees India through 'the educated vision' of the West,[10] Greene may be said to perceive Africa with a 'civilised' Western liberal conscience. It is misleading to argue, however, that Greene's Africans are either hospitable, generous, incurious, uncomplicated natives or civilised contemptible creoles; that the former are objects of pity, the latter of derision when seen, as Ogude reiterates in his incisive essays on Graham Greene's Africa, by 'the heartless perfect eye of the white man'.[11] This comment quoted from *Journey Without Maps* if taken too literally loses its point of bitter irony. As a master of understatement, Greene explores the relationship with subtle indirection to reveal structures of power and their effect on human experience. The white man's stance with which he starts out is progressively discounted during the length and breadth of travel and experience by a liberal conscience whose insights create a pervasive sympathy and understanding of the aspirations of the subject race.

European writing on Africa can rarely escape the psychological effect of the historical perception of the continent. Greene's work struggles between inherited perceptions and a process of unlearning through which he reaches out to the basics of human life. The result is a juxtaposition of various kinds of exploitation and oppression. The divide of race, creed, class and ideology is explored in a search for values which suggests that such forms of exploitation are both a matter of prejudice and of economic survival. His attempts to clarify these subtle relationships are underpinned by otherworldly hope which is less a compromise than an understanding of the deepest motives and impulses that govern human intercourse.

Passages in *Journey Without Maps* discussed earlier attempt an integration of spiritual ends and a condemnation of received views of Empire, religion and civilisation. Although the travelogue validates the work of some missionaries it reserves judgement as to 'whether what they brought with them in the shape of a crucified God was superior to the local fetish worship' (p. 82). Greene returns to this question in a tangential way in *The Comedians*. The juxtaposition of the two cultures, on occasion simplistic and superficial, reveals Greene's own preoccupations: a desire to evolve a synthesis of a Western missionary culture transmitted through imperialism and the indigenous pristine faith that has given identity and vitality to its believers.

*   *   *

Many of the ideas contained in the travelogues are inevitably transmuted in the novels though in none of those dealing directly or indirectly with African peoples does Greene confront the colonial situation directly, an omission that lays him open to the charge of evading an important issue of our time. Orwell, for instance, made the following comment when *The Heart of the Matter* was published:

> Why should this novel have its setting in West Africa? Except that one of the characters is a Syrian trader, the whole thing might as well be happening in a London suburb. The Africans exist only as an occasionally mentioned background, and the thing that would actually be in Scobie's mind the whole time – the hostility between black and white, and the struggle against the local nationalist movement – is not mentioned at all. Indeed, although we are shown his thoughts in considerable detail, he seldom appears to think about his work, and then only of trivial aspects of it, and never about the war, although the date is 1942. All he is interested in is his own progress toward damnation. [12]

In retrospect, from the vantage-point of today when colonialism is virtually an event of the past, it is easier to appreciate Greene's strategy which grapples with the main issue of exploitation within a network of human relationships rather than as a confrontation between the rulers and the subject-race with a liberal conscience arbitrating the dialogue. *The Heart of the Matter* has for so long been discussed as a Catholic novel that it is quite possible to entirely overlook its subtle representation of the relationship between the colonial officer, the intermediary and the colonised. Interestingly, however, Terry Eagleton compares the novel with Orwell's *Burmese Days* which has always been regarded as a classic of colonial confrontation:

> The resemblance lies not only in remarkable congruencies of setting and narrative detail – the seedy colonialist context, the machinations of a corrupt native leader, the arrival of a young English girl, the culminating suicide – but in the instructive parallels between Flory and Henry Scobie.[13]

There is also a very significant difference. While Greene had his eye on the main issue it was Orwell who was confused. The latter's is indeed the headlong onslaught against Empire but the power of his arguments is considerably undermined by a narrative strategy that inexplicably obfuscates issues and subverts the very points he seems to wish to make. As Eagleton points out, *Burmese Days* is widely known as 'an assault upon Anglo-Burma but what is less often remembered is its half-convinced apology, through the focus of the self-doubting Flory, for some of the regime's worst aspects'.[14]

Eagleton also illustrates the awkwardly narrow line on which *The Heart of the Matter* has to tread

> between the objective reality of goodness and a subjective un-awareness of its presence. Scobie's impotent passivity, his chronic incapacity for decisive moral action, is a criticism of his behaviour; yet it is lessened in force, not only because the mood and comment of the novel co-operate in confirming the intelligence of this stance . . . but because it is precisely his passivity, his desperately pragmatic scepticism, which leads him to a cour-ageous act and at the same time shields him from any destructive belief in its value. Because Scobie is caught up by his very pragmatism into an action which both transcends that process and yet is also its last, logical step, the novel is able to validate and criticise this ethic at the same time. He is led, by decent, 'rational' behaviour, to a kind of courage which outstrips the behaviour of the decent rationalist.[15]

Alongside this important analysis it is therefore necessary to recall that *The Heart of the Matter* comes very close to the realities of imperialism though it appears, on the evidence of its story-line, to be skirting the issue. Greene's attempts to 'totalise' and 'transcend' the immediate pressures of colonial society by revealing that experience in a wider perspective should not be dismissed as a spiritual movement beyond history and culture but discussed as an assimilation of spiritual directions within a historical perspective.

Scobie is the Assistant Commissioner of Police whose business it is to preserve order and civilisation with duties that range from the wartime importance of prevention of smuggling to arbitration in squabbles between landlord and tenant. That the law protects those that make it and those who bribe or render favours to the custodians of the law as a refrain in the main narrative as well as in the brief account of Pemberton's tragic suicide. The irony of the lesson is that Scobie and, by implication Pemberton, are good, humane and exhausted by their zeal for justice. This is a weakness in Greene's fictional representation of the colonial encounter. His colonial protagonists are portrayed as helpless cogs in an exploitative machine with its centre in London, and working with the middle man, the intermediary in the field – here it is Yusef – as part of a corrupt system. The colonial officer is absolved of the sin though he is not free from guilt. In Scobie's case the human predicament implicates him in the corrupt system more damagingly.

The novel's careful structure in three parts is based, in the main, on Scobie's relationships with his wife Louise and his mistress Helen Rolt. Part I concludes with the departure of Louise on holiday to South Africa. The holiday, paid for with a loan from the smuggler Yusef, creates an unholy bond between the upholder of the law and the trader with a reputation for corruption, between the colonial and the intermediary. It also suggests, as does *Burmese Days*, the difficulties of life in the outposts of Empire with 'heat, meanness and malice' which compel the sensitive colonial to turn to the intermediary for solace or financial help. While Orwell's structure does not present an economic link between the two groups Greene implies that Scobie's corruption is prompted by humane rather than materialistic considerations.

Another aspect of Greene's structure is that the intermediary is not African but Syrian thus introducing the juxtaposition of the Anglo-Saxon, the Mediterranean, and the African which recurs in a later novel *Travels with my Aunt*. Orwell's novel has two intermediaries: an Indian, Dr Veeraswami who is a professional within the larger colonial framework, and the Burmese U Po Kyin, subdivisional magistrate of Kyauktada in Upper Burma, who manipulates for personal advancement the authority conferred on him by the Empire. Thus Orwell's most serious allegations are reserved for the Burmese. The Indian doctor is ingratiating and a toady; the English are racist, bumptious fools, cowards; the Burmese will stoop to anything.

Forster's Aziz, another intermediary as professional, oscillates between injured pride and an ingratiating manner, between hatred for imperialism and love of English culture which in his mind parallels that of the Mughals from whom he claims descent. The personality that emerges is that of an endearing but weak man in whom Forster perhaps sought to merge various elements of culture and sensibility. Through him Forster attempts an interaction and a confrontation between the rulers and the ruled at the level of culture with the economic issue safely ignored. Professor Godbole, the pristine Indian, keeps aloof from the ruling race and finally resigns from the College run by Fielding, through whose liberal conscience Forster approaches the reality of India. Godbole's step is deliberate – a movement away from the colonial set-up to a new life to start his own school in an environment that is still free from the inroads of colonial civilisation. Forster grasps these levels of struggle and attempts to enter Professor Godbole's Hindu world, but the discourse ignores the economic aspects of exploitation.

Orwell's Flory admits that his only reason for staying on was initially to make money at the timber factory where he works though he finally realises, regretfully, as does Scobie, that it is too late to go back. Flory's suffering and destruction, induced mainly by his inferior social status within Raj hierarchies, are explained as the result of a corrupt system where, in the final analysis, the morals and culture of the ruled come off worst. There is little sympathy for the Burmese and the horror expressed is at the moral implications of the colonial encounter on English character.

The two approaches to colonial encounters in English literature as illustrated above are beset with limitations and lack of understanding: Forster's approach, apparently liberal and humane ignores the economic and political effects of colonisation. His attempt to suggest a synthesis of cultures, or liberal traditions of the West and the spiritualism of the East was already being foredoomed by the realities of the time. Orwell's approach is that imperialism debases the instruments of empire; he leaves the reader with the lurking suspicion that the cultures of the ruled are too debased to merit improvement, and so better left alone. Greene's approach transcends the categories of the rulers and the ruled and their confrontations; it is almost Kafkaesque in its despairing recreation of the absurdities of life.

For Greene the crux lies in the economic complexities of imperialism as reflected in the seediness and squalor of colonial encounters and administration of imperial outposts. He turns language and culture on its head so that when the intermediary, Yusef, quotes Shakespeare with genuine sadness – 'I am the base Indian who threw away the pearl' – as a joke against himself when blackmailing Scobie, the incident indirectly draws attention to the nature of the transactions of Empire. Not for Greene the neat middle-class moralities of Forster's humanism and Orwell's querulous criticism of the imperial ethic.

The narrative recognises the vitality and purity of indigenous cultures and unites the ruler and the ruled in a searing vision that removes distinctions of race and colour in an understanding of human nature which is expressed in a sense of religion and politics that is transcendental. Greene seems to be trying to say that original sin, for instance, is a condition of all men. At this most fundamental level, it gives equality to all: the seediness of the human condition with its vapours of corruption and survival carries with it a sense of sin and guilt which implicates all mankind.

Forster and Orwell can both be accused of cultural imperialism, not in the sense of an active participation in the racial hypocrisies of the regimes they indict but as unable to transcend the structures they wished to expose. The norm even for Forster who so actively embraced metaphysical questions outside his own ethos remained that of 'the educated vision'. Greene's novels are less grand in design but transcend the categories of cultural imperialism or racism by bringing up a dimension that makes a mockery of these categories. By staying close to the 'seediness' shared by all men, his perspective contributes to an understanding of the colonial encounter in human terms – not as a conflict between races and establishments but in human confrontations with the issue of exploitation always in the foreground. The weakness in Greene's analysis is that the Anglo-Saxon – although not the system of which he is a part – is absolved. Greene's villain usually has a foreign name – Colleoni, Sir Marcus, the *mestizo* as the Judas figure, and here Yusef the Mediterranean. It is only in the later fiction that the Anglo-Saxon is shown as not free from the taint of conscious exploitation. The courage of a vision that spares no one, including those who represent Greene's class and culture, gives his approach considerable moral power. This later development is best represented in *Travels with my Aunt* and *The Human Factor*.

In *The Heart of the Matter* the over-reliance on the Catholic viewpoint helps to create the necessary inwardness in Scobie. The political context is understated but its deepest economic structures suggested through interpersonal relationships. Part II develops the character of Scobie through his affair with Helen Rolt. The return of Louise, the tensions that follow, and further dealings between Scobie and Yusef occupy most of Part III which is, indeed, a poignant illustration of the collaboration and collusion between the colonial and the intermediary to promote each other's interests at the expense of the colonised. The victim at the end and the one most seriously betrayed is not Scobie who commits suicide but his loyal servant Ali, an African, who is less an intermediary than a representative of the colonised.

Flory, Scobie's counterpart in *Burmese Days* also commits suicide and his is the greatest tragedy in the novel which examines the issue of class, of civil servant versus boxwallah, of pukka sahib versus the brown sahib but rarely leaves the world of sahibs. *The Heart of the Matter* has only one victim, the innocent African. Scobie's heroism consists in his complete awareness of this betrayal for which he expects no absolution. Sadly, the strength of the psychological influence of inherited perceptions and Greene's own spiritual dilemmas overshadow the underlying structure: Ali who had served Scobie with dedication, loyalty and affection for fifteen years is knifed to death in order to safeguard Scobie's own reputation and that of Yusef. Ali is thought to know too much. Though he would probably derive no benefit from his knowledge, nor had he ever given any cause for distrust, his possession of such information is considered a threat to the existence of the colonial and the intermediary. The knowledge confirms collusion between the two. This is analysis of the colonial encounter at its most fundamental but worked through indirection rather than as direct confrontation.

Yusef, whom Orwell in his review of Greene's novel dismisses with half a sentence, is integral to the structure.[16] It is through the Syrian trader that Greene approaches the exploitative nature of colonial relationships and the network of economic bonds and covert actions. *A Passage to India* and *Burmese Days* illustrate the hypocrisy and xenophobia of the ruling race with the Club as centre. This was the social aspect of Empire and the extracurricular nucleus of forces used to subdue and carry on the business of economic exploitation. Greene's text presents an economic transaction, albeit personal and less detrimental to the character of the colonial than to that of the intermediary. In doing so it goes beyond the nastiness of the Club and the hypocrisies of the rulers in order to suggest the realities of colonial encounters.

In this sense the character of Yusef comes alive in his relationship with colonial structures far better than Forster's Aziz and Orwell's Dr Veeraswami, for instance, whose most signal quality is their ingratiating manner and admiration for English literature and culture. Yusef is open about exploiting the situation for his own economic ends. Shakespeare and romantic poetry are part of the scene but Scobie is not taken in by Yusef's protestations of admiration for English culture whereas Forster's 'good' English characters no less than Orwell's Flory thrive on the cultural connections. Ali's death in *The Heart of the Matter* embodies the burden of the subject-race who do not have the wherewithal to climb to the level of successful intermediaries.

Greene's novel does more than suggest the collusion between intermediary and coloniser. It illustrates the innocence of the colonised. They are pawns in the games being played by both groups and the fact that both employ boys as agents heightens this dimension: boys who survive by earning a living performing menial tasks which include snooping for information which they do not understand but which helps to advance the interests of their employers. The text balances the shrewd and calculating character of Yusef who swears friendship to Scobie and yet sets a boy to spy on Helen Rolt with parallel conduct from Wilson who has his own methods of spying on Yusef and Scobie. Both colonial and intermediary speak the same language of subtle connivance and exploitation.

In fact by making Wilson a representative of the Field Security Police directly responsible to London with power over those in the Empire hierarchies at the outpost Greene makes a distinction between colonials who served and developed a feeling for Africa and its people, and the heart of Empire in London which ruled by remote control with no thought for, nor understanding of, the realities except contempt and revulsion both of which were balanced by the profit of enterprise. Throughout the novel a latent racism colours Wilson's perception of his surroundings. His visit to the brothel where he is led, the narrative suggests, in spite of himself, reveals that he cannot truly feel attracted by a black girl whereas the first fact revealed about Scobie is that he loves Africans – 'he even sleeps with them'. It is a mark of distinction conferred on him by the author and equally the cause of his initial degradation within the British community.

Conrad's Marlowe reaches the base heart of the colonial encounter but conceals his knowledge when he returns to the centre in London, to the norm of civilised and moral conduct, to the idealism enshrined in Kurtz's relationship with his fiancée. Forster and Orwell face the realities of the relationship more consciously but remain imprisoned by norms set by a liberal conscience. Greene's novel moves at a different level, closer to Conrad's moorings, and succeeds because it subverts the norm, albeit the non-establishment norm of Catholic orthodoxy. The novel disregards obvious colonial realities such as those suggested by Orwell in the passage quoted from his review of *The Heart of the Matter* but the human experience of living within a colonial set-up unravels the cold logic of the imperial idea, a game in which Scobie himself is a pawn, with Ali as the most vulnerable of the group.

Some of these insights suggest Greene's efforts to extend his perceptions beyond the limits of 'the foreign novel of Africa' though it is possible to argue that in one sense *The Heart of the Matter* falls inescapably into this category: it does not – indeed cannot – embody national aspirations, nor a purely African point of view. The realities of Ali's life cannot be perceived by Scobie, nor could Greene participate in any sense in the larger reality of the life of his carriers in Liberia and in the experience of the boys who served him later in Freetown. Masks of survival protect the subject-race and prevent the colonial from perceiving the inner life of any of the colonised, even when the contact is as close and long as that between Ali and Scobie.

Such perceptions may have been possible if members of the urban middle class with skills of communication with their Western rulers and involved in freedom struggles were allowed to enter the text. As in *A Passage to India* and *Burmese Days* characters from the metropolitan centres of Empire are absent from Greene's novels of Africa though they do enter the centre of the narrative in *The Comedians* and *The Honorary Consul* as articulate members of the oppressed group. The closest portrayal of an African with a viewpoint of his own and the verve to express it is that of Wordsworth in *Travels with my Aunt*. At best he is Greene's idealised version of the half-educated, whom he actually professes to despise and calls 'creoles' in *Journey Without*

Maps. The African presence is registered forcefully but it is still an unequal presence and produces, necessarily, an unequal balance. Perhaps that is the point of the novel.

The fact that Greene frequently reiterates his love of Africa in terms of 'Africa of the Victorian atlas, the blank unexplored continent, the shape of the human heart',[17] with details of sights and smells provides easy pegs with which to nail the fiction down as the expression of a writer with a commitment to the idea of Empire and civilisation whose creations carry on the Victorian ethos of Rider Haggard's novels where a sense of adventure sustains the characters. Such arguments disregard the essence of Greene's fiction – as seen for instance in the characterisation of Scobie, Dr Colin and Querry – and indeed the fact that he has often explained that foreign locations enable him to explore Western traditions and English character in situations where the individual is deprived of the resources of familiar surroundings and supportive links with society.

A Burnt-Out Case (1961), set in the interior of the Congo, presents the *colon*, the intermediary and the African in a set of relationships in the shadow of Empire, perhaps suggesting a continuance of commercial and missionary activity in post-colonial societies. The central metaphor of the novel's title reveals characters within dimensions of a world-view that posits faith and the lack of it, pristine pleasures and material success, the village and intrusions from the outside world. The theme of wholeness and disintegration falls into place appropriately within the context of the leproserie. The narrative emphasises more than once the fact that 'leprosy is a psychological problem'.

The *colon* is introduced by references to the Otraco Transport Company, 'a monopolist of the river'. He is defined by colonial voices and codes in the town – Luc – where Querry conducts business to help his hosts the missionaries and Dr Colin of the leproserie. The characterisation of Rycker, manager of a palm-oil factory, whose illusions of intellectual superiority make him despise the bourgeois culture of his social group, presents aspects of the life of the *colon*. His wife Marie belongs to a family of *colons*, generations whose courage and tenacity she cannot emulate.

Characteristically Greene relates her sense of uprooting and discontinuity from an ordered life in France to the irrecoverable loss of Deo Gratias, the boy who is a burnt-out case and has stumps for hands. Both are described as looking for '*Pendélé*', a word used by Deo Gratias to explain what he seeks. The word is variously translated:

a place with dignity and independence which could also be pride and arrogance; a time of joy; a desire to dance and shout and run and sing. For Marie it is said to mean, perhaps, 'a dance at a friend's house, a young man with a shiny simple face, going to Mass on Sunday with the family, sleeping in a single bed'. The difficulty of translating the word suggests the untranslatable nature of what is lost, a loss that is never compensated, and though both Marie and Deo Gratias make a new life as 'translated' human beings, the wholeness is irrecoverable and specially so for Deo Gratias whose mutilation has deeply tragic consequences.

Deo Gratias works for Querry. The mutilations of leprosy seem to run less deep in him than those affected by change of environment and loss of a familiar and safe world. Both he and Marie are little more than children without defences against the outside world though the concluding section presents Marie as having greater resources for survival. She tells lies to secure freedom. Deo Gratias cannot communicate and is therefore robbed of this weapon.

Normally silent, Deo Gratias becomes inarticulate with excitement and words rush out when he tries to describe *'Pendélé'* to Querry. The urge to recover identity prompts escape for both Marie and Deo Gratias with Querry embroiled in both though anxious to remain uninvolved. This is particularly so in the case of Deo Gratias who has so far had no existence for the European except in terms of the menial tasks the boy performed. The long night in the forest when Querry goes in search and finally finds Deo Gratias 'cures' Querry of his self-absorption; it is 'a night when things begin' whose potential is never fully realised: Marie's plans for her own escape intervene with the kind of coincidence that contributes a dramatic poignancy to Greene's narrative.

Although the novel's main concern is the experience of Querry, ideals of selfhood are illustrated through juxtapositions of cultures and traditions of the *colon* and the African within a wider context provided by the arrival of Parkinson. The journalist brings in the wider world and Western cultural assumptions. That the dimension of cultural interaction and the disorientations and displacements brought by colonialism are never far from the creative consciousness is clear in the episode at the end of the novel when the building of the hospital designed by Querry is completed and the community celebrates the event with a mixture of European and African rituals and ceremonies. Modern technology will soon control pain, disease and death which means this should have been a festive occasion for all. Not everyone is happy, however, with this development. A dissident group is described as claiming superior knowledge, status and power. Though presented through the European perspective as 'trouble-makers' and outsiders from the coast their aspirations are endorsed by Dr Colin and by the fact that Deo Gratias, who has earlier escaped from the mission in search of *'Pendélé'*, moves slowly towards them and sits between the two groups. He is the only one who can understand their language:

> Nobody cared that a small dissident group who had nothing to do with the local tribe sang their own hymns apart. Only the doctor, who had once worked in the Lower Congo, recognised them for what they were, trouble-makers from the coast more than a thousand kilometres away. It was unlikely that any of the lepers could understand them . . . The proud song of superiority went on: superiority to their own people, to the white man, to the Christian god, to everyone beyond their own circle of six, all of them wearing the peaked caps that advertised Polo beer . . . Only Deo Gratias moved some way towards them; he squatted on the ground between them and the hospital, and the doctor remembered that as a child he had come west from the Lower Congo too. 'Is that the future?' Querry said. He couldn't understand the words, only the aggressive slant of the Polo-beer caps.
> 'Yes.'
> 'Do you fear it?'
> 'Of course. But I don't want my own liberty at the expense of anyone else's.'
> 'They do.'
> 'We taught them' (pp. 173–4).

The point is made: material needs, health, food, shelter, are not enough. Nor is faith if not rooted in identity. The text thus explores ideals of identity, disintegrations effected by the processes of history, and life lived with recognition of spiritual forces.

The intermediary in *A Burnt-Out Case* is the missionary. It is he who mediates between the ruling élite in Luc and the African in the village bringing to him the benefits of modern science – of which Dr Colin is a representative – with an effort to integrate them within valued tradition. The missionary as part of the colonial machine does not enter the scene in Greene's novels of Africa; he presents, instead, the missionary who is at pains not to destroy altogether the fabric of the villagers' lives, and the conversations between the wise Superior and the conscientious Father Thomas illustrate the two views of proselytisation.

The demands of routine are used to recall the fact that there is no communication between the African and the *colon* except within the activities of the mission. For instance, Deo Gratias and Querry stop for the night on their way to Luc where they go on behalf of Father Superior:

> The first night Querry stopped the truck at a turn in the road where a track led off towards the Perrins' plantation. He opened a tin of Frankfurters, while Deo Gratias put up a bed for him in the back of the truck and lit the paraffin cooker. He offered to share his food with Deo Gratias, but the man had some mess of his own ready prepared in a pot wrapped in an old rag, and the two of them sat in silence with the truck between them as though they were in separate rooms. When the meal was over Querry moved round the bonnet with the intention of saying something to Deo Gratias, but the 'boy' by rising to his feet made the occasion as formal as though Querry had entered his hut in the village, and the words, whatever they were, died before they had been spoken (pp. 30–1).

A parallel situation can be found in *The Heart of the Matter* when Scobie makes the long and tiring journey into the interior to investigate the suicide of Pemberton. However, Ali is more than a mere companion on the journey: he cares for Scobie, attends to all his needs in the long hours of discomfort when he suffers from malarial fever. The relationship between them is an active one largely because Ali has acquired the skills of communication that help both of them to survive and to develop a measure of understanding of each other.

Such a link begins to develop between Querry who grows less self-absorbed and is to his immense surprise first curious and then concerned about Deo Gratias. Querry, the exile, learns from the intermediary, the missionary, and from Dr Colin who mediates through action that is directed outside the self. Father Thomas's scruples, his abstract theorising and conventional ideas about religion and sanctity are gradually undermined and rejected within the narrative. The novel does more than use Africa to examine stages of belief, half-belief and non-belief: it expresses the aridity of material civilisations. In doing so it takes into account the fact that the European has often used Africa, as indeed other colonies, for his own spiritual needs. Hence the brief discussion on leprophils and the nun who fears that science and medicine will wipe out disease and deprive her of her sense of purpose. Finally, although the missionary as intermediary is revealed as necessary and useful his utility is undermined by the rationalist Dr Colin who has no belief and therefore, perhaps, no hope: 'These people here are all dying – oh, I don't mean of leprosy. I mean of us. And their last disease is hope.' This indictment seems to convey that technology and commerce by themselves are not the cure for post-colonial societies.

*   *   *

Greene excels in narratives of pursuit and escape. In *Travels with my Aunt* (1969) and *Monsignor Quixote* (1982) the form is slightly modified into an episodic account of journeys and adventures which symbolically and in conversation present the dialectic of religion and its absence or subvert conventional moralities in the context of ordinary life. *Travels with my Aunt* has very little to do directly with Africa but it does have the most full-bodied representation of an African individual in Greene's work. More importantly it relates the politics of culture and economic survival in the post-colonial world by immersing the novel in a flux of international connections and events that link the African, the Mediterranean and the Anglo-Saxon in relationships that test the loyalties of the Anglo-Saxon.

This pattern of connections parallels the links illustrated in *The Heart of the Matter*. Visconti, the Italian in *Travels with my Aunt* and Yusef, the Syrian in *The Heart of the Matter* are both Mediterranean but the former is also European. The implication is much more significant than the more obvious fact that Greene has great fun mocking himself by deliberately providing parallels with Elizabeth Bowen's *Viper of Milan* whose villain is also Visconti. There are many such happy returns to past influences, first loves, scenes and obsessions – to Brighton, for instance, and to Sierra Leone. These are, however, surface details to mask the writer's probing of political realities that underlie Greene's most entertaining novel.

The characterisation of Wordsworth, the African, in *Travels with my Aunt* is reminiscent of Joyce Cary's Mr Johnson with the important difference that Greene's hustler is not a 'native' in his country but an expatriate in England. He is half-educated, charming, lovable and loyal. In his own version of events he is first seen by Aunt Augusta, the ageing Englishwoman, when working as a doorman at the Granada Palace in London. She is quite taken up by his exuberant presence in the uniform he wears and claims him as her 'Emperor Jones', as a 'child of joy'.

Much of the power of characterisation rests on Wordsworth's ambivalent status – he is everything and nothing, invaluable and dispensable depending on contingencies. His first appearance as 'a large middle-aged negro wearing a butcher's apron' is quickly qualified with the revelation that he enjoys a higher status than a valet: 'He looks after my wants' says Aunt Augusta who clearly indicates that he is no mere valet and talks to him 'as to a child or lover' (pp. 18–19). Such complex characterisation reveals less an individual than the intense relationships that could exist between intermediaries and colonials; its interest lies in what it implies of the past through an examination of the relationship within contemporary existence. Aunt Augusta colludes with Wordsworth – together they make a formidable team of hustlers – and discards him when her existence, both economic and sexual, is better served by Mr Visconti who is introduced as part of an older and stronger bond.

Greene first meets Wordsworth in fact in Liberia and there are three separate versions of this man as well as a confession of the ruthless, if artistic, use which the writer makes of random encounters on his travels:

> odd assortment of characters . . . one collects through life, vivid grotesques, people so simple that they always have the same side turned to one, damned by their self-consciousness to be material for the novelist, to supply the minor characters, to be endlessly caricatured, to make in their multiplicity, one's world.[18]

In some ways Wordsworth emerges as the epitome of the African image in English social and literary tradition. Ogude rightly emphasises this point:

> Perhaps what firmly establishes Wordsworth's racial character-istics from the point of view of European tradition is his capacity for love. The tradition, of course, did not begin with Othello – Shakespeare merely put the seal of authority on a popular belief. Thus essentially, most Africans were conceived of in English literature as fantastic (and faithful) lovers and extremely jealous

husbands. It all dated from the period when Europeans confused Moors with Africans . . . Greene makes the point, rather forcefully, when Wordsworth and Henry are introduced: 'This is my nephew, Wordsworth', my aunt said. 'You be telling me the whole truth, Woman?' 'Of course I am. Oh Wordsworth, Wordsworth!' In his roles as valet and romantic lover Wordsworth appears to be merely carrying on a tradition.[19]

If it has to be said that Wordsworth lacks the dimension of indigenous African character it has to be remembered that Greene's is an outside view which does not pretend to delineate characters rooted in non-Western cultures. The argument that Greene's rendering of Africa and African characters is patronising, romantic and stereotyped misses the point that Greene's approach attempts an understanding in a spirit of atonement; the issue of exploitation as endemic to the human condition is approached from various perspectives and at many points in the history of his time; what is achieved is an indictment of all forms of exploitation, and a validation of his own tradition whose values underlie the narrative.

In Wordsworth the novel manages to convey the vitality and power of an individual with a history and tradition which he proudly articulates even when he mistakenly considers himself superior to these traditions since he has acquired the skills of 'civilisation'. It is important therefore to balance the presence of inherited cultural perceptions and prejudices with Greene's characterisation of Wordsworth who is brought to life with a great deal of bounce and aplomb.

Until introduced by Aunt Augusta and her friends into a world of hilarious if dangerous adventure Henry Pulling, her nephew, represents the quietist, conventional option: an innocent, uninvolved bachelor existence as retired banker cultivating dahlias in suburban England. The text is harsh on such orthodoxy: 'never presume yours is a better morality . . . You looked after people's money like a nanny who looks after other people's children. Can't I see you in our cage, stacking up little fivers endlessly before you hand them over to their proper owner?' (p. 111). Greene's novels have always declaimed against a passionless existence even when the declaration of feeling involves betrayal of country to protect a friend or human life. Human connections are primary though in *Travels with my Aunt* the economic nexus emerges as the strongest bonding-material of social structures. If Wordsworth loses in the end it is because skills acquired along the coast in Sierra Leone have given him only half a language. He can never be 'in the same league.'

The portrayal of Wordsworth attempts to put together every aspect of the colonial encounter and its carry over into post-colonial experience. Since Greene has no knowledge of life in the new African nation-states he appears to have decided to look at the migrant to illustrate, at one level, the web of geopolitical relationships; at another more personal level Greene explores what it is to be free yet dependent; to have once been proud, knowledgeable and strong, and to find newly acquired skills of 'civilisation' inadequate in the new field of battle. It is important, however, to stress that at no point in this novel or elsewhere in his work does Greene suggest the inadequacy of the man in full possession of his culture and tradition, or of those educated in Western traditions without having compromised respect for their own. These perceptions are explored in *The Comedians* (1966), a deep and profound novel despite its title.

Travels with my Aunt is Greene's most successful comic creation not least because the absurd comic posturing of Aunt Augusta and Wordsworth and the grotesque but passionate romance between the 75-year-old Englishwoman and the 80-year-old Italian unmask 'the injustices, the cruelties and the meanness' that are so cleverly hushed up in the world of international hotels, boardrooms and power games. The situation of Wordsworth as migrant is brought home with particular poignancy when Aunt Augusta decides he is dispensable but, being fair, wishes to pay him off. Although the narrative tone is always warm and affectionate there is little ambiguity in the verdict on Aunt Augusta's action:

'I am not your bebi gel, Wordsworth, any more. Understand that. I have kept enough money for you to return to Europe. . . '
'Ar no wan your money,' Wordsworth replied.
'You've taken plenty of my money in the past. The CTCs you've had from me and all my friends. . . '
'Ar tak you money them times because you love me, you slip with me, you lak jig-jig with Wordsworth. Now you no slip with me, you no love me, I no wan your damn money. . . !' (p. 222).

Wordsworth is dispensable to Aunt Augusta who pretends to believe that a CTC is sufficient to balance his loss; the reality is poignant:

'She wan me quit . . . She wan me for come bring you, and then she wan me quit. She say, "I give you biggest CTC you ever saw, you go back Freetown and find a gel" but I no wan her money, Mr Pullen, I no wan Freetown no more, and I no wan any gel. I love your auntie. I wan for stay with her like the song say: "Abide with me; fast falls the eventide, the darkness deepens: oh, with me abide . . . Tears have no bitterness" but man, these tears are bitter, that's for sure' (pp. 210–11).

Thus slighted, humiliated, and finally killed accidentally by one of Visconti's men, even as Ali had been earlier killed by one of Yusef's men, Wordsworth's departure releases Aunt Augusta from the burden of his loyalty and affection so that she can operate in peace with Visconti and Henry. That the new area of interest is Latin America illustrates once again Greene's acute instincts as to where the next scene of confrontation with imperialism, exploitation and superpower politics would lie. This is brought into the open in later novels such as *The Honorary Consul*. Criticism of the complicity of England and Europe in what is called American imperialism is implicit in all his work.

Visconti is described in terms of past exploits, his links with the underworld, and Aunt Augusta's romantic passion for him. Hints of his connections with Fascist Italy and Nazi Germany suggest a resumption of old ties with an unsavoury bedfellow who seemingly captivates a not-so-innocent Augusta. Adventurous and unconventional, her accomplices often prove unreliable for she has once been duped by a Frenchman and later by Visconti himself. Yet, when the latter returns into her life all set, it appears, to do it again, Augusta welcomes him back. Her all-abiding generosity of spirit forgives the Europeans but she is ruthless with Wordsworth who is now a liability. Less sophisticated and worldly-wise than the company Augusta now seeks, Wordsworth is, paradoxically, the only one with any real feeling for her. He dies undefended at the hands of Visconti's man; when a shocked Pulling brings news of his death Aunt Augusta brushes him away and continues to waltz in the arms of Visconti in semi-darkness, perhaps to hide her tears in much the same way that Scobie drinks in the darkness in the company of Yusef until Ali's agonised cry rouses him into a guilty search for the scene of the crime. In Wordsworth's case even this token gesture is denied.

The picaresque form of *Travels with my Aunt* allows Greene room for anecdotal exploration of human motives that bind relationships. In clubbing the Anglo-Saxon and the European together at a time when England debated entry into the EEC, and in then taking this group across the Atlantic into Latin America, the narrative suggests the directions of Western capitalism within a froth of entertainment and near-ribald humour. Through Wordsworth and his elimination the narrative explores the plight of the migrant who has half-assimilated a Western way of life and rejected his own traditions. The process is death.

At the close of the novel the grandly adventurous, enthusiastic and optimistic Augusta is rather a frail creature in the embrace of Visconti. Is the scene a metaphor for Britain's entry into the EEC which, when it was first being debated in the 1960s, was perceived by many as the reversion of Great Britain into Little England? The marriage of Henry Pulling with the local Police Chief's daughter in Paraguay perpetuates the links except that now the intermediaries and the *colons* have been taken out of the boundaries of acknowledged imperialism into a world of shady deals and the CIA. Greene does not abandon the imperial vision which he seems, in fact, to reiterate by abandoning the old formula of cultural superiority and exploiting and enshrining it in values for joy and justice in life, a theme that recurs in *Monsignor Quixote*. The novels discussed above are not a nostalgic evocation of the imperial past but a reaffirmation of the simple heroism and moral code of the human, unworthy, and forgotten instruments of Empire in its outposts.

*   *   *

The condition of exile as a condition of life for the *colon* occurs early in Greene's work in *Journey Without Maps*. Graham Greene and his cousin Barbara Greene have five fellow-passengers on the cargo ship – two shipping-agents, a representative from an engineering firm, a doctor on his way to the Coast and a woman joining her husband. One of the agents sings 'The Old Homeland';

> everyone felt English and exiled and wistful, everyone except Younger, who climbed carefully up the stairs, clinging to the banister 'I'm going home by rail'. He was more English than any of them; the north country was in his heart. He was firmly local and unsentimental and bawdy and honest. He drank because he needed a holiday, because he had heavy work before him on the

Coast, because he loved his wife and had desperate anxieties. He had more cause to drink than anyone. The boom years were in his heavy flesh and his three chins; one couldn't at first sight tell how the depression lay like lead in his stomach. If one were to paint his portrait in the old style of tiny landscapes and Tuscan towns one would have given him as background an abandoned blast-furnace or the girders of a great bridge left a perch for birds (pp. 26–7).

Conditions of economic survival are crucial to Greene's exploration of exile in his fiction as also the distinction as made above between the individual and the group. Younger is a product of the boom years and now of the Depression on his way to Africa on business. The other members of the group 'knew the Coast; they knew the same people; they had a common technique of living enforced by common conditions'. Younger, more English than the others, is rather special; more sensitive, even innocent; his words 'had the merit of children's art; they were vivid, unselfconscious, uncorrupted' (p. 27).

Exile, the loss of self and the search for recovery of self, derives much of its substance from Greene's own recall of the lost innocence of childhood. It acquires a resonance from the gritty, spare soil of the political realities and values explored in the text. Conversely, the visible universe of the narrative draws its literary and moral power from an inner self which Greene retrieved and developed from childhood. In *A Sort of Life* he describes these:

If a sinister atmosphere lay in my mind around the Crooked Billet, a sense of immediate danger was conveyed by the canal . . . the menace of insulting words from strange brutal canal workers and blackened faces like miners, with their gypsy wives and ragged children at the sight of middle-class children carefully dressed and shepherded (p. 13).

Aspects of the theme of exile – alienation, homelessness, rootlessness, and isolation – are expressed with a poignancy that suggests deep personal experience. Early boyhood divided between the horrors of boarding-school and the peace of home-life spent in the company of eccentric but loving aunts, uncles, brothers, sisters, amid rabbits and croquet lawns and rambling gardens is mythologised by the artist into the external landscape of life and the internal one of ideals.

The delicate dividing line between the visible universe and the private vision defines the moral life within a changing sociopolitical scene recreated in the novels as borders, and frontiers; as countries compelling divided loyalties and betrayal; as innocence and guilt, exile and home. The experience of two countries, home and school, enclosed within a single space, as it were, deepens the fictional representation of impermanence, homelessness and exile. The 'seedy' detail of an area of 'endless abandonment' acquires painful dimensions with the homeless state of the characters.[20]

Isolation is suggested most often in a representation of the individual in urban surroundings. They lack tradition and live in homes whose chief characteristic is impermanence and change. Professionals such as Scobie, the Assistant Commissioner of Police in *The Heart of the Matter*, Mr Pineda, the ambassador in *The Comedians*, and Fowler, the newspaper correspondent in *The Quiet American* change homes as often as their jobs demand it. Scobie's situation is perhaps the most poignantly realised: 'a table, two kitchen chairs, a cupboard, some rusty handcuffs hanging on a nail like an old hat, a filing cabinet: to a stranger it would have appeared a bare uncomfortable room but to Scobie it was home' (p. 15).

Relationships are tenuous and when they are good they are constantly under threat. Querry has no family; Fowler has a mistress whom he is in danger of losing and a wife he would like to divorce; Doctor Fischer is a widower with a daughter but he seems incapable of human ties; she finds happiness but dies within the year; Brown and Dr Plarr, both bachelors, have a formal relationship with a mother who is remote. Communication between people is a cherished value, rare and fleeting, and when it takes the form of love as in the case of Sarah and Bendrix in *The End of the Affair* and Sarah and Maurice Castle in *The Human Factor* it is presented as a precious, natural gift whose growth is curbed by powers beyond their control.

Some of these protagonists wander through life like Gabriel Marcel's problematic man; each of them has 'become for himself a question without an answer'. Spiritually dead, they have neither the capacity to love nor appear willing to be loved. Exiles either by choice or circumstance, they can detect innocence, appreciate goodness and admire courage. For instance, the relationship between Brown and Dr Magiot, and the young poet, Philipot; between Dr Plarr and his childhood friend, Father Rivas. The lucidity of these lonely individuals is best rendered in the characterisation of Doctor Fischer who is cynically aware of the motive – greed for material possessions – that draws his guests to his eery dinner table.

Rootlessness is most palpably defined in *The Comedians* in the character of Brown, the hotelier, whose business is destroyed by the reign of terror in Papa Doc's Haiti. The most alienated of all Greene's exiles, he reflects:

> There are those who belong by their birth inextricably to a country, who even when they leave feel a tie. And there are those who belong to a province, a country, a village, but I could feel no link at all with the hundred or so square kilometres around the gardens and boulevards of Monte Carlo, a city of transients . . . transcience was my pigmentation, my roots would never go deep enough anywhere to make me a home or make me secure with love (p. 223).

Whereas Fowler (*The Quiet American*), Dr Plarr (*The Honorary Consul*) and Querry (*A Burnt-Out Case*) are detached observers until compelled to act, Brown resorts to role-playing as does Jones. They change roles to suit each contingency, and Brown's final role as a partner in a business of undertakers seems to belong in the region of black comedy which life in Haiti, as the novel reveals, indeed is.

Dr Plarr lives in exile and tries to find a sense of purpose in his profession. His rootless existence suggests a spiritual death – he has come to the end of himself. The only feeling left is a dull leaden despair at 'the long impossible future beside the Parana'. Yet he still has sensitivity left to recognise and be jealous of Charley Fortnum's capacity for love. Life as burden and trap is the more anguishing with his daily inability to feel involved in his ministering to the needs of his patients – their oppression intense and apparently irremediable only serves to exacerbate his sense of futility.

It is in this sense that he envies his father, an Englishman, who has died a political prisoner. It seems to him that he was 'already his father's age, that he had spent as long in prison as his father had, and that it was his father who had escaped'; in fact the father had sent his young son and his Paraguayan wife into exile in Argentina to safeguard them from political reprisals. Finally and in spite of himself Dr Plarr gets involved. The plot thickens, as it were, when the political situation is made to interact with Plarr's own 'bored' self-reflection. The structure of the plot and the psychological condition of the character converge as shadow and substance. The two parts of the story integrate through memories shared of childhood, dreams, the idealisms of fathers, and the future that the sons struggle to build or, like Plarr, would prefer to ignore until memory compels action.

His death, violent and futile, carries with it the effect of a *coup de grâce* just as the bitter irony with which his funeral is portrayed accentuates the novel's complex concerns. The chief mourners are his mother and the members of the establishment, all of whom remain unaware of Plarr's private inner world and are blind to the realities that disquieted him. They would never understand either his motives or the tragic waste of his brief involvement in guerilla activity.

Though uninvolved in the great moral dilemmas being confronted by his childhood friend, Father Rivas, Eduardo Plarr understands idealism and has despaired at the horrors of oppression that surround him. Like Fowler and Brown he too finds himself drawn into a vortex of political turmoil and initiates a process of 'homecoming' by deciding to risk his life to save Fortnum's. Plarr's experience of meaninglessness may be compared to that of Querry who says 'I suffer nothing. I no longer know what suffering is. I have come to the end of all that too . . . To the end of everything' (p. 16). The contingencies of life in the leper colony where he first resists all involvement eventually open a new dimension in his life when he learns to be less self-absorbed.

Social injustice as cause of homelessness in the early novels takes the stark outline of Kate Drover's tenement (*It's a Battlefield*). It is detailed in Raven's terror-stricken memories of the orphanage in which he grew up (*A Gun for Sale*), in women with hard, bitter faces, fathers who are brutal, children as victims of this squalid situation. It is most pervasive in *Brighton Rock* where Pinkie and Rose share the sacred bond of having grown up in Paradise Piece with 'its flapping gutters and glassless windows, an iron bedstead rusting in the front garden, the smashed and wasted ground in front where houses had been pulled down for model flats which had never gone up' (p. 90). And Mr Prewitt's house 'shaken by shunting engines; the soot settled continuously on the glass and brass plate . . . there was nothing anywhere to keep out sound' (p. 208).

It is a dismal world whose oppressive darkness is lightened by hope of peace and goodness even if these are rendered in terms of an after-life. *The Human Factor*, however, is a more despairing view: life is 'an unpredictable ambush'; the line of communication between individuals, societies, power blocs, is permanently severed.

Maurice Castle strives 'to conform' in order to avoid suspicion which could destroy his home. His professional life intrudes into the love and peace of home and family which necessitates 'chilling long silences'. To protect this haven he gets involved in action that severs the ties most cherished, separates him from his wife and child, forces him beyond national frontiers – a narrative that evokes menace and complete despair. Such a break in relationships is reiterated in the emblematic tale *Doctor Fischer of Geneva or The Bomb Party* with a slight difference: political power is replaced by the destructive lure of wealth; the irresponsible conduct and power games of the former novel are replaced by a portrayal of human weaknesses such as jealousy and greed.

Greene's lawless roads, journeys and borders are metaphors of psychological and spiritual exploration. The border is occasionally represented as a political frontier to be crossed as, for instance, by Jones and Brown (*The Comedians*) and by the Priest (*The Power and the Glory*). For them the border represents the dividing line between annihilation and security. To cross it means entry into a haven of intellectual freedom and peace that comes from self-realisation. In *Our Man in Havana* Wormold, who is quite unpolitical, acts as a secret agent for purely mercenary reasons: he needs the money to keep his daughter happy. The escapades that ensue with secret missiles sought in designs of vacuum-cleaners make fun of the Secret Service but reveal tragedy in individual lives. Wormold's personal code has to be compromised when he has to plan to kill the man who threatens his own existence and the security of his loved ones. As he ponders the course open to him he stands listening to his daughter and Beatrice, the woman he loves, chatting securely on the other side of the wall quite oblivious of the danger that surrounds them:

He stood on the frontier of violence, a strange land he had never visited before; he had his passport in his hand. 'Profession: Spy.' 'Characteristic features: friendlessness.' 'Purpose of visit: Murder.' No visa required. His papers were in order. And on this side of the border he heard voices talking in the language he knew (p. 184).

The experience of exile and loneliness embodies man's search for meaning which is dramatised in the permeation of interpersonal relationships with social and political realities. Freed of the religious framework the novels of the late 1950s and after are instinct with a deeper religious sense pervading a secular and contemporary relevance. Maurice Castle, for instance, reflects in *The Human Factor* that he would like

> to strike, like his childhood hero, Allan Quartermain, off on that long slow underground stream which bore him on towards the interior of the dark continent where he might find a permanent home, in a city where he could be accepted as a citizen without any pledge of faith, not the City of God or Marx, but a city called Peace of Mind (p. 107).

Existence thus becomes a city of dreadful night. The redeeming factor is the struggle through night's darkness.

This struggle is dramatised as confrontation. The law-abiding class, the widest possible category in which the characters may be grouped, is often set against the law-breaker, the social outcast and the political activist. The custodians subject themselves to unconditional authority of the State or Church. The rebel lives under the threat of death or extinction. Greene's morally correct man who risks nothing has distinctive features: he is often distinguished by mindless gaiety, and smooth, urbane sophistication. These characters have evolved from the insensitivity of Ida and the stranglehold of Colleoni in *Brighton Rock* to the cruel, self-righteous irresponsibility and menace of Dr Percival and Muller in *The Human Factor*.

Along the way we meet Wilson, Louise, Rycker, Parkinson – all of whom share degrees of hypocrisy. But they are not all 'happy' as are Ida and Dr Percival. The latter represents the final most subtle characterisation of 'evil in *propria persona*, walking down Bond Street, charming, cultured, sensitive – evil to be distinguished from good chiefly in the complete egotism of its outlook'. Scobie reflects: 'Point me out the happy man and I will point you out either egotism, evil – or else absolute ignorance.' Rose chooses Pinkie and risks complete damnation rather than Ida's protection because she distrusts Ida for whom the world is 'all dandy'. These may appear oversimplifications but the concepts become flesh and blood of individual characters in situations that are deeply felt and realised in all their complex reality.

The outlines of these concerns are first visualised in *It's a Battlefield* where institutional authority is represented: 'Thin bureaucratic body . . . justice with a file of papers . . . assurance, eyes on the pavement, safe in London, safe in the capital city of the Empire, safe at the heart of civilisation' (p. 161). Ida and Dr Percival, Rycker and Muller in *The Human Factor* are presented as oppressors in varying degrees. Here the oppression is different from that encountered, for instance, in Haiti, in *The Comedians*, where the Ton Ton Macoute do not pretend to be anything other than what they actually are – the instruments of oppression. They even dress the part. But most oppressors in Greene's fictional world shelter themselves behind the structures of ethical authority and the law and are largely ignorant of guilt and suffering. In contrast, Pinkie and Rose in *Brighton Rock* feel 'shut out from an Eden of ignorance'. All they have is experience, and it is this that provides the added dimension of life. Perhaps the most ironic rendering of ignorance is in the character-isation of Alden Pyle, the 'quiet American' of the title, who wreaks havoc with the best of intentions, always remaining a very decent man, even when he is responsible for tragic devastation.

The theme of exile and the homeless wanderer suggests another pattern. The exile seems to be a wanderer from a postwar world, not merely after the Second World War and decolonisation but from an England forever lost after the First World War. It is significant, therefore, that Younger, a real-life figure in *Journey Without Maps* is 'more English' than the others. Over and over again confrontation leads the Greene hero to face the new realities, to bring them into proper perspective with reference to traditional perceptions and then to relate them to values that could ultimately create a better world. Whether this is ever possible is a question that may be answered only in terms of personal solutions and individual action.

The search clearly begins in *England Made Me* which posits tra-ditional values and the beginnings of change, Anthony Farrant, feckless and lovable, running away from things and yet capable, at moments, of honestly facing himself, is the first of a whole line of entirely credible characters – Englishmen away from home: exiles in the physical sense but more importantly exiles in time present seeking time lost. In a sense, they represent the quest for the lost childhood which is the driving force of all Greene's work. The following passage from *England Made Me* encapsulates an important perspective from which lost region the exile defines home, security, justice and peace in the contemporary world:

he [Anthony Farrant] saw himself and Minty clearly as one person; the exile from country and his class, the tramp whose

workhouses where Shanghai, Aden, Singapore, the refuse of a
changing world. If Minty were to be envied at all, it was that he
had chosen his dump and stayed there. They hadn't the vigour to
resist. They were not fresh enough, optimistic enough, to believe
in peace, cooperation, the dignity of labour, or if they believed in
them they were not young enough to work for them. They were
neither one thing nor the other; they were really only happy when
they were together; in the clubs in foreign capitals, in pensions, at
old boys' dinners, momentarily convinced by the wine they
couldn't afford that they believed in something; in the old country,
in the king, in 'shoot the bloody Bolsheviks', in the comradeship
of the trenches . . . He thought: it's because I'm not young
enough and not old enough; not young enough to believe in a
juster world, not old enough for the country, the king, the
trenches to mean anything to me at all (p. 180).

Greene is more or less a product of this time but rather than retreat
into a shrinking and closed world of his class and ethos he uses its
myths to sharpen his sensitivity to the political aspirations of non-
Western nations and his perception of historical process is worthy of
note. It has led him away from class and race and the 'provincialism
of the English novel' into the condition of all men 'outside the pale'.
These are not inhabitants of Greeneland, a country of the mind,
remote but spiritually true, but victims of a social order which the
novels have consistently tried to expose. His restless spirit and his
gifts for rapportage provided him with the opportunity 'to move
around and perhaps to see English characters in a setting which is
not protective to them, where perhaps they speak a little differently,
a little more openly'. The political dimension of this experience is
ultimately responsible for a movement towards the themes of
personal faith and political struggle.

6
Hegemonies

Greene undertakes his journey into human experience without and beyond the cartographer's directives. He seems to have discarded these props early in his career to push forward limits of perception and demolish barriers between races, creeds, and ideologies in order to reveal the essentials that bring grace to human life. This is not to say that he universalises various cultures. The novels do not, in fact, describe or define indigenous culture but reveal human experience within the flux of history.

Greene travels with a sense of freedom and a critical morality that does not ignore colonial consciousness but confronts it and works through it to liberate himself eventually from it. As discussed earlier this approach occasionally weakens the radicalism of his perception and yet his novels contain the only frank recognition of colonialism and its aftermath so far expressed within the mainstream of English fiction. Like Orwell he confronts the colonial facets of authority, responsibility, hierarchy, power and evangelism. Unlike Orwell he does not confine his critique to dominant middle-class perceptions. In his search for liberated selfhood he discards Kipling's myths of aggression, achievement and moral strength and finds the courage to look within. His exploration gains considerable moral power because he works with a critical Christian tradition. By identifying himself wholly with the oppressed in the societies where his novels are set, Greene looks at his own ethos and remains the true Englishman. *Monsignor Quixote* (1982) brings the scene back to Europe and represents the apotheosis of a search begun in *Journey Without Maps* (1936) and *The Lawless Roads* (1939). *Monsignor Quixote* which is the last of the novels to be published reveals civilisation and humanity in a rural environment. The novel celebrates non-modern, non-technological values, and expresses a sense of justice and faith by subverting religious and political thought. His long journey has sometimes brought him close to Kipling territory which he illuminates with moral conflicts that restate traditional as against colonial values.

In the process his work also illustrates that the genuine creative impulse in the world of today, in particular, cannot remain detached from social reality or escape historical compulsions, a point also recognised by George Orwell:

> The invasion of literature by politics was bound to happen. It must have happened, even if the special problem of totalitarianism had never arisen, because we have developed a sort of compunction which our grandparents did not have, an awareness of the enormous injustice and misery of the world, and a guilt-stricken feeling that one ought to be doing something about it, which makes a purely aesthetic attitude towards life impossible. No one, now, could devote himself to literature as single-mindedly as Joyce or Henry James.[1]

In his analysis of this passage Raymond Williams comments on the cultural assumptions that limit Orwell's understanding of the subject matter of literature. He points out that Joyce wrote as he did through poverty and exile, and that there is nothing particularly new about social awareness in writers since novelists from Dickens and Elizabeth Gaskell to George Eliot and Hardy were aware of injustice and misery. The important change came with Henry James in England when an opposition between the 'social' and the 'aesthetic' was widely attempted. Williams summarises the restrictiveness of this dichotomy:

> Not only was social experience seen as content and literature as form; also, and more dangerously, social experience was seen as only general and abstract, with the result that the definition of literary content was itself narrowed down to an emphasis on abstracted 'personal relationships' . . . The quarrel between James and Wells – between a composed, pure, essentially passive art, and new kinds of projected, committed, essentially purposive writing – came at a time when the development of the novel was very much at issue. A deeper awareness of psychological complexities was present at the same time as a deeper awareness of social complexities. What was common was a sense of crisis, but alternative ways or describing it were in practice, each in its own way, leading to radical changes in literary form, yet each pulling in quite opposite directions.[2]

Greene's work attempts to do away with this dichotomy and to interpret the interactions of the social and personal in a wider perspective where he is sometimes both explicitly religious and an urbane social critic. Nevertheless it can be said of Greene as he said himself of Henry James whom he admired: 'neither a philosophy nor a creed ever emerged from his religious sense. His religion was always a mirror of his experience'.[3]

Travel and journalism have helped the creative writer's exploration. When asked about his urge to travel Greene explains it as a sub-conscious movement towards death. Haunted by its spectre, per-haps even attracted by it, he tries to understand and confront it through the processes of life. Encounters with surface phenomena, the processes of history, the immediate and the transient heighten perception of the immanence of higher values. The novels that have followed each such confrontation attempt a mediation between the private and the public, the individual and the citizen, the state and international communities, religion and politics, life and death.

The more direct engagement with issues such as American and Russian hegemonies, the failure of *détente*, the menace of repressive dictatorships and the threat of racial alignments organised for the survival of capitalist interests is at the core of novels written between 1955 to the present day. These suggest his recognition of a global situation where the claims of individual freedom are irrelevant and where the human factor is sacrificed in the interest of the preservation of the balance of political power.

In his capacity as a journalist Greene has travelled to troubled places to report on revolution, social change, individual and col-lective suffering thereby opening himself to experience both physically dangerous and morally disturbing. He has emerged from this wide and deliberate travel with an oeuvre that nails down, interprets and thus orders his experience into a reflection on the connection between faith and action, the private conscience and the public act, man the individual and man the citizen. After exposure to religious persecution in Mexico, to the pristine cultures of the interiors of Africa and journalistic assignments reporting colonial war, oppression, revolution and social change in Indo-China, Cuba, Kenya, Haiti, Poland, Chile, Paraguay, Panama and Nicaragua, Greene reveals experience in regions where politics is a question of life and death.

The overt political perspective of *It's a Battlefield* reappears in *The Quiet American* (1955) a novel that grew out of experience of the war of decolonisation in Indo-China. His fictional world draws on the reality of journalistic experience to mediate between thought and existence. 'What', he asks, 'is a Christian civilisation in terms of human characters, human acts, and the daily commerce of human lives?' When Dr Magiot in _The Comedians_ (1966) spells out ideals that connect a _'mystique'_ and a _'politique'_ he defines, in effect, Greene's vision of faith understood as a radically historical mode of being.

Basic to Greene's politics is his loyalty to human rights and individual freedom, untrammelled by constraints of Church or State, dogma or orthodoxy – a value that provides the writer with an artistic form. The novels present an anarchic and heretical order of values such as has been the concern of great literary figures in the past. It is in this spirit that he indicts the conservatism of the early Shakespeare, 'the supreme poet . . . of what is now called the Establishment',[4] and celebrates the mature poet, the creator of two characters which Greene prefers to see as one composite character, Timon–Caliban:

> If only [Shakespeare] had lived a few more years, so that we could have seen the great poet of the Establishment defect to the side of the disloyal . . . to the side of those who by the very nature of their calling will always be 'troublers of the poor world's peace' – Zola writing J'accuse, Doestoevsky before the firing squad, Victor Hugo following Dante into exile, the Russian writers in their labour camps . . . It has always been in the interest of the State to poison the psychological wells, to encourage cat-calls, [sic] to restrict human sympathy. It makes government easier when the people shout Galilean, Papist, Fascist, Communist. Isn't it the story-teller's task to act as the devil's advocate, to elicit sympathy and a measure of understanding for those who lie outside the bound-aries of State approval? The writer is driven by his own vocation to be a protestant in a Catholic society, a catholic in a Protestant one, to see the virtues of the capitalist in a Communist society, of the communist in a Capitalist state. Thomas Paine wrote 'we must guard even our enemies against injustice.[5]

Well-defined views on the connection between literature and politics provoke his distinction between fiction that is engaged and direct political comment, between personal experience and the effect of public events that seep into the creative consciousness. An enlargement of perspective and his search for spiritual values within the processes of cultural change differentiates Greene's work from that of François Mauriac, the French novelist with whom he has often been compared.

Mauriac's political writing was confined to journalism in which he recalled traditional imperatives at times of national crisis. His novels remain, to the end, enclosed in the static and deeply conservative world of provincial Bordeaux. Greene's fiction bears witness to historical processes not because he believes that artists can affect political developments but because history provides the only real expression of moral issues. Paradoxically, Mauriac's view of his journalism – during the Resistance and after – as a natural extension of his fiction describes the work of Graham Greene far more aptly. The latter has not, however, sought to relate the two aspects of his work except to say that if one has anything direct to say about politics and society one should channel it into journalism.

In an interview in 1957 on the theme of *The Writer in Society* Greene disclosed that if he were to write a novel on the situation in Kenya despite his sympathy for the Mau Mau 'the hero and villain might well turn out to have their roles reversed'.[6] Propaganda finds no place in his conception of the writer's role: 'the writer's task is . . . to be a piece of grit in the State machinery . . . to draw his own likeness to any human being, to the guilty as much as to the innocent . . . to enlarge the bounds of sympathy in readers'.[7] In this age of unbelief, Greene explores the possibilities of a code that connects human dignity and transcendence with specific social realities.

Pivotal to all his writing is his recognition of forces of exploitation in their geopolitical context. To say that the location of his fiction is Greeneland is to deny the reality of the post-colonial world, of political processes and their consequences. The following section examines his despatches,[8] letters to the press (a selection of which are presented in an appendix), and the memoir *Getting to Know the General* (1984) to illustrate the context of historical facts, analysis of culture and society, and the world-view that underlie *The Quiet American* (1955), *Our Man in Havana* (1958), *The Comedians* (1966), *The Honorary Consul* (1973), and *The Human Factor* (1978).

* * *

Greene's despatches illustrate his consistency in supporting indigenous political movements with a popular base. He distrusts solutions foisted from above by power blocs in collusion with upper- and middle-class intermediaries, as in Vietnam, whose machinations of superpower politics are directed towards undermining a genuine nationalist movement of liberation:

> Is there any solution here the West can offer? But the bar tonight was loud with innocent American voices and that was the worst disquiet. There weren't so many Americans in 1951 and 1952. They were there, one couldn't help being aware, to protect an investment, but couldn't the investment have been avoided? . . . I suggested to a member of the American Economic Mission that French participation in the war might be drawing to an end. 'Oh, no,' he said, 'they can't do that. They'd have to pay us back.' I cannot remember how many thousand million dollars. The policy of our own representative in Hanoi was to combine a wise sympathy for the new nationalism of Vietnam with a recognition that France was our ally who had special responsibility and more important, perhaps, a special emotion after the years of defeat and occupation. Who knows, if that policy had been properly followed, whether the goodwill of Ho Chi Minh and of Sainteny might not have led Vietnam toward a gradual and peaceful independence?[9]

Greene's despatches emphasise the justice of the option of a peaceful transfer of power to a genuine President rather than to an emperor of doubtful qualifications without the grass-roots base and popularity of Ho Chi Minh, whose qualities Greene persistently describes. Vietnam's leader sought freedom and directed the struggle essentially for the nationalist aim of a united country with commitments – when he first started at any rate – to the country's many religious minorities – an aspect that no doubt contributed to Greene's admiration for Ho Chi Minh.

Greene contemplates with horror the American guarantee of twenty-one divisions, a disastrous solution that would have abandoned many non-Communist nationalists to the mercy of extremists. He describes how with each passing day it became clear that Ho Chi Minh was being forced into a solution by violence which he had long opposed: 'My own rational answers would be uniformly pessimistic. I believe the moment of Independence has been delayed too long.' Much later he reports Ho Chi Minh's tears when he meets the Bishop of Hanoi, tears for his failure to prevent the flight of the peasants: 'one need not imagine they were an actor's tears; he had been deserted by the very poor for whom he had fought. They were the tears of human nature at the inadequacy of great success.'[10]

Deep concern for the villages inhabited by Catholic peasants, all nationalists whose religion predated French colonialism, is characteristic of the sort of causes espoused by Greene. His position on this question led to a revealing exchange of correspondence with Kingsley Martin, then editor of *New Statesman and Nation*. The issue debated was the proposed solution by partition at the 17th parallel. Greene objects to this solution:

> Practicable possibly, but I doubt whether morally defensible. Such a line would hand over to the Vietminh the real nationalists of Vietnam, those almost independent States of Bui Chu, Phat Diem and Thai Bin . . . The Christians of Tongking are not 'colonial' Christians: they were converted by Spanish missionaries before France ever came into Indo-China, and the great-grandfathers of these men now fighting the Vietminh for their country and their religion with home-made mortars survived the persecution of the Emperor in the 1850s . . . The word 'partition' is now glibly used without any understanding of what it entails to human beings.[11]

His imperatives – freedom of religion and sovereignty – sometimes result in contradictions which lead to descriptions of him as being right-wing. Kingsley Martin, who eventually published Greene's letter, at first objected to the argument and tried to convince Greene of the implications of publicly expressing such a position. Greene, less concerned with political strategies than with clarifying the complex human issues involved, remained firm and stood by his argument which is true to facts rather than to political exigencies. Kingsley Martin does not seem to realise that for Greene, the real and only leader of Vietnam is Ho Chi Minh, and that partition would jeopardise religious freedom as well as compel Ho Chi Minh to take up extreme positions which is what eventually happened when the division took place. Kingsley Martin writes:

> If you really wish to say that you oppose some sort of partition, and that the Vietnam are the real nationalists, who should rule the whole country, then you must go on, under the present circumstances, to say that you think this is worth a full-scale war. I don't believe that you can mean this, but the inevitable retort to your letter would be that you want, on the grounds that some

villages are Catholic, to adopt the policy of the more extreme American group which is willing to start a war.[12]

Greene's letter to *The New Statesman and Nation* and Kingsley Martin's reply illustrate Greene's analysis of a political situation in all its ramifications, always with an eye to the will and the good of the people, and less concerned with statesmanship and exigencies of diplomacy – his letter was written when the deliberations in Geneva for the division at the 17th Parallel were taking place. In the light of these despatches Kingsley Martin's suggestion that Greene's position is similar to that of the more extreme American group is very strange indeed.

Although Greene's despatches reveal admiration for Fidel Castro and affection for Omar Torrijos, Ho Chi Minh appears to be the leader most admired; yet he likes to point out that his despatch was entitled *The Man as Pure as Lucifer* which is not entirely complimentary:

Dressed in Khaki drill, with thick dark woollen socks falling over his ankles, Ho Chi Minh gave an impression of simplicity and candour, but overwhelmingly of leadership. There was nothing evasive about him: this was a man who gave orders and expected obedience and also love. The kind remorseless face had no fanaticism about it. A man is a fanatic about a mystery – tablets of stone, a voice from a burning bush, but this was a man who had patiently solved an equation. So much love had to be given and received, so many sacrifices demanded and suffered. Everything had contributed to the solution: a merchant ship, the kitchens of the Carlton Grill, a photographer's studio in Paris, a British prison in Hong Kong, as well as Moscow in the hopeful spring days of the Revolution; the company of Borodin in China.[13]

Clearly two important factors in Ho's life attracted Greene: his identity as a man of the land struggling to get it back; his vision of non-violent Communism with a human face which continues to be Greene's ideal. Ho Chi Minh combined nationalism and the revolutionary role of the oppressed peasantry (as distinct from industrial workers) with religious freedom. Most importantly his movement was not an expression of bourgeois nationalism which would lead to the displacement of one élite by another.

Greene appreciates the value of the prudent and humane awareness with which Ho sought a wider base of support for the demands made on the French. Ho Chi Minh's approach, important for Vietnam and for the wider international context, was no easy task to be accomplished surrounded as he was by extremists. The despatches emphasise that external interference alone came in the way of Ho's success. This insight underlies *The Quiet American*: 'What if the elections are not held?' he asks in a despatch dated 1 May, 1953. 'What hope is there of avoiding a night of the long knives?'[14] What followed is now history. Greene refused to go back to report on the scene after direct American intervention. He had already said it all.

During his fairly extended stay in Vietnam Greene perceived Ho Chi Minh's efforts at developing a national Communism and his ideals of land and people. His sketch of the leader evokes aspects of this personality in a quirky description which nonetheless reveals qualities of political leaders whom Greene admires. The closest definition of his ideal ruler seems to be a benevolent dictator:

> I am on my guard against hero worship, but he appealed directly to that buried relic of the schoolboy. When he put his glasses to read a paper, bending a little down and sideways, shifting his English cigarette in long, bony, graceful fingers, the eyes twinkling at some memory I had stirred, I was reminded of Mr Chips, wise, kind, just (if one could accept the school rules as just), prepared to inflict sharp punishment without undue remorse (and punishment in this adult school has lasting effect), capable of inspiring love . . . I regretted I was too old to accept the rules or believe what the school taught. He was working 14 hours a day, but there was no sign of fatigue . . . I could understand the loyalty of his pupils.[15]

Another element that stands out in Greene's despatches from Vietnam is his perception of the role of the Catholic Church both in the North where Catholicism 'is more native and ardent', and in the South where 'it helped to ruin the Government of Diem'. Diem substituted America as the colonial power, slipped into an inefficient dictatorship, introduced religious intolerance, and thereby left his tolerant country a legacy of anti-Catholicism. He was 'separated from the people by foreign advisors droning of global strategy when he should have been walking in the rice fields unprotected, learning the hard way how to be loved and obeyed'.

Greene is equally scathing in his comments on Church leadership in the North:

> When we consider the political use made of Catholicism the great
> flight of the northern peasants comes first to mind. It was led by
> three Bishops . . . No one has the right to demand heroic virtue of
> another, but the thought remains – if these bishops had stayed,
> would their people have left in such numbers and would there
> have existed in the North today strong areas of Catholic non-
> conformity? The Church has not ceased to exist in Poland.[16]

The claims of nationalism, justice, and religious freedom as expressed
in indigenous movements underlie Greene's political positions. His
fellow-travelling which began in the 1930s has carried on apace –
an uneasy but steady journey it has been. It is hence no surprise
that he feels the ideals of Catholicism are best expressed today in
the communities and among some of the leadership of the Church
in Latin America. His work explores and illumines neither orthodoxy nor ideology but the core ideals shared by Catholicism and
Communism:

> There was sadness and decay, of course, in Hanoi, as there
> couldn't help being in a city emptied of all the well-to-do. For such
> as I, there was sadness in the mere lack of relaxation: nothing in
> the cinemas but propaganda films, the only restaurants prohibi-
> tive in price, no cafe in which to while away the hours watching
> people pass. But the peasant doesn't miss the cafe, the restaurant,
> the French or American film – he's never had them. Perhaps even
> the endless compulsory lectures and political meetings, the hours
> of physical training, are better entertainment than he has ever
> known. We talk so glibly of the threat to the individual, but the
> anonymous peasant has never been treated like an individual
> before. Unless a priest, no one before the Commissar has ap-
> proached him, has troubled to ask him questions, or spent time in
> teaching him. There is something in Communism besides the
> politics.[17]

The plot of *The Quiet American* reveals some of these insights – the
narrative alternates between a personal problem and a public
disaster, national struggle and global politics, war fought ideologi-
cally and war striking death on the innocent. Gloria Emerson who
covered the Vietnam war from 1970 to 1972 wrote that at least fifteen
years after Greene had left Indo-China for good it was as if the place
still belonged to him:

He had always understood what was going to happen there and in that small, quiet novel, told us everything.[18]

* * *

Greene spent some time in Kenya during the Mau Mau agitation preceding the Declaration of Independence for Kenya. Although this experience has not been transmuted into fiction his despatches need to be discussed not least because they emphasise his predilections and blind spots. Greene writes with great sympathy of the Mau Mau, and with an understanding of the aspirations of the Kikuyu peasants who struggled to reclaim land expropriated by white settlers. He comments with sensitivity on the Kikuyu, their ancient and natural democracy, their deep faith; on the sterility of modern infusions such as a progressive agricultural policy and secular education: 'To take the place of the lost tribal discipline, the Kikuyu seek another discipline, and other sacraments in place of their own tribal sacrifices.'[19]

Despite his sympathetic understanding, however, he is outside the struggle and the barriers that keep him apart are recognised as limitations of his own ability to understand and get a measure of the situation:

> In moments of depression one wonders why one has bothered to come so far to be still so distant from the heart of the conflict. In Indo-China, even in Malaya, there was something approaching a front line; one could feel oneself sharing to a small extent in the battle. Here the war is secret: it happens the day after one leaves or the day before one arrives. It is a private African war, which can be hidden so easily from white eyes . . . But if we are still far from the real stage, we are far, too, from that gallery in London where we could hear only the voices of our fellow-'gods' telling how the play would end and of how it should have been written. What seemed plausible there seems so complacent here, and so ignorant.[20]

This passage and others in the despatches suggest Greene's habitual distrust of intermediaries particularly those who would like to carry on the ethos of Western liberalism within a traditional cultural framework. He argues vehemently against Jomo Kenyatta's return to Nairobi and seems convinced that the innocent peasants were manipulated; that Mau-Mau oaths were thought out by minds 'more erudite and complex than those of the leaders in the forest war'.[21] These were oaths that made ignorant villagers regress into a spurious and vicious tribalism which he feels could only have been devised by a man trained in anthropology as Kenyatta was at the London School of Economics. This view is shared by many of the colonisers and settlers but not by members of the Mau Mau who deny any direct link between Kenyatta and their radical methods.

It is true, however, that Kenyatta led the people of Kenya in a new militancy when he returned from England in 1946 and was greeted as a national hero. He represented a synthesis of modernism and atavism and was wholly attuned to the background of his people, their customs, their rituals; he was simultaneously a broadly informed man in the Western sense of the term. Perhaps Greene's distrust is linked to the fact that Kenyatta did not reject Western liberal traditions nor those of paternal benevolence represented by the imperialists but sought to mediate and introduce a Westminster model of Government and administration to suit the realities of Africa. In all his writing Greene subconsciously attacks such mediations, seeking radical change and the purity of traditions. The trouble with Kenyatta, as far as Greene was concerned, seems to have been that he spoke the language of his people and was equally articulate in the framework of the colonisers which could lead to another form of exploitation.

An examination of Greene's despatches reveals qualities shared by leaders whom he supports in their struggle with existing colonial structures. He has given his unquestioning support, for instance, to Ho Chi Minh, Fidel Castro, Omar Torrijos, the Sandinista revolution and the directions of its struggle at the moment. All these represent a complete break with the colonial structure and post-colonial parliamentary democracy with the introduction of a Marxist model or, as in the case of the government of Omar Torrijos, consensus policies. He has never commented on developments in India, and although he says this is because India is too large and complex and defeated him one suspects that India has retained too much of the British structure to have warranted his interest, or indeed, affection. Lastly, perhaps it ought to be said that Greene looks for justice and for a practical experience of idealism at work in new structures and appears to prefer leaders who work within a folk-based critical tradition, which would steer clear of the failure of justice implicit in modern liberal ideology.

After Vietnam and Kenya the focus of attention has been the Caribbean and Latin America where the mixture of races and religions has presented Greene with the base for exploration of his ideals of justice and freedom which includes the freedom of religion. His comments on Fidel Castro's Cuba in 1963 are an eloquent expression of what he seeks on his travels. When he visits the Country Club in Havana, once the haunt of millionaires and presented as such in *Our Man in Havana* (1958), he finds the situation vastly changed:

Now the children of the dramatic school are eating a free lunch on the terrace and the new schools of music, ballet, folk-dancing, and of the plastic arts rise among the soft, green slopes, once a golf-course. The schools of painting, sculpture and murals, designed by the young architect Ricardo Porro, resemble an African village built in brick . . . It is like a village hidden among the hills and it reminds the visitor that Cuba is African as much as it is Spanish, and that the African has at last been freed – segregation is over.[22]

Greene writes of Castro with affection and with great hope in the early days of the Cuban republic – a continuing debate, an open-minded approach to problems, a new voice in the Communist world:

The arts have never been so encouraged (Socialist realism is a joke and not a threat); there is small danger of a Pasternak case with the state publishing house directed by a novelist of world reputation, Alejo Carpentier; Marxism here seems to be shedding much of its 19th Century philosophy.[23]

In subsequent discussion in 1984 Greene expressed regret at some aspects of Castro's dictatorship but makes allowances for political positions which he feels are a direct response to intransigence from the USA.

The border, an important symbol in Greene's writing, separates the Mexican revolution in 1938 from American capitalism; the Cuban revolution from Mexico under American influence; Haitian poverty and its machinery of tyranny from Santo Domingo where businessmen and politicians feel at home among the fruit machines and the swimming pools. The talk at the next table in the luxury hotel 'is all of dollars and percentages, but neither business nor politics has any relevance in Haiti. Haiti produces painters, poets, heroes and in that spiritual region it is natural to find a devil too'.[24] This passage illustrates the movement of Greene's prose from contingencies to the timeless, from action to reflection. It is in this spirit that Fidel Castro is 'the revolutionary brain visibly in action', 'so Pauline in his labours and in his escapes from suffering and death', 'a Chestertonian man who travels at home as though it were a foreign land' to educate himself.[25]

Comparison and contrast is frequent in the despatches and Cuba provides the contrast to Chile where Allende requires less the heroic charisma of Castro than 'extreme political prudence, a sense of humour and unspectacular courage'. Greene's despatch from Chile published more than a year before the coup captures the tension of the time. He sets out the contrasts between Cuba's solidly based revolution and Chile's aspirations beleagured by external threat and enemies from within. These include the bourgeoisie as well as the wealthy miners from Chuquiacama who feel threatened by the very notion of equality, and have little sympathy for the condition of the workers in Lota. The region of contrasts extends to climactic conditions so that God and destiny appear to be against the people of Lota: nine months of perpetual rain, a solitary cinema like a flea-pit and nothing to do after work but drink while Chuqui lies all year long in the sun of the desert; it has one of the best hospitals in Latin America; its houses are well-built, brightly painted; there are cinemas, churches, and shops full of goods.

The most important feature of the despatches from Latin America is that in all of them Greene builds upon the fact that there is no inherent opposition between Marxist economics and Catholicism which is why he argues with Castro for cooperation between Communism and Catholicism. Greene's perception of the role of the Church in this region began with his analysis of the religious persecution in Mexico during what he calls the 'phoney revolution' in 1938 when he recognised the depth of the faith of the peasants. Since then he has feared the potential power of the American church to destroy religious freedom in this region and to subvert the legitimate political aspirations of the people:

> through the radio the church in America continues to poison the wells . . . Perhaps it is a fortunate thing for the world that Fidel Castro was educated as a Catholic and knows that the voice of the

American hierarchy is not the voice of the church. It is too often the voice of the Cold War.

I write 'fortunate for the world' for here in Cuba it is possible to conceive a first breach in Marxist philosophy (not in Marxist economics) that philosophy as dry as Bentham and as outdated as Ingersoll.[25]

The novels explore the separation of church hierarchy from its priests in the field and from the community, of theology from life and humanity. 'The church is the barrio' says Father Rivas in *The Honorary Consul* and much earlier, in *The Lawless Roads*, Greene suggests that the Catholic Church should learn the language of revolution. His understanding of process in Central and Latin America has given him insights into developments in the Church in this region such as those eventually described as Liberation Theology. The interpretation of orthodoxy by Latin American theologians has only recently been recognised by the Church in Rome, although its radicalism has not been validated. Greene consistently pleads in favour of the new movements in the Latin American Church because they represent the faith and reality of those communities and it is Catholicism with such roots that has more to apprehend from its hierarchy than from its so-called enemies like Castro:

> Just across the water lie the great impoverished areas of South America – poverty and riches in revolutionary juxtaposition – vast opportunities for Communist expansion denied to Russia in Europe. Catholicism in Cuba has always been a religion of the bourgeoisie and so without deep roots. The religion of the peasant is Afro-Christian – Ogoune and Erzulie and Legba share their altars as in Haiti with a Christian god. But in South America, with the possible exception of Brazil, the Catholic Church is the natural religion of the peasant, and if Communism is to be imported from Cuba, Fidel will not appear in South America as the persecutor of the Church. Nor would it be his wish. The enemies of the Church in Cuba are not the Communist leaders: they are Cardinal Spellman and Bishop Sheen, those doughty champions of cold war and counter-revolution, churchmen for whom Pope John XXIII seems to have lived in vain.
>
> As Russia drifts towards state capitalism and China towards some fantastic variant of her own . . . . Cuba may well become the real testing ground of Communism.[27]

Although Catholicism does not have much of a following in Cuba, Greene realises the importance of Castro's role for the future of religious freedom in the area. Castro, too, aware of cultural traditions strongly rooted in spirituality has been careful to keep the options open. In a speech to the Jamaican Council of Churches in 1977 Castro went further than article 54 of the 1975 Cuban Constitution and said that there should be a strategic alliance between religion and socialism. He suggested that this was possible because 'there are no contradictions between the aims of religion and the aims of socialism'.[28]

Those opposed to the transformations taking place in Nicaragua, for instance, argue that these links between religion and Marxism are only short-term means useful to consolidate Marxism after which all vestiges of religious worship will be safely dumped. This view sees all Marxists as atheists, whereas the priests now holding important positions in the Nicaraguan government do not consider Marxism and Christianity as mutually exclusive. They realise that Marxism can be used as a tool to analyse society and to change it. Such a view does not accept that religion is being used merely as a tactical measure to strengthen the development of a Marxist state. Greene's own view seems to be that constant economic and military aggression from the USA is the power that will drive these societies to hard line Marxism. Though Castro's Cuba is no longer what it was in the spring of Cuban revolution, it is difficult to point to repressions without simultaneously relating these to external pressures.

In all Greene's despatches from Latin America, the role of the church is a constant preoccupation. In Chile, the church is progressive; the Christian Left is active but so are the Christian Democrats and the Pentagon 'who may feel impelled to exhibit its undiminished power in what it considers its sphere of influence'.[29] In Paraguay Greene distinguishes between the historically honourable record of the Jesuits who protected the Indians from the Spaniards so that Guarani is still a living language here and others who allow themselves to be used by General Stroessner's ruling elite. Contrasts dominate the landscape yet again:

> If you can afford that old colonial house, with a cook, a housemaid and a gardener for 40 dollars a month, it's just as well to carry a red handkerchief when you walk in the street that day and forget the troublemakers in prison and the malnutrition you might find among the scrap-heap huts perched on the red cliffs of Asuncion

in the shadow of the white Shell bastions like the hovels which clung against the walls of a medieval castle.[30]

Harold Pinter spoke of such contrasts in a recent interview when he discussed the politics of his work in relation to his latest play, *One for the Road* which is on the subject of torture.[31] Pinter commented on the difficulty of creating art when the writer's point of view is already committed to a particular end. The turning-point in his own mind towards a more direct commitment, says Pinter, came when a democratically elected government in Chile was overthrown by machinations from outside. Greene's letters to the press, insistent and frequent, and activities about which he is reticent except in marginal references in his memoirs and conversations, reveal a lifelong concern with political issues into which he has been drawn for moral reasons. A writer must, above all, face up to reality which includes political reality. Greene's technique in this regard is unique: he successfully juggles the balance to emphasise a moral sense rather than a political solution. The ambiguities that follow from such strategy exasperate hardliners who see him, perhaps, as emotionally attracted by revolution but intellectually conservative. What needs to be remembered is that Greene is first and last an artist committed to his vision of humanity.

The main theme of *The Honorary Consul* brings together these contrasts and concerns with great power. One of the protagonists, Leon Rivas, an ex-priest, appears to be modelled on Camillo Torres, a priest who was shot with the guerrillas in Colombia. Greene calls Father Torres 'the Catholic equivalent of Che Guevara'. He sees his own ideal of the role of priesthood as supporting, inspiring and directing movements for justice and human rights, as is being put into practice in Nicaragua. Greene supports the presence of the three priests as Ministers or Advisers in the Government – positions of worldly authority and power – as a temporary phase and as beneficial in guiding hard-won and fragile freedoms. Conscience demands engagement with the aspirations of the people of Nicaragua, which is how the priests see their role. They exercise the Christian presence within the reality of the people's movement. Though called a revolution, it is not a Marxist-Leninist model that is at work, says Father Cesar Jerez, Rector of the University of Central America. People gave their blood in the cause of Christian principles which drew them into the struggle.[32]

Since Greene's work attempts an expression of humanism

through an understanding of the relationship of Christianity to political process his enthusiasm and involvement with social change in Central and Latin America should come as no surprise. The radicalisation of faith and the radical structural transformation of society that is taking place in Nicaragua is, in a sense, an expression of Papal encyclicals he quotes in *The Lawless Roads* 'which have condemned capitalism quite as strongly as Communism' (p. 28). Understandably, he is very critical of the pronouncements of Pope John Paul II on the Church in Latin America. For Greene – as indeed one would venture to say for the majority of the Catholic population spread across the world – revolution in Nicaragua is a manifestation of faith. The priests in government think they can better serve the poor in this way and ensure a Christian face to the revolution so that abuses can be criticised and anti-religious directions can be avoided. Their argument goes beyond the scope of canon law to suggest that their position in government is a manifestation of their obedience to God since they view the project of the revolution as an expression of the message of the Gospel. Their allegiance is not to the *magisterium* of the Pope but to the 'people's Church' and to 'the God of the poor'. Greene's consistent emphasis on the importance of these priests in positions of authority to safeguard the ideals of justice and faith is, in fact, paralleled by the structure of his novels where the orthodoxy of Catholicism is deliberately subverted in order to reveal the living expression of justice and love.

A touching tribute was the presentation of the Order of Ruben Dario in April 1987 by Nicaragua to honour Greene's 'fundamental contribution to contemporary literature which is recognised by all of humanity and also for his struggle against imperialist domination'. In his short but emotional speech Greene said he was touched by the award but also felt a certain feeling of shame that it was being presented to an Englishman:

> I am well aware that England, like France, has done very little for Nicaragua in her difficulties. Therefore, I don't feel as an Englishman that I deserve this declaration . . . I see Nicaragua not only as a small country fighting a bully in the north. I see you even more as being in the front line of the trenches in a world wide conflict between civilisation and barbarism.[33]

The fusion of religion and politics was first attempted by Greene in *Brighton Rock* (1938). *The Lawless Roads* (1939) combines insights into a fundamental aspect of society – that in man everything is mediated politically, with the awareness that original

Christianity did possess the political dynamic. The novels reveal this ideal by indirection, through the experience of individuals in given circumstances, and suggest the matrix of a political community engaged in concerted, responsible and sustained action. The 'theological' framework of novels such as *Brighton Rock* (1938) rooted in practical experience, reveals that justice is the condition of love and the basis of the spiritual life. Greene's imaginative rendering of the concept of sin encompasses the social sin of injustice and oppression, and this understanding underpins the 'evil' actions of Pinkie. An intuitive, despairing and terrified comprehension of all these dimensions by Rose compels her loyalty to Pinkie and gives the novel its spiritual power, an element that is further developed in *The Power and the Glory* (1940) and *The Honorary Consul* (1973), where Greene juxtaposes religion and politics more directly.

A fascinating aspect of the development of the novels is to see them in relation to changes within the Catholic Church since Vatican II, and the Conference of Latin American Bishops held in Medellin, Colombia, in 1968 and Puebla, Mexico, in 1979 when, finally, the Church declared itself unequivocally committed to 'the option for the poor'.[34] *The Power and the Glory* expresses this need in the confrontations between the power of the socialist government and the humiliated representative of the glory of the kingdom of God. Religion and politics are integrated in ideals of faith and action expressed through simple, humane actions when Carol shelters and feeds the priest, and in the perceptions that underlie the meetings between the lieutenant and the priest.

The dynamism of Greene's vision is, in a sense, expressed in the process at work in Nicaragua today where the ideals of peace, commitment to the poor, revolution, the kingdom of God and national pride are combined as faith rather than as ideology. A new Catholicism has developed through priests, nuns and lay people working in basic communities in Central and Latin American society who, radicalised by their experience, interpret the Gospel with a political dynamic and work for revolutionary social transformation. The government of Nicaragua is working towards a system which clearly articulates the process as involvement in an integral way in Christianity and in the revolution, an ideal sought by Greene in *The Lawless Roads* (1939). The concluding section of this book examines *Monsignor Quixote* (1982) where belief, faith, ideology, the systems that represent these, and human experience are brought, as it were, face to face.

From 1976 to 1983 Graham Greene visited Panama five times and attended the signing of the Panama Canal Treaty as a member of the Panamanian delegation along with Gabriel Garcia Marquez. As with other leaders in whom Greene has placed his faith, General Torrijos's appeal lay in his courage and willingness to risk a great deal in his negotiations with America. In this sense the Canal is important only as a symbol of colonialism just as Panama represents more than the isthmus: it is Latin America.

General Torrijos was not a typical military dictator and Greene likes to emphasise that he did not assume the title of President. His government attempted to substitute grassroots democracy for the rule of the oligarchy. He was, in Greene's view, a patriot and an idealist without a formal ideology;[35] a lonely man without the base of a political party but with the right kind of politics: a friend of Fidel Castro, of the Sandinistas, who gave much support to the guerrillas from San Salvador.

The ideals shared by Communism and Christianity in developing societies tend to be overshadowed by the connection between communism and Soviet power. This connection obscures understanding of the commitments of Christian humanism. All national movements that seek freedom from American hegemony, and release from participation in the economic system of the USA are seen as a threat to the security of the USA. Fears of Soviet power underlie its relationship with Central and Latin America. That this is well understood by Torrijos is illustrated in his conversations with Greene.

Greene's memoir *Getting to know the General* is an account of his friendship with General Omar Torrijos, who ruled Panama from 1968 to 1981, when he died in a plane crash which many believe was an act of sabotage by the CIA. His travels in the region are spent educating himself and sharing the dreams of the General for his people. Their conversations are often comic and illuminating and one can imagine the approving twinkle in Greene's eye when Torrijos discusses American fear of communism in Angola: 'I told Andrew Young that Africa is more a danger to your vanity than to your security.' The book combines elements of the travelogues, journalism and fiction. With commitment and compassion and without sounding propagandist, Greene reveals his ability to look at the world and human experience with an awareness of every nuance of the strategies of survival.

The account of travel in Panama is enlivened by the presence of Chuchu who is acknowledged as friend, philosopher and guide. José de Jesus Martinez, better known all over Panama as Chuchu is a man of many parts: a Marxist professor of philosophy, mathematician, poet and linguist, security guard to the General as well as Greene's interpreter, chauffeur, pilot and fellow rogue. As ever in Greene's factual accounts, reality merges with the transcendent, the public mask with the innermost self so that he perceives in Torrijos a man 'whose eyes expressed sometimes an almost manic humour, an affection, an inscrutable inward thought, and more than all other moods, a sense of doom' – qualities that could well describe the novelist himself and elements of his fiction.

Getting to know the General, perhaps quite intentionally, reveals less the General than Greene's own commitments. General Torrijos functioned as a beneficent dictator with a remarkable ability to steer the path of consensus policies and keep both labour and capital happy. Since his death Panama is still looking for a leader who can carry on his progressive stand which captured the deeply felt national aspirations of a small but strategically important country. His hopes for the non-aligned movement suggest Greene's own vision of a humane and interdependent world free from domination by the two super powers. Greene is much happier with the concept of non-alignment than with the idea of a Third World.

My discussion of Greene's journalism illustrates insights gained during his years of unmapped but quite deliberate travel which helped him explore the relationship between imaginative creation and political radicalism. For a Christian no one strand of the web which links the three corners of Church, literature and politics can be touched without affecting the others, says Terry Eagleton in *The New Left Church*.[36] It is easier, he suggests, for a Christian than for others to move between church, culture and politics; what the church, politics and the arts have in common is that they offer basic descriptions of what it is to be human and the descriptions they offer are finally synonymous. In a broad sense this may be applied to Greene's work with the clarification that his 'church' is one that includes any culture rooted in spiritual traditions, and that is free to carry on as a living tradition. He has sought creative responses to the new challenges of our times with a story telling technique where life is rooted, is strong in experience, and is supremely human.

Although Greene's work presents modern society as composed of soulless masses and spiritual vacancy it is not to suggest a return to feudalist aristocracy or innocent, starving peasants. Kipling loved peasants too, and villagers, and the loyal warrior. He despised Westernised Indians in much the same way, it could be said, that Greene castigates the creole in his travelogues. But this would be to miss the point. Whereas Kipling hides his true self behind the might of the Empire he proclaims, and finds himself in the Indian countryside, Greene exposes the underside of Empire and restates original values that his own tradition has lost while pursuing the myth of aggression, progress and technology. His is a vision of landowning peasantry so that what he asserts theologically and morally makes sense politically. His work moves beyond middle-class liberal conformism to understand revolution and conceptualise possibilities 'outside the enclosed network of liberal paternalist deadlock'. His individual finds fulfilment within a sense of community and history which results in an overlap between religion and nationhood as is happening, for instance, in Nicaragua today. *The Honorary Consul* and *Monsignor Quixote* are specially important. They express the development of insights first realised in *The Power and the Glory* to reveal a vision of the Church within social structures, not in duplicated structures; the focus of the Christian community is that of the natural community as is happening in Central and Latin America where priests work alongside and within the general social movement towards a better society.

*   *   *

The novels discussed in this section illustrate the following propositions: (i) to be human is to be political, and (ii) the politics of today is inseparable from living, from the essential issues of freedom and dignity basic to life. They proceed on the very assumptions of civilisation and in the process expose the hypocrisies of power blocs and establishments to reveal the fleeting, precarious and inestimable value of freedom and dignity. In a way the so-called gentle reader is jolted into recognising the threat to his own reality. In *The Quiet American*[35] the situation where confrontation of basic issues moves at several levels is Vietnam. It is a novel set in the context of national liberation emerging from the death-throes of the old imperialism only to be nearly exterminated by the new and more insidious imperialism of the superpowers.

Fowler is the English newspaper correspondent who reports the scene and takes it to the centre of the war. Although all the novels discussed here attack American foreign policy directly or tangentially, individual Americans are presented as naive or innocent, and as unable to appreciate the dangers of official ideology. Thus the power of *The Quiet American* rests on the innocence and decency of Pyle, the American of the title, who is completely convinced of the morality of what he believes; he is not devious nor underhand as the Englishman is; he is honest and direct; his idealism is manipulated by the system he represents.

The subject of Greene's satire has always been American foreign policy which pretends to protect the 'free world' but wraps materialistic doctrines in the language of spiritual aspiration, and then uses the package to spread its power throughout the world. Talk of the 'free world' in fact often means only one objective: American interests, her security and trade, and the dissemination of cultural modes dedicated to feverish consumerism. Communism is distrusted without regard to some of its ideals. More to the point is the fact that talk of the 'free world' does not really concern itself with democracy and justice in its satellite nations.

A running theme in Greene's work – the promise of socialism – is first expressed with compassion in *It's a Battlefield*. The novel exposes the devious working of an establishment which would like to brand every worker asserting his rights a Red. *The Quiet American* and subsequent fiction focuses on the need for revolutionary mobilisation against foreign intervention and domestic tyrannies. The novels discussed illustrate how every Government that seeks a degree of autonomy from American hegemony is branded a liability, its sovereignty given short shrift, its power destabilised.

The fact that Greene takes sides against American hegemony has less to do with his being pro-Communist than with his commitment to ideals of dignity and justice for societies where politics are the realities of hunger, degradation and death – the kind of repressions normally associated with Communist regimes by members of the 'free world'. More than once has he said that his interest in politics is not where elections and votes determine the degree of income tax, but where the issue is life and death.

For the writer who interpenetrates the temporal with the spiritual, the city of man with the city of God, and in particular for the 'Catholic writer', the demands on artistic expression are not easy – the supernatural has to be conveyed in terms of the natural order. Anthony Burgess considers this situation generally as one where the Catholic writer expresses the vision of the supernatural order in terms of a conservative and pristine framework of the natural order. In Greene's fiction, however, it is the natural order that tends to be subverted:

once a Catholic lays open his soul to the corruption of the great world of commitment, he must accept a kind of empiricism if he is not to be damned, drawing from the natural order what may conceivably further the terrestrial ends of the supernatural order. In Greene's fiction, however, there is little flavour of empiricism

. . . There are instead paradoxes and anomalies – the sinner who is really a saint, the philanthropist who is really a destroyer.[37]

Burgess has correctly conveyed the situation of the religious or indeed Catholic writer. But he tends to interpret the natural order as one of dogma and ritual, the sacramental conveying by a kind of allegory the ineffable or the divine immanent in reality. Hence by this definition the frame of reference of the natural order is coterminous with religious dogma. Both have to be fixed so that the progress of plot and characterisation proceed through an ordered aesthetic. By this definition a religious writer has to be conservative and orthodox like Evelyn Waugh and François Mauriac. A contrary view that a revolutionary and heretic can be a religious writer with an aesthetic that is valid can also be held if the touchstone applied is that both categories of religious writers – the orthodox and the heretical – use religion as a means towards unfolding a vision of reality and truth that transcends dogma and ritual.

It is true that the religious writer projects the supernatural through the natural order but this does not mean that the natural order which he accepts is one of conservatism or of orthodoxy. In fact religious writers like Greene and Waugh do convey a unified sensibility of the soul struggling in isolation for grace and redemption – Sebastian Flyte in *Brideshead Revisited* and Querry in *A Burnt-Out Case*. Where Greene has advanced the argument is in his use of the natural order in its wider cosmos of politics and history. He moves away from the traditional reference points of the landed gentry as in Mauriac and Waugh to the experience of professionals and the urban proletariat, the ex-colonial officers, the new power groups and those 'outside the pale' whose experience defines the religious sense.

The novels describe the world of today in the widest and narrowest sense of the term as comprising nation-states, power blocs, communities, cultures, and individual human beings. It concerns itself with survival rather than class struggle, with the bare limits and precarious existence of the many for whom 'life is gaol'. Lack of freedom and dignity is explored at an individual level as also at a national level with nations controlled by an unseen iron fist that lends its power to repressive regimes which are, in turn, mere pawns in global strategies.

In this sense Russian hegemony has an edge: it does not pretend to be disseminating the idealism of a 'free world'; more importantly, it has in this century created a less unequal society; the fact that spiritual values are openly and actively resisted under Communism saves it from the bigger hypocrisy committed by an ideology which admits freedom of religion yet produces societies immersed in materialism with soul-destroying vigour. To call Greene anti-democratic or pro-Communist is to simplify the issues that engage him: power and responsibility: moral choices for individuals and governments; not forms of government but the quality of human life; not confrontation between superpowers but the repercussions of the endless Cold War on people's lives.

In *The Quiet American* Greene sets the Vietnamese scene as consisting of groups or camps: the Chinese quarter of Cholon whose inhabitants plot quietly and work unobtrusively but with passionate dedication to the cause; Vigot, the police inspector at the French Sûreté who is unable to protect the civilian quarters from the hazards of the battlefield; the front line as seen from the relative safety of headquarters at the battlefront; and the rice fields nearer to the action when Fowler manages to slip further than authorised. These are concerns of an ingenious narrative that come to a head not merely in the scenes of devastation like the canal at Phat Diem or the bombs in a public square, but in the tiny space of a watch-tower where Fowler, Pyle and two Vietminh guards seek refuge. The long conversation here between the two outsiders about the fate of Vietnam is particularly poignant: the outsiders survive and the Vietminh guards get killed.

The Quiet American suggests with controlled indignation the point of view of the Vietnamese, both human and national. 'How many dead colonels justify a child's or a trishaw driver's death when you are building a national democratic front?' (p. 163). Although the narrative exposes political realities through the perspective of Fowler's 'objectivity', it slips into a pattern of male paternalism in the account of the relationship between Fowler and Phuong, the Vietnamese girl, who has been a hostess at the Grande Monde until she moves in with him.

Phuong exists as others see her yet neither Pyle nor Fowler can ever fathom her and she is described as 'owning herself completely' (p. 32). Both she and her elder sister who works for the American Embassy appear to take their ideals from Western models of consumerism and materialism. Phuong knows Piccadilly, and the Empire State Building; these constitute her dreams of escape. Her sister's most cherished ambition is an American husband for Phuong. The dominant point of view, however, remains always that of Fowler who defines her in terms of his need:

she was the hiss of steam, the clink of a cup; she was a certain hour of the night and the promise of rest . . . To take an Anamite to bed with you is like taking a bird: they twitter and sing on your pillow. There had been a time when I thought none of their voices sang like Phuong's. I put out my hand and touched her arm – their bones, too, were as fragile as a bird's (p. 12).

No glimpse of her inner life is offered and yet her character serves a purpose beyond the obvious one of the story-line. Phuong accentuates the nature of the relationship between the subject-race and the outsider. When they come together as human beings the level of the relationship expresses the political situation: entertainer and entertained, service loyally rendered and affection protectively bestowed. Phuong's mask of survival is foolproof. She glides in and out of Fowler's life and back again revealing no hint of her emotions though the narrative suggests that she enjoys the company of Pyle and the promise of escape he represents. Though Fowler's actions and motives are utterly selfish in his personal life, he is remarkably sensitive to the aspirations of the Vietnamese in the public context.

Phuong in one sense represents the urban intermediary at the lowest level of the power structure, manipulated and exploited by all, including Fowler, but better off than the peasant in the rice field whose reality is more stark. Her cultural baggage is well concealed, her literal baggage non-existent; she poses no threat to anyone and has learnt to survive yet preserves her innocence through an age of experience gained in her young life. Her innocence embodies, indeed, the main point of Greene's narrative: 'She might lie from politeness, from fear, even for profit, but she would never have the cunning to keep her lie concealed' (p. 82).

Fowler relies for inside information on Dominguez, his assistant who, as a fellow-Asian, has the trust of the Vietnamese community and thus enjoys a freedom denied to Fowler. Sources of information can sometimes be innocent, such as Fowler's conversations with Phuong who collects gossip on her daily encounters in shops, on the streets, or among old women who chat at doorways. This is how she inadvertently confirms Fowler's suspicions about the real nature of Pyle's work. Although ostensibly employed in the American Economic Mission he represents interests that wish to substitute French colonialism with a Third Force for Democratic Freedom to be supported by American aid – a move designed to stifle Vietnamese nationalism which has aligned itself to Communist leadership for a base. Fowler attempts to educate Pyle in the realities of Vietnam:

They want enough rice . . . They don't want to be shot at. They want one day to be much the same as another. They don't want our white skins around telling them what to do (p. 94).

Dominguez as intermediary is less vulnerable than Phuong. His aims – not mercenary as are those, for instance, of Yusef in *The Heart of the Matter* – are linked to ideals described in terms of indigenous religion and culture, a reality frequently validated in Greene's world view. Dominguez combines in his character the qualities of gentleness, humility, love of truth, and respect for life. Aspects of his personality are traced back to Dominguez's original religion, Hinduism, to the influence of Buddhism and these – the cultures of their birth – create a bond between Dominguez and Mr Heng, an ally of the communists. They share a distrust of outside elements seeking to infiltrate the struggle. In this context Dominguez and the Catholicism of the peasants of Phat Diem are valued and differentiated from the Church hierarchy.

Greene's journalism describes the hierarchy as dominated by the USA; the novel pays less direct attention to the Catholic Church than to General Thé, once the leader of the Caodaists whom the Americans try to instal, in the narrative, as leader of the Third Force. Although the character of the intermediary at this level of power is not explored the text defines the nature of the role in the hierarchy of exploitation. Fowler's perception holds these various strands together although his credibility as a witness is flawed. His jealousy of Pyle colours his motives and this too is no simple matter. In danger of losing Phuong to Pyle he is, nevertheless, fair enough to recognise that Pyle has more to offer her: youth, marriage, security. The whole affair becomes more poignant when Pyle saves Fowler's life. Such irony deepens the plot into a humane exploration to reveal dimensions of experience that lift the novel to a level other than that labelled by critics as anti-Americanism.

The narrative represents Pyle as the more caring and concerned for Phuong though in a simple-minded, conventional way; Fowler is selfish, but aware of complexities and depths. Pyle is the romantic idealist, Fowler the cynical realist who manages to slip into condescension:

It's a cliché to call them children – but there's one thing which is childish. They love you in return for kindness, security, the presents you give them – they hate you for a blow or an injustice.

They don't know what it's like – just walking into a room and loving a stranger. For an aging man, Pyle, it's very secure – she won't run away from me so long as the home is happy (p. 104).

Such perceptions are clouded by benevolent paternalism which persists in Greene's work despite the progression in subsequent novels towards articulating the hopes and aspirations of the ruled and the oppressed. Thus, in *The Honorary Consul*, Fortnum marries the prostitute Clara to protect her. He has no one else and settles for unrequited love. Maurice Castle the English double agent in *The Human Factor* (1978) marries Sarah who is black and from South Africa. They love each other deeply. He risks his reputation and career to save Sarah, to express solidarity with her people, and to do whatever is in his power to help the struggle. In so doing he loses everything including the home so jealously guarded.

Peace, justice and freedom in Greene's world are ideals sought and simultaneously negated by worldly powers. In all these novels members of the oppressed class or race are described with sympathy but in a relationship of dependency. This is particularly obtrusive where women of subject-races are concerned until *The Human Factor* where Sarah, a black woman from South Africa is liberated from such dependency by her stoic capacity for love and sacrifice. A measure of independence and dignity is realised in the character-isation of men – Father Rivas, Aquino, Dr Magiot, the poet Philipot, the awareness of Wordsworth, as indeed in the character of Domin-guez and the brief glimpse of Vietnamese workers such as Mr Heng whose knowledge is contrasted with Fowler's complete ignorance in their midst. Here he is led and guided and the point of view of the narrative is subtle in its ability to convey Fowler's perception of what, on the face of it, seems like chaos, confusion and dirt, and his simultaneous acceptance that this is a reality he does not know but would like to comprehend. Pyle does not seek such knowledge; his innocent ignorance and misguided sense of purpose cost him his life. The death of Pyle serves only personal ends:

And, waking that morning months later with Phuong beside me, I thought, and did you understand either? Could you have antici-pated this situation? Phuong so happily asleep beside me and you dead? Time has its revenges, but revenges seem so often sour. Wouldn't we all do better not trying to understand, accepting the fact that no human being will ever understand another, not a wife a husband, a lover a mistress, nor a parent a child? Perhaps that's why men have invented God – a being capable of understanding. Perhaps if I wanted to be understood or to understand I would bamboozle myself into belief, but I am a reporter; God exists only for leader-writers (p. 60).

The reporter who stubbornly announces his objectivity comes to realise that a grasp of reality precludes comforting illusions, and breeds in him distrust of motives disguised by good intentions. The only novel that shares the 'secular' but spiritual and tragic sense of this reflection on life and death is *The Human Factor*.

Greene has found the film technique enriching and often transposes from this medium the intense focus of the close-up. The relaxed narrative that precedes and follows such direct scrutiny allows the ideas accentuated to sink into the reader's consciousness. Such a scene takes place in the middle section of *The Quiet American* when Fowler and Pyle take shelter in a watch-tower already occupied by two young Vietnamese soldiers who are terrified by the intrusion. The conversation between Fowler and Pyle in the quiet of the night as they worry about their chances of survival develops into a passionate and ironic discourse on motives and values. The novel comments on the domino theory: 'I know that record. Siam goes; Malaya goes; Indonesia goes. What does 'go' mean?' (p. 95). It often attacks Western liberalism but at its best it illuminates human experience:

who cared about the individuality of the man in the paddy field – and who does now? The only man to treat him as a man is the political commissar. He'll sit in his hut and ask his name and listen to his complaints; he'll give up an hour a day to teaching him – it doesn't matter what, he's being treated like a man, like someone of value. Don't go in the East with that parrot cry about threat to the individual soul. Here you'd find yourself on the wrong side – it's they who stand for the individual and we just for Private 23987, unit in the global strategy (p. 97).

The politics of Greene's fiction should be linked to the ideals of conservative Liberals in the early years of this century. There began a distrust then of the compromises being made by the Liberal left to placate the younger generation who sought more radical solutions. An interesting insight into the situation is revealed in Claud Cockburn's autobiography which discusses the deep conservatism and radical idealism of his father who worked in China, Korea and Japan. His account is specially interesting when it distinguishes between his father's candid rejection of the hypocrisies of the colonial encounter and his stubborn loyalty to the idea of Empire. Claud Cockburn was a fellow-student at the school Greene has mythicised in his fiction and a favoured student of the headmaster for his skills in chess. The headmaster, of course, was Graham Greene's father – Charles Greene – whose historical insights into life and literature have been described with affectionate understanding and loyalty by both Claud and Graham.

The early sections of Cockburn's autobiography, *I Claud*, recount the values of the fathers, their sense of a crumbling, chaotic, disintegrating world dominated by Bolsheviks and the new liberals. The comforting options of the latter group seemed to them to dispense with cherished values in the search for a new order, and this choice tarnished the dream. With such influences in their formative years some of the sons – Cockburn and Greene among them – sought the moral life in political journalism and art. Cockburn became a Communist and stayed the course. Both he and Greene joined the Communist Party while at Oxford, and Greene later joined the ILP but membership of both for him did not last more than a few weeks or months. To constrict the politique of Greene's fiction into right-wing or left-wing moulds is misleading. His writing reveals a radically conservative mind which seeks realisation of human potential in the most humane and liberal sense of the term. 'Conservative' here refers to the preservation of life-enhancing values, not to party politics.

Greene has expressed his admiration and affection for Kim Philby qualified by criticism of Philby's intrigues to supplant Coghill, his chief in the British Secret Service. One suspects that it is Philby's courage to 'go the whole hog' and to risk everything for a belief in an ideal that enthuses and holds Greene's enduring loyalty. Philby quoted from Greene's *The Confidential Agent* to explain his own actions and choices. In his introduction to Kim Philby's *My Silent War* Greene says it contains no propaganda but a dignified statement of his motives and beliefs in which the end justifies the means:

> this is a view taken, perhaps, less openly, by most men involved
> in politics, if we are to judge them by their actions, whether the
> politician be a Disraeli or a Wilson. 'He betrayed his country' – yes,

perhaps, he did, but who among us has not committed treason to something or someone more important than a country? In Philby's own eyes he was working for a shape of things to come from which his country would benefit.[38]

Greene's emphasis on the motives for Philby's choice reiterate ideals defined by conservative liberals of their fathers' generation:

he demands fairly enough what alternative there could possibly be to the bad Baldwin–Chamberlain era. 'I saw the road leading me into the political position of the querulous outcast, of the Koestler–Crankshaw–Muggeridge variety, railing at the movement that had let *me* down, at the God that had failed *me*. This seemed a ghastly fate, however lucrative it might have been'.[39]

The difference between Cockburn's representation of the dream and Graham Greene's is that the former is unfailingly realistic. Cockburn is baffled by the separation in his father's consciousness between the immorality of exploitation and the grandeur of the dream. His father's defence, he says, of the ultimate perfection of colonial expansion, for instance, while quite aware of its realities and methods, was like the pleasure that may be derived from listening to a strange symphony – one of such beauty and grandeur that the morality of the composer and the conductor was irrelevant:

About the personalities and forces . . . which motivated and directed the imperial machine, he had, as they say, no illusions. He found them comical, subjects for savage ribaldry. Or pathetic. Or sordid. And often simply ignoble. The machine, on the other hand – that was admirable and good: a fine bit of work, satisfactory and even inspiring to tend. Perhaps his reference to music was the clue. He was listening, perhaps, to some strange symphony. The rest was as irrelevant as would be the fact that the composer took dope and the conductor lived on the immoral earnings of women.[40]

For Greene too the manipulations of Empire were ignoble; he upholds the idealism of the men of action at the outposts and condemns the machinations and the hypocrisies of those in control. His summation of Philby's position is as follows:

How many a kindly Catholic must have endured the long bad days of the Inquisition with this hope of the future as a riding anchor. Mistakes of policy would have no effect on his faith, nor the evil done by some of his leaders. If there was a Torquemada now, he would have known in his heart that one day there would be a John XXIII.[41]

Alan Bates as Guy Burgess expresses a parallel sentiment in Alan Bennett's script of the film *An Englishman Abroad*. Bennett makes Burgess less the repulsive figure than the disreputable and lonely exile. The character reveals, with a mixture of frivolous panache and despair, an abiding love for England not as fatherland but as repository and instrument of ideals and dreams that could create a better world for all men. The search has led many of this generation on a long and distant journey, often bewildering and tragic. Greene's fiction encapsulates these dreams and although there is no escaping their genesis in the imperial myth it is important to acknowledge that his novels struggle with courage to renew the myth in terms that respect the cultural and spiritual integrity of all the peoples of the world.

The novels that followed *The Quiet American* reveal the many-sided enquiry into life that underlies Greene's work. *Our Man in Havana* and *Travels with my Aunt* are comic accounts that do not lose sight of the serious questions present more overtly in *A Burnt-Out Case*, *The Comedians* and subsequent fiction. Though Greene knew Havana well enough in Batista's day *Our Man in Havana*[42] has little to do with the Cuban revolution. When the novel was being researched Havana was a 'bizarre, corrupt city with its brothels, cheap drugs, gambling saloons, all owned by Las Vegas. Everyone went there for a good time.' It was only in the mountains, where Castro's rebels were already gathering that the situation was serious. Greene's novel does not reach this critical point but explores a region no less serious – that of the Cold War. Structured as an entertainment, its fun highlights realities such as the CIA concern over concealed missiles in Cuba. Greene discounts the historical accuracy of the fantastic plot as 'pure fluke.'

Our Man in Havana mocks the British Secret Service with affection: derision and distrust are reserved for the CIA. Espionage appears as a game played with little grasp of reality and with a fanatical rigour for the drill and rules of secrecy. These and Wormold's own bag of tricks devised to cope with a spendthrift daughter take on a surreal quality when the fantasy he invents as the man from MI6 in Havana inexplicably assumes life and shape. The novel reiterates the theme of *The Ministry of Fear* which is set in wartime London: 'It sounds like a thriller, doesn't it, but the thrillers are like life.' There are times, says Greene, when he is inclined 'to think that our entire planet gravitates inside a fog-belt of melodrama'.

Unobtrusive and lonely, Wormold's life in Havana is very private and has little to do with political issues until these intrude. At this point he defines his choice without any compromise, and betrays hegemonies to protect human beings:

> Wormold said to himself, At least if I could kill for a clean reason, I would kill to show that you can't kill without being killed in your turn. I wouldn't kill for my country. I wouldn't kill for capitalism, or Communism or social democracy, or the welfare state – whose welfare? I would kill Carter because he killed Hasselbacher. A family feud had been a better reason for murder than patriotism or the preference for one economic system over another. If I love or if I hate, let me love or hate as an individual. I will not be 59200/5 in anyone's global war (p. 186).

The police chief Segura, known as the Red Vulture, with a reputation for cruelty, is closer to the realities of the 'torturable' than the intermediaries of the spy game who fly in and out taking in beach and night-club as they plan global strategies. Though Segura is symbolically the wielder of repression his conversation with Wormold reveals a humanity lacking in their employers.

No such awareness disturbs the ruthless control of Haiti by the Ton Ton Macoute, instruments of Papa Doc's dictatorship illustrated in *The Comedians*. The most important aspect of *The Comedians* is that for the first time in Greene's fiction the voice of the non-European articulates its own point of view. Admittedly Dr Magiot and the young poet Philipot, who define the tragic reality of Haiti in terms of a revolutionary vision, are in one sense intermediaries: they are products of European culture and education. Their strength lies in their awareness that cultural dependence is a weapon of neo-colonialism and that skills must be acquired from a grass-roots base. The difference in their ages captures the history of Haitian struggle and the desolation at the end suggests the intractable realities of oppression.

The Comedians illustrates courage rather than hope. It explores the reality of struggle and the agonising powerlessness of those trapped by external power allied to internal tyranny. The novel has much

that is based on real events, not least the character of Dr Magiot
directly inspired by a personal friend, a physician and philosophe
who was Minister of Health in Paul Magloire's government. He late
had to resign, and die in exile in New York. He was never a Marxist
but Dr Magiot is described as a Marxist and defines his own creed ir
terms that suggest the closest Greene has come to a definition of
personal philosophy:

> I have grown to dislike the word 'Marxist'. It is used so often to
> describe a certain economic plan. I believe of course in tha
> economic plan in certain cases and in certain times, here in Haiti
> in Cuba, in Vietnam, in India. But Communism . . . is more than
> Marxism, just as Catholicism . . . is more than the Roman Curia
> There is a . . . mystique as well as a politique. We are humanists
> you and I . . . Catholics and Communists have committed grea
> crimes, but at least they have not stood aside like an established
> society, and been indifferent. I would rather have blood on my
> hands than water like Pilate (p. 286).

Dr Magiot and Papa Doc function as representative figures of th
forces of change and stagnation, freedom and repression, com
passion and corruption. The terror of Papa Doc's regime stalking th
streets is watched equally, even if less successfully though not ir
vain, by the patient courage and dignity of Dr Magiot. Within thi
reality Greene places a group of outsiders: Brown, rootless and
cynical, of uncertain nationality and parentage; Jones, an Englisl
hustler on the run; Mr and Mrs Smith, well-meaning American
who preach the gospel of vegetarianism and world peace. The
engage themselves with Haitian experience for selfish or naiv
reasons. The contact redeems them in ways none of them envisage
or believed possible except perhaps Mr Smith.

A long record of idealistic enterprise that led him to contest th
Presidential election in the USA also makes him aware that wars ar
made 'by politicians, by capitalists, by intellectuals, by bureaucrats
by Wall Street bosses and Communist bosses – they are none o
them made by the poor' (p. 22). Brown and Jones operate on th
fringes of this power group. They are portrayed as parasitic influ
ences that depend as much on elements within Haitian society fo
success as on their own hustling waywardness. The entire discours
takes place within a historical context.

The characterisation of the Smiths like that of Pyle comprehend the courage and good intentions of individual Americans as also their misplaced, ill-judged and simplistic attitudes to life and the world. The scenes at the Post Office and in the ghost city, Duvalier-ville, where Mr Smith empties his purse and flings coins to the beggars is less an ironical comment on Mr Smith's action than intended to expose the irrelevance of individual charity when insti-tutionalised aid itself buttresses imperialist activity. The Big Bat-talions of exploitation are described time and again:

> Papa Doc is a bulwark against Communism. There will be no Cuba and no Bay of Pigs here . . . Papa Doc's lobbyist in Washing-ton is the lobbyist for certain American-owned mills (they grind grey flour for the people out of imported surplus wheat; it is astonishing how much money can be made out of the poorest of the poor with a little ingenuity). And then there's the beef-racket. The poor here can eat meat no more than they can eat cake, so I suppose they don't suffer when all the beef that exists goes to the American market – it doesn't matter to the importers that there are no standards here of cattle-raising – it goes into tins for under-developed countries paid for by American aid, of course. It wouldn't affect the Americans if this trade ceased, but it would affect the particular Washington politician who receives one cent for every pound exported (p. 232).

The only hope left for the oppressed of this region and in Latin America is the American people – they must be made aware. This is a point stressed by Ernesto Cardenal, Minister of Culture in the Sandinista Government in a recent interview. The Americans, he said, must be told the truth and made to understand realities that will compel them to bring pressure on their government. Mr Smith acquires such knowledge and understanding of the truth about dollar diplomacy and human nature. He goes back a disillusioned man but with a new strength to his sense of purpose.

Another American enters the narrative briefly to reiterate the weight of capitalist enterprise from which there is no escape. He finds a place in the story in a juxtaposition of scenes that explore further the realities of tyranny and freedom. Brown escapes from Haiti into Dominica and hopes to find a job at a mining firm. The immense bauxite concession in the Dominican Republic is run by Mr Schuyler Wilson. Molly Mahood locates the novel very specifically in 1963 to show that this was a time when it was still possible for the

USA to display in its dealings with Duvalier 'the idealism and integrity of the Smiths rather than the crass materialism represented by Schuyler Wilson'.[43] It is more likely, however, that the Smiths are intended as a deliberate foil, the innocents in the face of American foreign policy particularly since the narrative does not, at any point, hold out much hope for Mr Smith's idealism and alternative world view.

The brief scene between Mr Schuyler Wilson and Brown illustrates a less tragic but no less insidious relationship than the one prevailing in Haiti. After the violence of Haiti, Brown finds spacious, well-laid-out streets in Santo Domingo. These are not haunted by the spectre of the Ton Ton Macoute and lead to Mr Wilson's enclave which he is 'free' to enter. Here freedom is protected: barbed wire, barricades, armed bodyguards, silence, a private port and a private landing strip; Mr Wilson, genial with Coca Cola in hand, is happy to employ those who believe like him that every insurrectionist is a Communist and that those who wish to educate his workforce are troublemakers or cranks.

The Comedians recreates a social panorama where culture has been destructured, is closed and fixed in the colonial status – caught in the yoke of oppression. Freedom from slavery in Haiti has introduced another form of tyranny. The colonisation of culture has further hardened original strengths, confining people's minds and diverting their attention from the true meaning of liberation. The anguish of Philipot, the poet, proceeds from his consciousness of what Fanon has called 'cultural mummification' which leads to a mummification of individual thinking. He knows that his verses are, at best derivative; they smell of *Les Fleurs du Mal*.

Philipot's self-consciousness – his realisation that he is no less a comedian than Jones and Brown – is at the heart of *The Comedians*, and gives the novel its rich sociopolitical resonances. He understands that his generation has been softened by bourgeois comforts and has played at culture by learning to sing, paint, and write in Paris while Papa Doc's reality emerged powerful, tyrannical and supreme. These later novels illustrate the role of the intermediary in contemporary forms of exploitation. The narrative underscores a history of slavery, of cultural destruction and the modern phenomena of propaganda. Brown may think that the tourist industry which he exploits is good for Haiti; Philipot knows that none of its financial gains reach the poor.

The climax where Philipot takes the leap to faith and the search for freedom by aligning himself with revolutionary groups in the mountains and spiritual movements rooted in a living tradition is rendered with a despairing sense of his anguish at complicity in events, and the need to be cleansed. The ceremony itself is a synthesis of traditional and new religions, Voodoo rites and Catholic rituals; the participants pray for deliverance from an evil that encompasses the slavery of the past and Papa Doc's cruel present.

Graham Greene's novel remains within the perspective of struggle even though the narrator, Brown, is alternately selfish, uninvolved, uncomprehending or unimpressed. He thinks Philipot's decision to join the struggle in the form which exists is regressive: if Philipot, whose poems had been published in an elegant limited edition, bound in vellum, who had been educated like Brown by the Jesuits and had been to the Sorbonne, is one of the initiates, 'what a triumph that would represent for Papa Doc as he dragged his country down' (p. 180).

The narrative validates Philipot's action in a paradoxical representation. Greene's art consists in his ability to reveal the validity of Philipot's consciousness, through his narrator, who keeps himself clearly outside the framework of struggle. The strategy enables him to enter the scene in Haiti as closely as is possible for a sympathetic outsider and simultaneously to reveal Brown's condition of exile. Brown's loneliness, his incapacity for any total involvement – this is made clear in his relationship with Martha – is intended as contrast at various points in the novel and his comments are meant to illustrate a process in his own evolution rather than a judgement of Philipot's choice. The heroic stature accorded Dr Magiot and, within the context of the struggle, his successor Philipot, endorses Philipot's turning to the gods of Dahomey for strength.

Within this discourse, Jones, a child of colonialism and its culture, attempts to survive on the peripheries of power. Born in India, the son of a tea-planter who abandoned his wife and child, Jones hustles his way to his dream. The material dream of colonials shorn of all values has been handed down to him, and he seeks his heritage denied him by the disappearance of his father: sahib house and golf. A genial companion, he has the capacity to believe in his dream whereas Brown's disquieted conscience finds strength in cynicism. Jones may seem dishonest as an arms dealer with no loyalty except to money, who ends up helping the guerillas because he has no option. This factual side of him is negated by the

paradoxical representation of him as the more humane. The two
characters complement each other as bastards of the colonial en
counter, 'thrown into the water to sink or swim'.

The novel touches cultural and moral questions that underlie the
colonial encounter and carry over into neocolonial relationships
The economic realities of foreign investments and aid are under
scored not least in the discussion between Mr Smith and the
Minister in Papa Doc's government, as well as in Dr Magiot'
request to Brown. The latter inherits the Hotel Trianon from hi
mother, a woman he hardly knows, having run away from boarding
school and more or less fended for himself since then. Dr Magio
advises him to sell the hotel to Marcel, his mother's lover. The
reason is simple: Marcel is Haitian. Marcel enters the narrative very
briefly. The confrontations between the two men illustrate the
materialistic, cold, and impersonal objectives of Brown and the
hopelessly involved anguish of the Haitian. The cynicism of Brown
who wishes to exploit his inheritance for his own advancement and
comfort with little thought for Haiti and its people, counterpoint
the involvement and despair of Marcel whose suicide very early in
the novel introduces the tragic sense in *The Comedians*.

The characterisation of Brown's mother is equally brief. She is a
player like her son but takes risks, gets involved, is loved and
respected by Dr Magiot. Her hotel has never been what Brown
succeeds in making it perhaps because she was within the reality of
Haitian struggle in a sense that Brown never wished to be. There i
no better choice of metaphor for economic and cultural exploitation
in *The Comedians* than the descriptions of Hotel Trianon in its
heyday: the disparities between the naked girl cavorting in the
swimming pool, business tycoons and tourists who carelessly
dispense dollars contrast with the realities of hunger and cruelty or
the streets. The narrative refines the dimensions of exploitation and
the meaning of liberation to its furthest point when Dr Magiot says
that in spite of everything, he would fight on the side of Papa Doc i
the Marines came. Internal solidarity is the first step to nationa
integrity and liberation just as traditional cultural strengths are the
basis of personal freedom. The bedraggled guerillas in the fina
section of the novel seem to be Greene's comment on the might of
the Big Battalions that pace the world.

The Honorary Consul brings the concerns of Greene's work together
in its epigraph: 'All things merge with one another good into evil
generosity into justice, religion into politics.' His exploration o

social change which began with *It's a Battlefield* and *Brighton Rock* continues in *The Honorary Consul* with a positing of the role of faith in the struggle for dignity and freedom. The novels recover the religious sense within contemporary situations. Without a spiritual dimension, Greene has often said, there is a flatness in the projection of characters in fiction however good the technique or craftsmanship may be:

I think that the flatness of E. M. Forster's characters, and Virginia Woolf's or Sartre's, for example, compared with the astonishing vitality of Bloom in Joyce's *Ulysses*, or of Balzac's Père Goriot, or of David Copperfield, derives from the absence of the religious dimension in the former. Mauriac's characters are equally endowed with this strange substantiality. In *La Pharisienne*, when one of them – a very minor character – crosses a school yard, we have a sense of having seen him in flesh and blood, while Mrs Dalloway doing her shopping leaves one indifferent. She moves out of our minds as easily as she moves out of Harrods.
Along the same lines I should say that very few good writers have emerged from the Communist world, with the exception of a Solzhenitsyn or a Pasternak or a Sinyavsky, who have in fact retained their sense of the religious. The Welfare State has driven God off the stage, just like the devil, but it has failed so lamentably that I have the impression God is making a timid reappearance. History tends to prove that Faith is reborn from its own embers. Would a Solzhenitsyn have existed if Communism had met with a more obvious success?[44]

Greene's passionate commitment to the liberation movements in Latin America springs not only from sympathy with their politics of independence but has to do with their convictions that they should be left alone to work out their survival free from superpower interference. It would be facile to structure the national cause and commitments in terms of conventional ideologies or hierarchies. The Nicaraguan Government has priests as its members and avoids the language of ideology. Here the Church is not a place to reflect on life and death but a centre of struggle for liberation and for the celebration of freedom. The scene in *The Honorary Consul* embraces these ideas and is brought even closer to America's backyard than in *The Comedians* to expose the fundamental distrust and dishonesty in the relationship between cold war superpowers and its self-deceiving satellites.

The novel is set in a small town in Argentina whose importance lies in its strategic situation on the border with Paraguay on the banks of the Parana. More importantly, the text establishes the context of the struggle: 'South America is our country . . . Not Paraguay. Not Argentina. You know what Che said. "The whole continent is my country" ' (p. 105). The landscape is clear and the map drawn true to historical realities: Paraguay where doors, even internal doors are locked, not against robbers but against the police, the military, and the official assassins.

The novel opens with the idea of exile, with a politics that is identified with need, a politics that is indeed life. The opening section also announces the visit of the American ambassador, a pivotal presence whose physical absence as a character both here and in *The Comedians* only serves to emphasise the burden of his authority. The narrative establishes a direct link between consumer-capitalism and undernourishment, poignantly juxtaposed as Eduardo Plarr's insatiable cake-consuming mother and the malnutrition of his patients; the aristocratic splendour of Leon Rivas's palatial home and the gnawing hunger of his congregation. Although Greene has said that *The Comedians* is the only novel where he set out very specifically to make a political point and to expose Papa Doc's repressive government, there is an equally overt suggestion in *The Honorary Consul* of the links between paternalist aid, underdevelopment, and the collusion of the ruling establishment.

It is simplistic to argue that Greene's view of the world is a naive option between communism and capitalism. His deep understanding of international affairs and insights are invaluable when transmuted into his novels as the reality of experience. To discuss his work as that of a Catholic writer, of a superb craftsman, with little reference to its political, humanist dimensions is to do great disservice not merely to his art but to the world it represents. Can these concerns be the proper subject matter of art? Their dichotomy and ambiguities seem to be the stuff of life itself in the world of today. The prevailing ethos is defined by David Hare and is quoted here to illustrate assumptions that are also questioned in Greene's work:

An interest in foreign affairs has for some years been out of fashion in England. The modern newspaper employs as few foreign correspondents as possible; for they are, in the best possible sense, out of control. They bring unwelcome news of a world which is difficult, and whose diversity and vitality contrast with the politics of selfishness which is now the orthodox practice of the West . . . News of how little everyone else in the world is getting can only confuse and disorient the domestic electorate. The suggestion that the battle-lines may be redrawn between the old ideologies is vigorously resented. Dismantling the cold war represents a real challenge to the brainpower and imagination of our rulers . . . Too close an examination of the map may only reveal where Nicaragua actually is.[45]

As Hare suggests, the Western world is alive to the repressions of Communist regimes but prefers to cover up its own support of loyal intermediaries whose repressions are tolerated to preserve the balance of power and spheres of geopolitical influence. News of such realities gets a mere side-glance since a closer look would disclose the role of the politics of Western powers in perpetuating the cold war. Except for a few courageous exceptions, the voices of freedom and dignity from such 'peripheries' are ignored by the mainstream media, by writers, and journalists. When they do get a hearing it is as hungry masses in need of aid and loans which governments can ill-afford to repay.

Graham Greene's work is a passionate expression of these realities ignored by Western politicians and writers in their relationship with their own voters and readers. The world of Greene's novels reveals this experience. It encompasses the unemployed in England and Europe, the exploited and oppressed in post-colonial societies, and the machinations of power blocs. However, these are the very realities which lie outside the frame of reference imposed on the public, as Hare suggests, and literature that falls outside this frame of reference – like several aspects of Greene's novels – is dismissed as Catholic or Marxist or just simplistic, without of course tending to detract from the reader's enjoyment of the craftsmanship and the entertainment value of 'Greeneland'.

The frame of reference described by David Hare has affected most analyses of Greene's fiction which has often been segmented into categories that skirt the realities and deny aspects essential to its vision. When he visited Mexico in 1938 Greene described the disparities as exhibited in consumer-waste and the starving poor; the faith of the peasants undiminished by a socialist revolution that promised equality without religious freedom. He then pleaded for a Church that could learn the language of revolution. His own conversion to Catholicism appears to have taken root, as it were, only after his experience in Mexico. In subsequent work Green expresses the spirit of freedom and self-realisation in a framework i which action is ultimately a search for transcendence.

Such action evokes the theme of responsibility and illustrates the expression of faith in *The Honorary Consul*. The novel establishe links amongst the lives of those in authority, those 'outside the pale', and men like Rivas and Plarr – sons of the privileged classes who feel compelled to take sides. It has been suggested that the character of Leon Rivas is modelled on Camillo Torres of Colombia Greene denies the likeness for superficial reasons: Rivas carries n gun, unlike Torres who died gun in hand. In fact Rivas and h fellow guerilla, Aquino, between them combine the essentials of Camillo Torres's life: he belonged to one of the rich and aristocrat families which has long produced oligarchies in this region; he late became a Dominican priest and taught at the University; when 1965 the US forces invaded Dominica with connivance from Colomb he resigned, took off his cassock 'to be more truly a priest', an declared that 'every Catholic who is not a revolutionary, and is n on the side of the revolution lives in mortal sin'.

Greene's novel has two protagonists. The first is Eduardo Plarr, doctor who has chosen to practise among the poor. As a boy he ha been sent to safety in Argentina along with his Paraguayan moth a woman whose character embodies all the vices of the urb bourgeoisie so that her self-indulgence, both emotional and materi contrasts with the austere idealism of her English husband wh stayed back in Asuncion to help in the struggle against repression These two are symbolic characters, emblematic in intention as a the characters of Doctor Fischer and his guests in *Doctor Fischer Geneva* (1980).

The other protagonist is Leon Rivas, Eduardo Plarr's scho friend; when they meet in adult life Rivas is an ex-Catho priest involved in the struggle which he brings, as it were, in Eduardo's bored, desultory and disquieted life. As in *The Comedia* the modern condition of alienation is explored in order to sugges movement away from self-absorption into involvement a awareness of human need. Rivas turns away in revulsion from rich home: a house with six servants; a father who threw ou gardener for stealing a few pesos lying on a garden seat; a fath untouched by repression since he contributes to the Genera party to be able to enjoy his privileges. The Church is guilty of worse betrayals:

> 'Sell all and give to the poor' – I had to read that out to them while the old Archbishop we had in those days was eating a fine fish from Iguazu and drinking a French wine with the General. Of course the people were not actually starving – you can keep them from starving on mandioca, and malnutrition is much safer for the rich than starvation. Starvation makes a man desperate. Malnutrition makes him too tired to raise a fist. The Americans understand that well – the aid they give us makes just that amount of difference. Our people do not starve – they wilt (p. 116).

Brief details of Rivas's past in a boyhood shared with Plarr suggest Rivas's fiery idealism since boyhood. He finds neither models nor authority at home where his father 'buys' freedom by donating handsomely to the Colorado party; nor is the Church as it exists in practice of much use to help him validate and translate these ideals. Frustrated, he rebels and enlists the help of Plarr, with whom he had shared his dreams of fighting as an *abogado* for the poor. Plarr's loyalties lead him, unwilling, into the centre of the storm; in the risks he takes to save the life of Fortnum and in his proximity with death Plarr finds the answers he sought in life when he was secure and a respectable member of society.

In the novels set outside England Greene seems to be reaching out to an element of genuine idealism which the text suggests did exist in the fathers' generation. Hence the characterisation of Eduardo Plarr's English father, though absent throughout the narrative as a physical presence, is overpowering as a moral force. This view of struggle could be disputed as Plarr's awakening is realised through the memory of his English father's idealism rather than directly through the disquieting experience of the poverty of his patients, disgust with the glossy world of his mother, and sympathy with Rivas's commitments. Is the narrative trying to suggest, yet again, a lost dream of justice and dignity as embodied in English character? Greene's answer would be, one suspects, that this is a strategy he adopts to help him approach a scene unfamiliar to him. It is his way of relating to experience outside familiar territory and culture. The fact remains, however, that over-emphasis on idealism linked with the past, and a romanticism which is inextricably linked with the myth of Empire undermine the sharp insights of the text.

Charley Fortnum, the Honorary British Consul, is an unsuccessful businessman, an alcoholic, too old to catch up with life but still capable of appreciating the need for dignity. He marries Clara, a prostitute, in order to give her security and to help her family of Tucuman Indians who depend on her earnings. Through her the narrative extends into the realities of hunger; it links her brother, who has suddenly 'disappeared', with the sinister silence that surrounds Plarr's father's whereabouts, and the realities of repression. The tales of torture recounted by Aquino define the imperatives that pervade the novel.

Conversations where Plarr tries to arbitrate for the release of Fortnum, kidnapped mistakenly instead of the American Ambassador, encompass questions of justice, law and order, life and death. In the hut where Aquino and Rivas hold their captive, Fortnum, Plarr's gradual awakening is completed. It is a process that is linked by memories of his father with his reactions to his mother and the fashionable bourgeoisie, his frustration at being unequal to the task of alleviating his patients, and finally his exposure to Charley Fortum and Leon Rivas who show him the capacity for love and involvement. Greene has said *The Honorary Consul* is his favourite novel because it captures the changes and development of the character of Eduardo Plarr. His inner life is recreated with great subtlety. It will probably surprise no one that this dimension of the novel, as indeed the reality of struggle and sacrifice, is completely absent from the filmed version of the text. Like most distortions of Greene's novels, the most notable being *The Quiet American*, the film misses the point of the book, makes of Plarr a macho lover and reduces Leon Rivas to insignificance.

The novel illustrates the changes in Plarr's consciousness imperceptibly. They often take the form of a poignant wish to understand his father's motives and courage for self-sacrifice. The development of introspective questioning in Brown and Plarr is comparable except that Brown maintains a protective shell of cynicism. He is finally left with a request from Dr Magiot, also a father-figure: 'If you have abandoned one faith, do not abandon all faith. There is always an alternative to the faith we lose. Or is it the same faith under another mask?'[46] Rivas describes his own faith redefined to suit the realities of life:

'Christ was a man', Father Rivas said, 'even if some of us believe that he was a God as well. It was not the God the Romans killed, but a man, a carpenter from Nazareth. Some of the rules He laid down were only the rules of a good man. A man who lived in his own province, in his own particular day. He had no idea of the kind of world we would be living in now. Render unto Caesar, but when our Caesar uses napalm and fragmentation bombs . . . I think sometimes the memory of that man, that carpenter, can lift a few people out of the temporary Church of these terrible years when the Archbishop sits down to dinner with the General, into the great Church beyond our time and place, and then . . . those lucky ones . . . they have no words to describe the beauty of that Church' (p. 220).

Leon Rivas says he is not a man of vision yet he is clearly pursued by a vision that makes him comprehend that the Church 'is this barrio, this room. There is only one way any of us can leave the Church and that is to die' (p. 200).

The theme of responsibility which also doubles as the search for a father or fatherhood runs through Greene's work. In *The Honorary Consul* this theme is emphatic: Rivas's bourgeois father whom he rejects; the Bishop as father of the Diocese – a role to which he shows scant sensitivity; Rivas as priest unable to shed this role after he joins a guerilla movement and who, even to Maria, who is now his wife, continues to be 'Father'; Rivas's responsibility to his flock; Plarr's father who dies for his ideal in contrast to Rivas whose ideals are betrayed by his father; Plarr's illegitimate child and finally Fortnum who assumes responsibility for the child, and acts with unexpected dignity and grace – the ideal restored by an Englishman who, throughout the novel, does little to preserve his own dignity or that of the country he represents as Consul. He loses his honorary job in the process, but emerges as true and honourable.

As always in novels set outside England *The Honorary Consul* has characters with English antecedents who are compelled to take moral positions. This is not to say that the reality of Latin America and its repressive governments function as a convenient base for European anguish. The perspective refers to man and the world; it deals with questions of politics and culture in national terms as well as in the context of international developments. The narrative tells a good story within which lie concealed imperatives that face every thinking individual, every responsible Government. The resolution sought is worked out within the context of the story line in terms of

action that mediates between contingency and values, and is ulti
mately transcendent.

These are some of the many themes orchestrated with the dis
sonance of skyscrapers and mean streets, posh cafes and mudd
wastes, the complacency of belief and the anguish of faith. ,
recurrent motif is: 'Life is absurd. Because it's absurd there's alway
hope.'[47] Greene dramatises the inadequacy of liberalism tha
assumes that man can achieve meaning and fulfilment solely throug
his own energy and merits. The early novels evoke authenti
existence as conflicting with abstractions such as impersonal human
tarianism, arbitrary justice, right and wrong. The theologic
dimensions of his later work, and not least the search of his lapse
Catholics and non-believers, is revealed in the struggle of man i
society. The two are not mutually exclusive. To discuss the refine
ments of the theology – Manichaeism, Jansenism, Pelagianism –
to move away from the essence of Greene's work which is life in o
world.

The Human Factor (1978) encapsulates in its title the concerns ar
questionings of Greene's fiction but places them in a 'secula
context. The novel brings together themes of his earlier work
underscore his life-long obsession with power and responsibili
and compels recognition of the subtle ways in which Greene h
enlarged the scope of moral and political questions in his fiction. Th
sum of his work is indeed a stirring discourse on the quest f
power, on the relationship between faith and action, the priva
conscience and the public act, man the individual and man th
citizen.

The Human Factor completes a circle begun with *Brighton Rock* ar
marks, as it were, the end of a search which has been at once ble
and illuminating. It drew Greene outside modern societies, outsi
the world of technology and 'civilisation' to Sierra Leone, Vietnar
Haiti, Cuba, Paraguay and Central America and back to Lond
where *The Human Factor* is set. This reading of the text emphasis
the absurdity of labels such as 'Catholic' and 'Third World'
applied to Greene's work for he is essentially concerned wi
expressing the need for a spiritual tradition and the sense th
injustice is the rule rather than the exception in our world. F
exploration of exploitation within an international framework dc
not obscure inequalities within individual nation-states nor a
these allowed to cloud understanding of international connivar
with the realities of repression and injustice. Since his fictio

structures are devoid of overtly political frameworks, and since the solutions to problems arising out of what may be called government policy are rendered in human terms, Greene makes himself vulnerable to accusations of political naiveté which reveal the ideological commitments of his detractors.

As an idealist, Greene's faith has always been strong enough to balance keen insights into contemporary realpolitik. It is important to acknowledge the power of both these elements in his work and the fact that absence of conventional forms of political analyses does not suggest a lack of understanding. What may seem naiveté is really an assumed innocence, a brilliant stance that enables him to juggle the balance between dream and nightmare, illusion and reality, hope and deep pessimism, and to analyse contingent situations with a cognisance of eternal destiny.

The Human Factor combines essential elements which we have come to expect of Greene's work – suspense, irony, wit – with a plot that moves with easy grace from the private to the professional life of individuals, flashing out codes and signals to communicate the theme of racial alignments and moral responsibility. With the British Secret Service as base, Greene creates a complex and mature blend of familiar themes: loyalty and betrayal, free will and destiny in a plot that is solidly rooted in contemporary history.

Maurice Castle, the double agent, has no ideology; like his creator, he cares about people. He is committed to his wife Sarah and her son Sam, who are black, and to her people in South Africa. He is, in fact, 'an honorary black' whose connection with Boris, the Communist agent to whom he passes on information, is one of gratitude for helping Sarah to escape from South Africa. It is a human connection. They are friends, not fellow-workers engaged in struggle for a cause. The cause materialises only towards the end of the novel and, as is to be expected in a Greene novel, it is a human cause. Castle takes his final and irrevocable step in his role as double-agent – thereby forfeiting personal fulfilment and the human connection he prizes above all else – after three interrelated incidents. He meets Muller, a member of BOSS, the South African Secret Service, the man most responsible for Sarah's earlier predicament and now planning further abominable strategies in defence of apartheid; he hears of these plans which threaten Sarah's people; he also learns of the 'elimination' of a good man, Carson, a lawyer who defended those taken into custody in South Africa. The twist Greene gives the plot to complicate human implications still further is to make Castle's actions lead to the death of his innocent colleague, Davis, his one friend within the office. In this bleak world there are no heroes, only victims in an endless chain of Being.

Love and compassion provoke Castle's last stand, and typically the gesture is seen as futile, as ultimately valueless in a world full of traps and controlled by the Big Battalions where such values are ineffective except in the context of individual self-expression. Subtle connections between choice and destiny, human strength and weakness, and the abiding power of love create a haunting resonance quite unlike anything Greene has written before. It is a novel devoid of hope. The silence at the end when the telephone line is cut and the conversation between Sarah in England and Castle in Russia is broken off midstream can be endured because of the intensity of their feelings for each other. That endures.

The narrative disturbs with the realities of apartheid, with tangential references to black experience in predominantly white societies, and transfixes the reader with Castle's restless, tormented search for peace. An effective juxtaposition of the lives and characters of Castle, his colleague, Davis, and the hierarchy who control the Secret Service establishment, facilitates mediation between the private and the public life of an individual. Castle finds shelter in suburban anonymity to safeguard a precious human relationship. Davis, clearly intended a contrast, yearns for a home and family; he is conspicuous for a flashy taste in clothes, for love of vintage port, for betting on the tote, for the Jaguar he drives. In fact, he plays so hard at living that he ends up a marked man despite his complete innocence.

The upper echelons are occupied by the two who control the establishment: Sir John Hargreaves, the Chief, and Dr Emmanuel Percival; also by Daintry, the new security chief, a conscientious guardian of morality and responsibility, lonely and uncomfortable in both his private and public self, yet sensitive to the 'total risk' with which Castle leads his life. The first two are connected by authority they wield and by what is apparently a consuming interest in gourmet cuisine, upper-class leisure activity, and a culture that puts even Daintry 'outside the pale'. The men at the top are confident and flippant; they chat about 'games' in a language he cannot share.

> Flippancy was like a secret code of which he didn't possess the book. He had the right to read cables and reports marked Top Secret, but flippancy like this was so secret that he hadn't a clue to its understanding (p. 34)

Above them hovers a network of power: governments with shared interests and policies; power as destiny.

The characterisation of Sir John and Dr Percival carefully details their past: Sir John, a District Commissioner 'in what was once the Gold Coast', now with an official position considerably enhanced with the added cachet of wealth from an American wife, recalls the paternalism and loyalties of his old job when faced with the ruthless logic and bloodshed of the present. Dr Percival, an urbane art collector, fancied himself a Communist and really believed in internationalism in his student days. Now he is 'fighting an underground war for nationalism'. He is quite open about his motives:

> I want to be on the side most likely to win during my lifetime . . .
> Enjoy. Only enjoy. I don't pretend to be an enthusiast for God or
> Marx. Beware of people who believe. They aren't reliable players
> . . . The player is as important as the game. I wouldn't enjoy the
> game with a bad player across the table (p. 163).

The novel is set in London and suggests Greene's unease with the role of Britain in superpower confrontation and his disquieting awareness of the inevitability of such involvement. 'The West', he said, when commenting on a review of *The Human Factor* 'cannot afford to see South Africa go down the drain. The news that apartheid in employment is being abolished will make it easier for the West to join in Uncle Remus'.[48] In the novel, Uncle Remus is the code name for an elaborate defence pact designed to protect South Africa in which all the major Western powers are implicated.

Greene's statements on this fact and the sharpness with which his insights are transmuted in the fictional merit comparison:

> I don't believe the fine anti-apartheid words of the United Nations
> and the West. Whatever the leaders may say, they could not stand
> by and watch South Africa slip into enemy hands. The country
> occupies a key strategic position on the Indian Ocean. If it became
> Communist like Mozambique, the Russians would be there, and
> no one in the Western camp can afford the risk of this happening.[49]

This perception underpins the fictional world of *The Human Factor*. Castle's guilt is discovered when he, who had previously passed on relatively unimportant information to the Communists, decides to leak details of the operation code named Uncle Remus. The nature of the plan – the tactical use of a 'reasonably clean' bomb in a region occupied by black South Africans – appals Castle. His links with the country are human unlike those of his boss, Sir John Hargreaves, for whom only West Africa, where he had served as a colonial officer, is real. His understanding of the proposal is solely in terms of economic relations:

> Have you ever wondered, Castle, what would happen to the West if the South African gold mines were closed by a racial war? And a losing war perhaps, as in Vietnam. Before the politicians have agreed on a substitute for gold. Russia as the chief source. It would be a bit more complicated than General Motors. Diamonds don't age like cars. There are even more serious aspects than gold and diamonds, there's uranium . . . Like it or not, we and South Africa and the States are all partners in Uncle Remus (pp. 54–5).

In a note to the novel Greene writes: 'The plot of Uncle Remus is purely a product of the author's imagination (and I trust will remain so) as are all the characters.' Nevertheless *The Human Factor* is yet another instance of Greene's remarkable sensitivity to political developments for the plot of his invention has been proved to exist. A few months after the publication of the novel, Zdenek Cervenka of the Scandinavian Institute of African Affairs and Barbara Rogers formerly of the British Foreign Office and a consultant to the United Nations and the Congressional Subcommittee on Southern Africa relying on hitherto-top-secret documents, informants and the Public Record Office, pieced together the story of the clandestine collaboration between West Germany and South Africa to develop operational nuclear weapons, the transfer of secret technological data and the ways in which other countries – including the USA, Britain, France and Israel – have been involved.[50]

It is misleading, however, to over-emphasise the political dimension in the novels in order to redeem the subject matter of Greene's work from descriptions of it as set in exotic and troubled places, or to make more fashionable claims that Greene is writing about the Third World. At one point in the novel Castle asks Muller the following question:

> Is Uncle Remus really practicable? I can't believe the Americans will ever get involved again – I mean with troops in a strange continent. They are just as ignorant of Africa as they were of Asia

except, of course, through novelists like Hemingway. He would
go off on a month's safari arranged by a travel agency and write
about white hunters and shooting lions – the poor half-starved
brutes reserved for tourists (pp. 155–6).

This deliberate and unnecessary reference to perceptions of a
novelist writing about a society outside his normal experience could
well be a subconscious expression of doubts Greene himself may
entertain – despite the rigour with which he sets about getting down
to ground level – regarding his own ability to do justice to the areas
he explores. His candour in this respect is reassuring. He would,
perhaps, be the first to acknowledge that there may be distrust, even
dismay among local readers since the work lacks the depth that can
only emerge from intimate local experience.

The lack of this dimension is compensated by the sharpness of his
global vision. The area is set in its geopolitical context and its
vulnerability or strength explored with a simultaneous plumbing of
shades of experience, and moral ambiguities. Thus the loss of
realism of one order and the fact that characterisation is often
subservient to the evocation of mood and feeling, are balanced by
Greene's unfailing grasp of games of power and the techniques of
survival devised by individuals and nations against brutal establishments and power blocs. It is quite normal, then, that a novel about
apartheid should be set in London: the theme of *The Human Factor* is
not the desolate world of South Africa's black population but the
moral responsibility of the world Greene knows.

An extraordinary aspect of critical estimates of Greene's work is
that, apart from general comments on his prescience regarding
international crises, so little attention has been paid to his understanding of historical process. Spiritual dimensions that deepen the
symbolic intensity of the fiction seem to draw the attention away
from what is more vital – Greene's great gift for recreating the reality
of human issues within a framework of world politics. The validity
of his work lies in the subtle interplay of the fate and workings of
nations and the fate of individuals, the connection between the
metropolis and the peripheries in global terms, and as ever, the
working of conscience or its absence in the private sphere of human
activity. To discuss the novels without these recognitions is to
undermine the complexity of his contribution.

The Human Factor much underrated and neglected perhaps because of the uncompromising nature of its structure which does not

permit critical digression into religious themes, nor acceptable discussion of repressive regimes, combines spiritual and political concerns into one closely woven texture whose strands cannot be disentangled. The theme is human relationships and moral responsibility at an individual, national and international level; not the Church and the State, nor the individual and the establishment though these concerns by implication permeate the whole. The passionate intensity underlying the urbane and chiselled prose is best illustrated in the metaphor chosen by Dr Percival, a character whose ruthlessness has been commented on by Kim Philby, whose own story is said to have inspired the novel. The metaphor is chosen to demonstrate the professional code that Daintry is expected to observe. He chooses a Ben Nicholson painting to bring home the point:

> Take a look at that Nicholson. Such a clever balance. Squares of different colour. And yet living so happily together. No clash . . . There's your Section 6. That's your square from now on. You don't need to worry about the blue and the red. All you have to do is pinpoint our man and then tell me. You've no responsibility for what happens in the blue or red squares. In fact not even in the yellow. You just report. No bad conscience. No guilt (p. 38).

Percival's actions – his cold-blooded elimination of Davis, almost as a game being played, his pursuit of Sarah after Castle's defection to Russia with the suggested threat that both she and her son are in his hands – are Greene's most graphic evocation of the themes of power and responsibility. Daintry cannot perceive his role in quite the same way, nor, one suspects, does Boris. The Communist agent confesses to Castle that he lives in a box as well and is kept ignorant of the connections and consequences of his action. In *The Honorary Consul* Rivas and Aquino follow orders from El Tigre, a leader they have never seen, but have no recourse of any kind when their plans misfire. Thus in Greene's view of the world, the evils of capitalism are not necessarily redeemed by Marxist praxis, both of which in various ways ignore the claims of human connections and dignity. *The Human Factor* illustrates what Greene does best: a plot that expresses human need, existential truth and ultimate values, a combination that creates fiction which appropriates some of the functions of philosophy. Such fiction reflects and explores; it is a process of discovery and interprets seriously the possibilities and consequences of human action.

Conclusion: Face to Face

In *Doctor Fischer of Geneva* (1980) and *Monsignor Quixote* (1982) Graham Greene abandons the narrative of action to present a distillation of his vision. With old men as protagonists he wrestles with the worlds of money and power. The life and death of both Doctor Fischer and Monsignor Quixote illustrate extreme commitments: selfish absorption with worldly goods and power on the one hand and on the other, a life shorn of everything except humanity laced with the innocent joys of living – friendship, conversation, wine, cheese. Anna Luise's rejection of her father's world, the simplicity and freshness of her relationship with people stands as antithesis to Doctor Fischer's avaricious quests and his caviare.

The deaths of the two protagonists – the one bitter, lonely and violent, the other a seamless transition that reveals illusion as the reality – work as finely honed symbols for the themes that underlie his work. Anna Luise's tragic death in the first flush of idyllic love evokes the precious and fleeting nature of such life-enhancing times. After her death, her husband Alfred Jones who narrates the story reflects:

> happiness is like one of those islands far out in the Pacific which has been reported by sailors when it emerges from the haze where no cartographer has ever marked it. The island disappears again for a generation, but no navigator can be quite certain that it only existed in the imagination of some long-dead look-out. I tell myself over and over again how happy I was in those weeks, but when I search my head for the reason I can find nothing adequate to explain my happiness (p. 43).

Indeed the brief union of Jones and Anna Luise is the most gentle, tender and idyllic recreation of love in Greene's novels. Without the passionate intensity of *The End of the Affair* and the anguish of *The Human Factor* the narrative nevertheless communicates a fragile and complex relationship. Anna Luise's extreme youth, her knowledge of life acquired through exposure to her father's world and her mother's suffering, Jones's own earlier widowhood, the loss of his hand and of his parents during the war – these are details that unobtrusively contribute to the reality of the story.

Commenting on the lack of song and fruitful laughter in Greene's work Kenneth Tynan explained this lack:

> hell is murky, and Dante, remember, escorted us through a long purgatory and a still longer inferno before, in the last Cantos of the *Paradiso*, he unfolded joy. The final test of a man's stature is his capacity for exultation: but we must wait ten years or more before deciding whether Greene's literary journey is going to bring him back across the Styx.[1]

The fruitful laughter of *Travels with my Aunt* and the innocent joys of the last two novels represent Greene's final crossing of the frontier guided by his compassion for human inadequacy.

The two novels face moral options and the inexorability of death. These are themes that permeate his work including an early novel *The Tenth Man* discovered recently and published in 1985 after languishing for forty years forgotten both by Graham Greene and Metro-Goldwyn-Mayer for whom it was written under contract. 'I regard it rather coldly' says Greene, 'It doesn't seem to belong to me but to MGM – a child I don't recognise.'[2] But the reader does recognise familiar elements. The novel suggests, for instance, that class, education and economic security in themselves are inadequate preparation for a life of hazard and risk, indeed for the courage to face death.

That the two late novels appear slight, even point-making, in comparison with Greene's major works does not weaken their power for the form is allegorical. Doctor Fischer's story is, in fact, emblematic as a morality play. Its poignancy rests in the dramatisation of Doctor Fischer's parties within an interlude of love. With a fortune made from Dentophil Bouquet, a toothpaste, and from a grand mansion that stands against the lake 'like a Pharaoh's tomb' where his staff adopt some of his arrogance, Doctor Fischer exudes power and contempt for all who surround him. Characters range from this bastion of economic security and status to the lowly clerk Steiner, a man whom Doctor Fischer destroys in revengeful jealousy. Alfred Jones occupies the middle ground in this hierarchy of wealth and power. A translator in a large chocolate factory, his modest life-style gives Anna Luise the security she could not find in the heartless excess of her father's house. The narrative conveys the dehumanising effects of material pursuits and the blight these cast on human relationships. For both the women in Doctor Fischer's life less is more: they spurn his kingdom for human love.

The familiar narrative tensions of Greene's fiction are absent yet the novel illustrates in a powerful but spare style the baseness of human greed and the void in those who enjoy worldly success. Jones is a shocked observer at Doctor Fischer's dinner-parties to which he invites a sycophantic group. By not participating in Doctor Fischer's games he forfeits an expensive gift which is the reward for humiliation endured. His ability to distance himself and preserve his dignity humiliates the toadies more than any of Doctor Fischer's manoeuvres. His presence in this ritual of power, arrogance, acquisitiveness and his own hatred for Fischer registers the absence in this world of the other dimensions of feeling – generosity, contentment, sincerity, and love which are part of the world he shares with Anna Luise.

The novel plays with the idea of the power of God – the almighty Doctor Fischer whose company is sought yet feared, whose largesse demands a nasty price; his daughter who believes he and his greedy friends can destroy her fragile happiness. Her instinctive desire to keep away from the group suggests the extent of their corrupting influence. She reassures herself when Jones decides not to be afraid and to attend one of the dinner parties: 'We don't depend on him for anything. We are free, free . . . He can't hurt you or me' (pp. 46–7).

Yet Greene's intention seems to be less to present Doctor Fischer as a malevolent force, a wanton God, than as an example of the effects of worldly success which leave him a lonely, bitter man who has lost the power to love and be loved. Details of his past are filled in: he had failed to respond to his wife's love of music. Completely disillusioned when he discovers that his wife finds companionship with so 'insignificant' a man as Steiner, his punishing hatred, his unforgiving scorn, has no limits and soon embraces the world. Her death leaves him with an even fuller possession of his sense of power and knowledge of its emptiness: 'I have no friends . . . These people are acquaintances. One can't avoid acquaintances. You mustn't think I dislike such people. I don't dislike them. I despise them' (p. 102). Greene's view of his character is sympathetic: 'I hoped that [the] correct description of him as a very sad man came through at the end, even through the hatred felt for him by Jones. I meant the reader to feel suddenly a sense of sympathy at the close'.[3]

The novel's evocation of worldly success is symbolic and factual. It is set, for instance, in Switzerland – 'a land of strangely knotted business affiliations: a great deal of political as well as financial laundering goes on in that little harmless neutral state'. When asked to translate a document brought to him by Mr Kips – one of the toadies and Doctor Fischer's lawyer – Jones finds technical terms connected with weapons:

> Apparently there was a firm called ICFC, Inc. which was American and it was purchasing weapons, on behalf of a Turkish company, from Czechoslovakia. The final destination of the weapons – all small arms – was very unclear. A name which sounded as if it might be Palestinian or Iranian was somehow involved' (p. 76).[4]

Although Mr Kips makes it clear that the document has nothing to do with Doctor Fischer this little piece of information enlarges the framework of the toadies' operations to comprehend many ramifications of power.

The world of *Monsignor Quixote* is more humane, less despairing. Graham Greene steps out into the open to look at faiths that have influenced him and the world. The result is a mellow and invigorating mixture of old themes finally resolved: the hunted but innocent man; religious faith and its expression in life in tones that shade into the idealism of Communism. The novel's protagonists are Monsignor Quixote, 'a poor priest-errant travelling God knows where' and Enrique Zancas (alias Sancho), the ex-Mayor of El Toboso and avowedly a Communist. Together they set off on a journey to escape from an authoritarian Bishop and the election victory of a right-wing opponent. They discourse along the way on life's constraints and its possibilities for freedom and their spirited dialogue is considerably enlivened by wholesome country wine and cheese.

Though disturbed by intrusions from the *Guardia Civil* and what look like members of the *Opus Dei* the measured pace of a conversation, filled with wisdom, verve and good humour is kept up till the last section. Here the abrupt entrance of Professor Pilbeam researching the life of Ignatius Loyola in the Trappist monastery where Monsignor Quixote finds refuge, introduces the world of 'intellectual speculation' only to give it short shrift.

Monsignor Quixote's parish of El Toboso, the town of which Zancas was until recently the Mayor, is not a place of desperate poverty and repression, as for instance the countryside where

Father Rivas's congregation lives. Yet the absence of dire realities contributes to the allegorical frame of the novel and enhances the journey of this 'holy innocent' into the modern world, along which he encounters enticements that he cannot even begin to comprehend: sex and money; a brothel, a blue film, a condom, religious processions where money buys a vantage seat on the journey to salvation.

The connections with Cervantes's classic are insistent: they travel in Monsignor Quixote's old Seat 600 Rosinante and their adventures recall, indirectly, the intentions of the original – to examine the essential nature of human life and man's greatest metaphysical problem, that of illusion and reality. Like its classic original Greene's novel, as indeed all his work, has a wide appeal and holds a deeper meaning for those that wish to see it. What emerges from this homespun combination is not ideology and orthodoxy but life viewed in its pristine beauty and bounty. The text expresses everyone's right to the simple and good things in an effective combination of funny episodes reminiscent of *Travels with my Aunt* with which it shares its picaresque form. Underlying the hilarity this time rests a difference: ideology is consciously set against human needs, theological argument against faith that transcends it. The bond between the travellers is strengthened by the implicit awareness that their respective faiths have:

> not done away with either nationalism or imperialism. It's these two that cause the wars. Wars are not merely for economic reasons – they come from the emotions of men, like love does, from the colour of the skin, or the accent of a voice. From unhappy memories too (p. 107).

What was a paradox in the 1930s when Orwell called Greene 'our first Catholic fellow-traveller' appears to be resolved here. Faith is expressed as realisation of life within the community in terms of its needs, as the realisation of humanity. The form of the novel as an account of a friendship and the endearing zest of the travellers makes the process of bridging the gulf that theoretically separates them appear a practical and entirely plausible affair. As they meander across the countryside of a remote district of Spain each interprets the beliefs and texts of the other in relation to the business of living. A tongue-in-cheek juxtaposition of the Gospels, the breviary and the Communist Manifesto, the Roman Curia and the Politburo, the Protestant and the Euro-Communist, Torquemada and Stalin, the Cross and the Hammer and Sickle, creates a devastating blend of humour and insights into life and the world. Greene succeeds admirably in what he felt G. K. Chesterton was trying to do:

> He restated original thought with the freshness, simplicity, and excitement of discovery. In fact, it was discovery; he unearthed the defined from beneath the definitions, and the reader wondered why the definitions had been thought necessary.[5]

The encrustations of theology and ideology obscure the fundamentals of religion and politics, and with the hair splittings motivated by selfishness and avarice, Greene also includes the posturings of the power blocs, explicitly that of the United States but implicitly that of the Soviet Union. His premise of doubt works as a creative strategy; it successfully challenges dominant modes and subverts ideological structures of injustice and oppression. The politics of faith, immanent and yet transcending continents and cultures, illumines his world with grace, charity and humanity.

Monsignor Quixote celebrates fundamentals of humanism perceived in *Brighton Rock*, and expressed in *The Power and the Glory* and *The Honorary Consul*. The novel is a moving apotheosis where fact and fiction, belief and faith converge into an acknowledgement of doubt as part of the fabric of belief, as the humanising factor that sustains and nourishes religious and political certainties, and rational solutions.[6] Such an apotheosis is also implicit in Greene's remarks in Moscow in February 1986 at the International Forum for a Nuclear Free World:

> Through my own fault I failed at the Round Table to bear witness to one thing. The old suspicions and antagonisms between Communists and Catholics in South and Central America have almost ceased to exist except among some rather isolated Roman Catholics who are nearly as old as I am. Communists and Catholics are fighting side by side in the struggle against Pinochet in Chile, the Contras in Nicaragua and the death squads in Salvador. My friend Tomas Borgez, Minister of the Interior in Nicaragua is working in close and friendly co-operation with Father Miguel d'Escoto, the Foreign Minister, and the Jesuit Father Ernesto Cardenal in health and education.
> May this co-operation be extended to Europe East and West,

Mr General Secretary, before I die I hope I shall see an Ambassador of the Soviet Union go to the Vatican.[7]

In his essay on Dickens, Greene describes the creative writer as one who perceives his world once and for all in childhood and adolescence and whose career is 'an effort to illustrate his private world in terms of the great public world we all share'.[8] Greene's own contribution to the development of the novel may be assessed from several crucial standpoints of time and history: When Greene began his career in 1929 it was difficult to speak of a literature of interiority divorced from global and historical realities and it was also a time when there was talk of the death of the novel almost contemporaneous with talk of the death of God. It was a time when private worlds were crumbling in the aftermath of world wars, the ebb of empires, a time that has since witnessed the interdependence of capitalism, socialism and resultant power blocs overriding national frontiers and parochial loyalties. The static world of fixed boundaries in the geography of moral, cultural and physical territory has changed to a flux. Here the power centre of a ruling class and dominant culture no longer holds. But with this loss Greene recognises the pluralism of cultures, and manifestations of the human intellect and spirit in systems and beliefs – be they political or spiritual.

It is Greene's achievement that he has extended the frontiers of the novel, to encompass the diversities of the human spirit, and to express them not in a regressive mode, not eschewing what theories of criticism may call the smudge and taint of political and religious discussion, hitherto considered the exclusive domain of the theologian and the journalist. He has used this rejected material as the corner-stone of the structure of his work. A sense of history and politics by itself could not have engendered the creative act if it had not been also for Greene's deep understanding of the human situation, not as human power and progress – ideas that were belied by the carnage of wars and the degradations of poverty and unemployment – but from feelings of loyalty, compassion and respect that spring from a deep religious sense.

Another significant aspect of Greene's achievement is his creative use in literature of liberating disassociation from what Edward Said calls 'the hegemony of an imperialistic culture.' Said defines this strategic articulation of power and knowledge:

If we believe that Kipling's jingoistic White Man was simply an aberration, then we cannot see the extent to which the White Man was merely one expression of a science – like that of penal discipline – whose goal was to understand and to confine non-Whites in their status as non-Whites, in order to make the notion of Whiteness clearer, purer, and stronger. If we cannot see this, then we will be seeing a good deal less than every major European intellectual and cultural figure in the nineteenth century saw. . . . What they saw was the necessary, valuable connection between the affirmative powers of European discourse – the European signifier, if you like – and constant exercises of strength with everything designated as non-European, or non-White.[9]

Yet, Greene continues the discourse through his work as the European signifier, albeit, in a broadly based cultural discipline. While he has achieved the incorporation of this discipline in the novel, his reiteration of European signification may be seen as detracting from an all-encompassing world view.

In his defence it should be argued that Greene interprets the world from territory that he knows and loves – the territory of his spiritual and cultural traditions which he certainly did not abandon in the ebb of imperialism. It can also be said in his defence that he recognises the pluralism of cultures, the integrity of traditions other than his own. For those who transgress the boundaries of establishments, cultures, traditions and hegemonies, there is very little hope of peace and fulfilment. They, however, share a mutuality of awareness, compassion, and even the faith which doubt and annihilation bring as in the burnt-out cases of Querry and Deo Gratias or in the pathetic picture of the drunken priest being led to his execution, or in the uncomprehending love of Rose for Pinkie.

In the ultimate analysis, however, the supreme act of love is beyond the capabilities of Greene's own faith and work. The recognition is there but somehow the fulfilment of promise fails even as, symbolically, the realisation of love between the English defector, Maurice Castle, in Moscow and Sarah, the black South African in London, is cut off by the telephone which goes dead. Yet, the inadequacy of Greene to reach the Dostoevskian vision may itself contribute to the permanence and endurance of work that has enshrined honest doubt as a mode of existence in a changing world.

Greene has liberated the English novel. Criticism, therefore, cannot, as Said says 'assume that its province is merely the text, not even the great literary text'.[10] Since Greene has himself shown so intimate an awareness of 'the greater stake in historical and political effectiveness that literary as well as all others texts have had' his work deserves to be read in this context. It is a liberation which Greene has achieved through a great sense of humility but also with a painstaking attention to his craft, comparable with the sense of faith, anonymity, and economic necessity of medieval masons carving in stone in a creative act where craftsmanship itself reveals the supreme vision of faith that endures.

Interview

MC: My analysis of your work rests on the premise that you were moved by Socialist ideals in the 1930s, that your politics has developed but has not changed. Did you belong to any political party?

GG: I would be inclined to agree with that. I did belong to a party for a short time. I joined the ILP, the Independent Labour Party around 1933 which was on the left of the Labour party and have always been on the Left, but I did not have much time to be fully involved and soon resigned. As for Catholicism, I haven't liked all that Vatican II did, but it was a breath of air, anyway. Since I am critical I am suspect from the Catholic and from the Socialist point of view; I cannot be wholeheartedly a Socialist according to a fixed Marxist standpoint or a Catholic by those who wish to extend the dogma of Papal infallibility.

MC: Orwell is a great polemicist but your novels come much closer to the realities of capitalism and imperialism. Do you like Orwell's writing?

GG: *Homage to Catalonia* is an excellent account of the Spanish Civil War and I admire *Animal Farm*, a brilliant allegory, but *1984* never seemed to me real; I did not think that was the sort of future one had to be afraid of, no more real than Aldous Huxley's *Brave New World*. I still don't think it is real and am not particularly convinced by the characters and those very unlikely love scenes. What he brings out correctly is change in the use of language. Even 'Social democracy' has become a bad word.

His literary essays sometimes irritated me. He wrote good plain prose but sometimes he was dead wrong. He wrote, for instance, that Dickens had never been appreciated on the Continent which is nonsense. Proust was one of Dickens's great admirers, but it didn't suit Orwell's book to say that or else he was simply ignorant of the fact that he was so popular in France.

MC: When this point of comparison between your work and Orwell's was made at a recent discussion,[1] Stephen Spender had this to say:

I don't think one can think of Greene as political in quite the same way as Orwell. Orwell had great political insights into the class system, and realised that everything in England really is class. I think he became rather hypnotised by this. The other thing he understood quite well was the possibility of an authoritarian kind of society controlling absolutely everything including the thought processes of the people who belong to that society.

GG: Well, I never went the whole hog like Auden, Spender, Caudwell. They joined the Communist Party. I joined it for a matter of weeks as an undergraduate with my friend Claud Cockburn as a joke though he later became a serious Communist. It is natural for some of those like Spender to be a little suspicious to find me getting closer and closer to positions they have abandoned. Their God failed. I suppose I am suspect because I have never involved myself in the ideology of politics. My ambiguity makes me suspect to the literary and to the Catholic establishment.

Cockburn saw much more of Spain than Orwell, Spender or Auden. He was a remarkable man and my friend at Berkhamsted and at Oxford but I didn't see much of him for the last thirty years before he died. He was the only real Communist. He had a position as *Times* correspondent in Washington which he gave up on principle. For the others it was only a temporary romantic attachment, never really serious. How anyone can take Spender seriously to this day I can't imagine. Auden yes, Spender no.

I was not part of any group. I am not alienated, nor an 'outsider' as is sometimes claimed. I like to work alone, in solitude, or at best in the company of one person who is close and with whom one can discuss and talk. Writing needs solitude. I could not ever function as writers do in France where they meet as groups and discuss each other's work. That would be the end. That's one of the reasons why I could not be with Auden, Spender and Cecil Day Lewis. Working in a group can be incestuous and one would feel the need to compromise, I think. I'd rather be with a group of businessmen than with writers. At least I'd learn something.

MC: Would you like to talk about the 1930s?

GG: For me it was the period of the Hunger Marches and the General Strike. It wasn't like the demonstrations now when on the whole the standard of living has risen a great deal. The hunger marchers were really hungry. I have been accused of betrayal because during the General Strike I had a certain loyalty to my paper, *The Times* and did not join the strike. If we'd stopped Churchill's would have been the only voice to be heard; no independent voice at all, only the official one. Not only had *The Times* to fight the strikers, it had to fight off Churchill as well. He was trying to launch his own paper, *The British Gazette*, with the support of the extreme right and a moderate voice was essential.

MC: Do you know you have sometimes been referred to as right-wing? Is it to do with your trip to Germany?

GG: That was during the Weimar Republic but how could I be called right-wing when the Weimar Republic was, if anything, to the left? Yes, I see that Bergonzi calls me right-wing and in a later chapter illustrates the influence of Auden on my work which I do not suppose he thinks is right-wing. Very strange. I went with Claud Cockburn to the Weimar Republic in our undergraduate days; it seemed a romantic adventure and there was no hint of Nazism then; Hitler had not appeared on the scene.

It was the fact that I did not join the strike which made the pseudo-left regard me as right-wing but Orwell came to my defence writing that I might prove to be the first Catholic writer in English to be a fellow-traveller. Later on with Franco, the fact that I was a Catholic did not help. Orwell was inclined to think that Catholics would necessarily support Franco, for example, which I never did. I did not support the Republican side either because there were things they did I didn't like any more than I could bear Franco. I couldn't take the romantic view of them as others did. The primary guilt was Franco's, but I couldn't feel wholeheartedly for the Republic although I could feel wholeheartedly against Franco and for the Basque Republic.

MC: In Orwell's letters there are references to you as part of the group around *The Criterion*.

GG: I never read it, nor was I part of any group. Orwell hated *The Heart of the Matter* for some reason. I don't care for it myself.

MC: There was an article on Anthony Blunt that said intellectuals of his generation were drawn towards Communism as a reaction to the materialism of the United States and its popular culture that was sweeping over England. Would you agree?

GG: No. I think it was a reaction to the crisis in England; the Hunger

Marches, real poverty, real hunger. The hunger marchers then were quite different from the trade-union rioters now. They were really people who had not had enough to eat and I think it was that that turned us all to the left. Burgess, Maclean, Philby were all at Cambridge about the same time and then the authorities began to wonder whether there might have been similar characters in Oxford in the twenties. I once received a questionnaire with a list of names of Oxford characters – I knew several of them. I've often wondered that I haven't been suspected myself.

I think Philby genuinely believed in Communism. In the SIS during the war we were a little group dealing with Iberia with Kim Philby at the head of our operation and he was much the most efficient man in the British Secret Service. Oh yes, I did admire him – he did his job extremely well. As for Communism, he was recruited by the Communists at the time of the Hunger Marches and I'm sure didn't commit treason for money. He lived out his belief and I admire him for that.

Philby's Communism had nothing to do with reactions against the policies of the United States which didn't seem such a danger as they seem today. Their policy in Central America is certainly driving me now to be more friendly towards Communism than I would otherwise be. They've driven Castro to choose Communism and are pushing the Sandinistas towards Communism. What's ugly about the United States – not the American people but the occupants of the White House – is their desire to have the whole of the American continent under their control right down to Chile.

MC: When you wrote *Getting to Know the General* some reviewers suggested you like dictators. In my book I've called them father-figures – Ho Chi Minh, Castro, Torrijos.

GG: It's exaggerating a bit to call me an admirer of Ho Chi Minh; the original essay I wrote is not entirely in his praise; it is called 'A man as pure as Lucifer' which is hardly complimentary. Castro has done a great deal for his country and there are undoubtedly enormous improvements there since the fall of Batista in education, in health. If authoritarianism has raised its ugly head it is not ugly in the sense of authoritarianism in San Salvador or Videla's in Argentina, or Pinochet's in Chile. But the United States are responsible for Castro moving further and further to the left. He's got no alternative; he's got to live and the people have got to live. Every overture he makes to the United States is rejected.

I was shocked when he supported the Russian invasion of Czechoslovakia because a few days before he had made a speech in which he had said that each country must make its own way to socialism. And then I met the Italian ambassador to Havana who told me that Castro had had no alternative: there was a whole *équipe* ready with Dorticos, then the President, to move against him if he said a word against Russia. I had always thought Dorticos a figure-head and the real power was with Castro but apparently Dorticos was the head of the group ready to take over and then we would have had a Communism more extreme than Castro's.

MC: In your recent interview for *The Sunday Times*[2] you spoke of Castro and Mrs Thatcher with the same sort of admiration.

GG: Did I say I admire her? Well, not all that much. Perhaps I said what is true, that is that I would have voted for her in the first election because we had had two Labour Prime Ministers in whom honesty was not a very strong point. On the whole a woman is more honest than a man, I think. But I wouldn't vote for her now. I felt that she might do some good when she came in after the long spell of Wilson and Callaghan but I certainly don't think she's admirable in all she does.

MC: Did you comment at all during the Falklands war?

GG: I wrote in an Argentinian paper that it was a stupid war and that the only good that could come out of it was the fall of the military junta. I think that Mrs Thatcher ought to come much more willingly forward to talk because it would help the new democratic Government. You know what Churchill said, 'jaw-jaw is better than war-war'. The war itself was a brilliant exercise, a very interesting one from NATO's point of view and I don't see how it could have been avoided under the circumstances but we were partly respon-sible for the circumstances. At the same time it was difficult to come to serious talks with a Government where 30 000 people have disappeared; so authoritarian that it was perhaps not possible to have reasonable talks with them.

Another silly thing is all this fuss about British citizens. The greater number of the Falkland Islanders were not full British citizens till after the War. They were employees of the Falkland Island Company, had tied cottages, and had to leave the Falklands when they reached retirement age.

MC: Your work gives the impression that you don't believe that democracy can work.

GG: It depends what one calls democracy. Some people say it works in the United States. But that's extreme capitalism, isn't it? I react against American consumer society, not American culture except in a sociological sense. Inside the country there's liberty and so on, maybe, but they don't admit liberty outside and one can't compare the USSR and Afghanistan with Reagan's Contras and Nicaragua. Afghanistan had been a Stalinist government and President Amin was responsible for the murder of the American Ambassador.

MC: Don't you think you can be accused of a simplistic attitude to American people?

GG: I am anti-White house, not anti- the American people. The United States came in at the very end of both our wars and took all the credit. They did not declare war on Hitler; Hitler declared war on them. I am closer to Communism than I might otherwise be because of America. I can only hope that Europe will be strong enough to stand between the two rather similar cultures – Russia and the United States.

MC: Do you regard yourself as European or English? I remember an article that said you fit more comfortably into the French pantheon.

GG: I regard myself as European, but Europe, like Communism, is being created by the United States. It created Communism in Nicaragua and Latin America and European reactions to America now are forming a Europe closer to Communism. What one would like to see is a reform of Communism in Russia rather on the lines which once seemed to be happening in Czechoslovakia. This would minimise the antagonism between Europe and Russia. And maybe then we would have a neutral Europe which could stand up against and modify the imperialism of the United States.

MC: How do you react to the suggestion that you romanticise the left?

GG: Maybe I do. But I don't think I romanticise the Communists. I have a certain sympathy and there's a link between Communism and Catholicism, the Curia and the Politburo. But there's not much of the real Communism left; it's becoming State Capitalism. In any case I'd rather romanticise the Left than romanticise the Right as Evelyn Waugh did.

MC: Do you agree that there is an element of Jansenism in your work?

GG: Those who say I am a Jansenist have not read theology. Anthony Burgess who is a born Catholic accuses me of Jansenism. Born Catholics are not strong on theology. I don't believe in such a thing as hell, for example. I have a hope that there is something beyond death certainly, but not hell. François Mauriac could be accused of Jansenism; I admire him, but he went too far and in that sense my work is not Catholic at all. I'm exactly the opposite of the Jansenist. I believe in 'between the stirrup and the ground'.

Gabriel Marcel, the French philosopher, and also a Catholic, claimed that I was an existentialist. I don't know what existentialism is except as a picture of life as it is but he claimed I was a Catholic existentialist and that I'd reduced hope to its smallest possible size. Original sin does not mean anything much to me any more than the Trinity does. The Church seems to me to be an attempt that was needed, perhaps, long ago, to explain a mystery. Once you try to explain a mystery you get things tabulated. But I certainly believe there is good and evil in the world.

I am sympathetic to a religious belief but I can't wholeheartedly be a Catholic, or wholeheartedly a Christian. As I get older and older I lose more and more my belief in God. I have always liked the Biblical saying 'Lord I believe. Help my unbelief.' I try to believe and what remains of my faith says that I'm wrong not to believe. I make a distinction between faith and belief. Faith is irrational and belief is rational. I would describe myself as a Catholic agnostic, not an atheist, and I feel a link with Catholicism. I feel no link with Anglicanism at all. When I became a Catholic and had to take another name, I took Thomas, after the doubter.

Christian Marxism? I don't know much about Marxism. In South America today we certainly see Christianity as it always should have been – with the Church actively involved in the struggle for justice. The Pope made a big mistake attacking the presence of priests in the Nicaraguan Government and he behaved badly there. He'd been wrongly advised, probably by Cardinal Ratzinger.[3] I think he made a mistaken parallel between Nicaragua and Poland in the fifties with the Pax movement, but the situations are completely different. The priests' presence in the government of Nicaragua is a kind of guarantee against a completely Marxist state. I was in Poland in the 1950s when the Russians were definitely trying to build a national Catholic Church through Pax and the head of Pax was a Fascist. He'd fought bravely against the Germans and the Russians by whom he'd been captured and everyone thought he'd been shot. But he'd been taken to Moscow and he came back with permission to open a Catholic publishing firm to sell holy statues, etc. It was an attempt to divide the Catholic church by making a national Catholic church as was done in China. But it didn't work. The Poles were too united. I think perhaps the Pope thought that the Catholic priests in the Government of Nicaragua, the foreign minister, D'Escoto, the minister of culture, Ernesto Cardenal, and Ortega, the Jesuit in charge of education and health, represented the same kind of thing as Pax, but the situation is completely different. Unlike Poland there had been a civil war. It was more like the position in France at the end of the war when Catholic and Communist resistants who had been working together were both represented in De Gaulle's government. It is desirable that they should continue to work together. That dreadful scene on television when the Pope waved aside Father Cardenal as he knelt to kiss his hand shows that he does not realise Father Cardenal's importance to his people. He is not only a priest, he is their greatest poet. No wonder there were disturbances at the Mass.

MC: Do you think the Pope has two standards when it comes to the involvement of the Church in politics?

GG: I don't say that. But I'm not an enthusiast. I admire his courage. He obviously has charisma. He wanted to be an actor and now he's got a leading part, and he obviously enjoys his role.

MC: I'm amused when you say that you don't know what Liberation Theology means.

GG: I am not a theologian. If it means that the priests are allowed to play their part in politics in defence of the poor then I'm all for it.

MC: Don't you think Liberation Theology suggests the overlap between Marxism and Catholicism?

GG: Yes. We've got the same structures in the sense that you can compare the Curia and the Politburo; both are bad. And I think the church today is concerned with poverty. Perhaps as the church becomes more concerned with poverty and human rights the Marxists become less concerned with poverty and there's nothing to show they are concerned with human rights. I find that the most interesting comments on my books have come from Catholics and Communists and that there is a parallel between the rather hesitant doubts of some of my Communist friends and my own doubts.

MC: That comes across rather well in *Monsignor Quixote*. Is it an idea you have developed over the years?

GG: I was looking into the *Carnets* of Camus and I find I had written all over the margins – in 1964 – what *Monsignor Quixote* is all about; it is strange because what I have written here about belief, not having a whole belief, the necessity of doubt which is what my book is about has nothing to do with what Camus is saying. So the idea was born a long time ago though I do not know what made me write on the margins at that point. What Camus has to say is this: [reads] 'Christianity is pessimistic about man and is optimistic about human destiny. Marxism is pessimistic about human destiny and human nature and is optimistic about the march of history.' This is a contradiction. I would say myself that I am pessimistic about the human condition and optimistic about man. But all this and what Camus is saying has nothing to do with what I've written now.

MC: And what did you write in the margins? In *A Sort of Life* you say that forgetting is important for the imaginative process to work. And it is this forgetting, perhaps, that led to *Monsignor Quixote*?

GG: I've written this: [reads] 'Marxists do not believe in persuasion or dialogue. As for the famous Marxist optimism it just makes me laugh; few men have distrusted their fellows more completely. Perhaps the most important historical point in the future will be when the Christian says "I do not always believe" and the Marxist agrees with him. A good future based on the failure always to believe. Comprehension and charity also follow. Violence comes when we are afraid to admit that we do not always believe. By violence we try to kill the doubt in ourselves.' Curious. This was written in 1964.

MC: How much was Father Rivas modelled on Camillo Torres?

GG: Not at all. Camillo Torres was a young man who found himself in a particular position but Rivas was a much older man and I had to invent a theology for him. My friend, Father Duran, says it is perfectly acceptable by the Catholic Church. Rivas was affected by certain things in Paraguay and by the fact that the head of the Church sat down to dinner with General Stroessner. Things went too far when a priest, Camillo Torres, actually carried a rifle in Colombia, shooting and killing. That's a job for the layman. I don't say it is wrong to kill. But I don't agree that priests should not take part in political situations as intolerable as Somoza's.

I visited the Jesuits in Paraguay. They were under strict surveillance, and their telephones were being tapped. The Archbishop of Santiago in Chile made a very good stand against Pinochet from the beginning, and he supported Allende. I went to a curious service in the Cathedral in the middle year of Allende's government; it was on the National day. The Archbishop presided, a Methodist and a Jewish rabbi said prayers, a Jesuit preached the sermon, the whole Government attended as also the Chinese from the embassy. A good ecumenical service, I thought. Quite recently his successor has been condemning Pinochet in the most outspoken terms and unlike Archbishop Romero in Salvador, he has so far managed to survive. The Church in Panama is practically non-existent and in Cuba it was always only skin-deep; it was an upper-class religion and didn't have its roots in the people as in Nicaragua. Voodoo is the real peasant religion in Cuba; I've attended two Voodoo ceremonies, in Cuba and Haiti.

MC: What draws many of us to your work is its openness. It is not very common, perhaps even un-English, to have this wide perspective, and yet your sensibility is very English.

GG: I happen to travel a great deal and much of my experience has been outside England. The great English novelists have, it is true, been local. But I am not a great English novelist. Hardy, Trollope, Thackeray, Dickens – there has been a tradition for the novelist not to write much about the outside world. But this is not necessarily narrowness. I wouldn't call Trollope a narrow man at all. He used his experience of England. It has been curiosity which drew me out of England, though there was a tradition with the young after the First World War, who hadn't had experience of the war, to travel – Evelyn Waugh went to British Guyana and Ethiopia, Peter Fleming to Manchuria and to Brazil. But Waugh was not a good observer and his travel books are not among his best, particularly the one on Mexico. I went to Liberia and Mexico following the same sort of motive. Today the motive is different. One breathes politics in the same way as belief and non-belief; politics are part of the air we breathe.

I have sometimes thought that my travels have been prompted by a death wish, or rather, an attraction towards death, a desire to get as close to it as I can which is not the same thing as wanting to die. The moth is attracted by the flame and wants to get near to it; it does not wish to die.

MC: Do you think that the sense of crisis was greater in the 1930s?

GG: Politics was very prominent; not merely the politics of unemployment and Hunger Marches but the international politics from 1933 to 1939. One was living under the shadow of war. I don't think the shadow is deeper now than it was then. When the war came one felt a sense of relief. Tension was very high. First the Depression and then Hitler. It couldn't be worse; even the nuclear threat seems distant compared to Hitler. Maybe the young feel differently but for me the tension now is less.

MC: Have you consciously tried to subvert the adventure form?

GG: Yes, oh yes, I wanted my novels to be in a sense adventure stories too. I have always liked adventure stories and I was consciously reacting against the Bloomsbury group. I did not like Forster's book on the novel: 'Oh yes, I suppose we have to have a story.' He was very superior in his attitude to the story. And so I felt let's go back to story-telling. I think there was also a certain pride in having R. L. Stevenson as my mother's cousin.

MC: How much did the theatre and film influence you?

GG: Film certainly. The Victorian novelists were influenced by painting; their descriptive scenes were static because they were thinking in terms of pictures. I belong to the age of the cinema. I have tried to make my descriptions with a moving, hand-held camera.

MC: You've said in an interview: 'I try to restrict myself to home-ground if I can, English backgrounds, London whenever possible. I've always made that a rule.'[4]

GG: That interview was given quite a while ago and I have gone out of England for my subjects more often than not. But I always try to have an English character. I spent long periods of time in Vietnam. I went there every winter between 1951 and 1955, the last time mainly to fill in the additional details which I needed. I had gone as a journalist and not as novelist but on my third visit a novel took hold of me and so my character became a journalist who had got involved as I had got involved. In a strange way I had a sort of sympathy for the French. I could understand their feelings; they had been the colonial power and believed they were fighting for something of value. A whole class of Vietnamese are as French almost as the French. I had also my sympathies for the Vietminh, but I could see no reason why the Americans should come in from half-way across the world to interfere. The French were defeated and I think if the decisions of the Geneva Conference had been carried out and the Americans had not interfered, there would have been elections and Ho Chi Minh would have come in with an easy majority in the South as well as in the North and a kind of Yugoslavia would have resulted – free from Russia and China. But the United States wouldn't have it and my sympathies were and are with Vietnam. When the American war came people wanted me to go back. I refused because I would have sympathy only for one side.

MC: And Cuba?

GG: *Our Man in Havana* is not really about Cuba; I wanted to make fun of the Secret Service and I chose Cuba as a setting for I had visited it many times before and after Castro. Haiti, Cuba, Central and South America I have visited many times. I have friends who are intimately involved both in the Government and outside though in Haiti my friends were all opponents of the Government and have disappeared or died in exile.

I've often been asked what draws me to these places and the only answer I can think of is that politics out there are not an alternation of political parties but a matter of life and death. I am interested in such politics and I write about such politics.

MC: You have commented on political developments all over the world. Why have you not written about India?

GG: I think India rather frightened me by its size. I have enjoyed myself very much during two weeks in Goa, but to write about India in a novel I would have had to live there over a considerable period of time and I think I was daunted by the problems. I am probably wrong, but I've always felt that Communism was in the end perhaps the only thing that could work in a country so divided – how was it going to rise from that extreme poverty? I know things have changed a lot but the poverty is still there. But then one has seen the failure of Marxism in Africa.

MC: I see what you mean but Communism would have to be a form we evolve for ourselves within our spiritual and cultural tradition. You've written very perceptively about the spirituality of Russia.

GG: I don't know Russia very well and am planning a visit again this autumn. One has a feeling that the religious element there is a deep unconscious thing. It will always be there and Russia will never be as materialist as the United States.

MC: Have you been back to Sierra Leone?

GG: Yes, and I was pleased to go back after Independence. They had got the Chinese to teach them how to grow rice, and Italians to advise on the development of fisheries. I felt that they were much more open to the world than in the days of what had been a good paternal government. The pattern of colonisation had been different there, not as it was in Kenya, with all those big farms owned by white men – a kind of Happy Valley atmosphere. No white man had been allowed to own land in Sierra Leone. Young and very idealistic men went out to act as district officers, tribal law was maintained, and if paternalism can be agreeable, it was as agreeable as it could be in Sierra Leone, though when I went back I welcomed the new openness to the world outside.

MC: What I find engaging about your work is your sensitivity to other cultures and civilisations. But your fiction does not confront British imperialism except by indirection and suggests that the British Empire was superior to American hegemony.

GG: I was never even a British imperialist. It was lucky probably that I went to Africa when I was young; if I had gone ten years later I might have had my fixed ideas and been looking for things which I had already somehow established in my mind. I said what I wanted to say in *Journey Without Maps*. The British Empire was coming to an end. Scobie in *The Heart of the Matter* did have great sympathy for the Africans and was uneasy about being part of the ruling side.

United States imperialism is something different, far more destructive than paternalism. How can they call it Third World violence when the violence is created by themselves?

MC: The reviews of *The Human Factor* found the plot unrealistic and your descriptions of London outdated, didn't they?

GG: One of the silly things I remember for which I was criticised was that I had shown a man doing up his flies as he walked across the yard of the King's Arms Hotel. Well, I have still got suits with flies because I have only bought one suit in the past twenty years, and the others all have flies. I am sure that a lot of people in Berkhamsted who have not got much money are also wearing twenty-year-old suits. As for the secret plot between West Germany and South Africa which was called Uncle Remus I found the evidence for it in [Rogers and Cervenka] *The Nuclear Axis* which appeared after my novel was published.

MC: To get back to Africa, I find your writing has compassion and a great sense of involvement but your criticism of the creole is not justified because the creole in many ways has combined two cultures and has identified himself with national aspirations. By creole do you mean Western-educated, or does it have connotations of colour?

GG: Not of colour. I've used the word in the sense used in West Africa of Africans who have lived for some generations in the West and have then returned to Africa as they did to Liberia and Sierra Leone from America. It does not apply to people who have not left their country and still belong to a tribal society.

My first encounter with the creole was in Liberia and I did not like what I saw. He had taken control of a tribal country and was not very nice to his fellow-countrymen, even, in the case of the Krus, selling them into slavery. I did not find this a serious factor in Sierra Leone among the educated class and when I wrote against creoles I was writing mainly about Liberia.

MC: Would you agree that your involvement with the world began with *Journey Without Maps*?

GG: If you live at all you become involved. My first political book was *It's a Battlefield*, a little before *Journey Without Maps*. It is the only book in which I have worked consciously with a cinematic technique, so it has never been filmed.

MC: Conrad and James are the ones you acknowledge as masters. Is there any philosopher or writer apart from these who has been a formative influence?

GG: Conrad and James I would say are the serious influences though Conrad was a bad influence and I had to stop reading him for more than twenty years. I have read two of Chardin's books, and

Hans Kung on infallibility is very good. I have a great admiration for Kierkegard. As a Catholic I'd say Newman was the important influence on me; he was dead against infallibility and he was a magnificent writer of English. I specially like his *Essay on the Development of Christian Doctrine*. He argues against a too-dogmatic church and demonstrates the evolution of ideas.

Travel did help me understand and appreciate other religious traditions but I don't think I was ever a thorough Catholic. I accepted Catholicism as an intellectual likelihood, that it was perhaps nearer the truth than other religions. I wanted to understand what my future wife believed in, but I wasn't prepared for that reason to become a Catholic. I went for instruction to understand, and then decided that perhaps Catholicism might be nearer the truth than other faiths. I had no emotional attachment to Catholicism till I went to Mexico and saw the faith of the peasants during the persecution there.

MC: I hope you are not going to be dismayed with some of the things I say about the novels. I feel, for instance, that *Travels with my Aunt* has to do with Empire.

GG: Does she travel anywhere in the Empire? Except England, of course. She only goes to Turkey, France and Latin America, doesn't she?

MC: I mean through the presence of Wordsworth and then the arrival of Visconti; old connections and responsibilities as represented by Wordsworth are thrown aside for an older involvement represented by Visconti. Why do you have Wordsworth killed off? Were you saying like Kipling that the East is East and the West is West and there is no meeting point?

GG: One has to have a bit of tragedy in a comic book. This was no revenge on the real Mr Wordsworth I told you about whom I'd met in Liberia. He looked after us very well! As the narrative went, the death of my character was inevitable. It had nothing social about it. He might equally have been an Yugoslav peasant, let us say. He had to die because the undesirable Mr Visconti had to be a winner.

MC: Why?

GG: Because he was the clever one. I really don't think I felt, even unconsciously, that Wordsworth was a loser because he was black. He was a loser because he was simple, honest and kind, in a different class from Mr Visconti who would have called himself a gentleman. It was the simple and honest who had to die.

MC: When I say black I mean in the sense of the new post-colonial nation-states; we've all joined the League very late and are still learning to survive in games of power; the Viscontis of the world are already familiar and your killing of Wordsworth makes it a very bleak conclusion.

GG: What's wrong with a bleak conclusion? Is a book to be judged by a happy ending? I like the novel very much. The English did not like it; it had very poor reviews. The Americans accepted it as also the French. But the English are always expecting me to be very serious.

MC: But it is a very serious book and my favourite in many ways. My comment on the bleak conclusion is not a judgement of the book except to say that it suggests a bleak view of world politics. The novel is, in a sense, the history of the modern world – Empire and post-Empire – full of the joy and sadness of being alive. Words-worth's death gives the novel a ruthless honesty that is frightening. It is a great novel precisely because of this honesty.

GG: Yes, but the narrative is comic. I even like Visconti. He is a villain, but a likeable man; he even learnt how to handle the truth machine and get away with it.

Appendix: Letters to the Press

A NATION'S CONSCIENCE

I spent the month of September in the Kikuyu areas of Kenya, and it was with small surprise, that I read of what happened on the Nyeri–Mweiga road. Too many similar cases have already reached one's attention: three bodies exposed for days in the yard of a police station where every passer-by could see how little respect there was for a dead African; the honourable record of certain regiments like The Buffs matched by the dishonourable record of other trigger-happy units who fire first as soon as curfew falls and look at papers afterwards. (The papers, we are told, of these dead Africans were not in order.) How many Africans' papers are in order? Four or five scraps of paper have to be carried around at one time – there is no proper system of passports to include all the necessary forms from tax receipts to travel permits.

'The dead men at Nyeri had taken the oath.' What of it? So have 90 per cent of the Home Guard. If this were ever to become a war between white and black, it would need more than three generals to wage the campaign. It is the Kikuyu who have suffered heavy casualties, not the white settler or the soldier (casualties from Mau Mau action are fewer than casualties from accidental shootings). There is not even the excuse of a terrible and costly war to explain carelessness and nerves.

The pictures of the Lari massacre have had a wide circulation, and very terrible they are, but if photographs were available of the scene on the Nyeri road it would be seen that the Bren gun can produce a result as horrible as the panga, *The Times*, 4 December 1953.

CUBA'S CIVIL WAR

The welcome success of Dr Fidel Castro in overthrowing the dictatorship of Batista reminds us again of the extraordinary ignorance of Cuban affairs shown by the British Government. If it had not been for the intervention of Mr Hugh Delargy, MP, this country would have gone on happily supplying the dictator with arms. When Mr Delargy first raised the question in the House of Commons Mr Selwyn Lloyd replied that, when the export permits were granted, the Government had no evidence of a civil war in Cuba. Yet at that very period the province of Oriente was already dominated by Dr Castro and a military reign of terror existed in Santiago.

Any visitor to Cuba could have given Her Majesty's Government more information about conditions in the island than was apparently supplied by our official representatives: the mutilations and torture practised by leading police officers, the killing of hostages. This was the situation *before* the British Government granted export licences for turbo-jets and tanks.

What kind of information, we may well ask, was the Foreign Office receiving from its representatives in Cuba? I was myself told quite untruly before visiting Santiago in November 1957, that Dr Castro was a Communist. It is strange that our officials in Havana had not learnt that Dr Castro was supported by the head of Catholic Action in Santiago and by the representatives there of the Protestant Churches, *The Times*, 3 January 1959.

CUBAN ITCH

As a Catholic and a recent visitor to Cuba I wish your reviewer would enlarge on his curious statement that Castro 'has despatched' the Church. Odd then that I could attend Mass; odd that Castro could be the guest of the Papal Nuncio when he celebrated the coronation of Pope Paul. Perhaps your reviewer has been misled by a misguided broadcast by Bishop Sheen, *The Times Literary Supplement*, 26 March 1964.

In your issue of January 18 you write that the Catholic population of Cuba 'has dwindled from 95% to a nominal 40%' I think that the word 'nominal' should have qualified both figures. The 'popular religion' of Cuba before the revolution was Voodoo, though as in Haiti the Voodoo worshippers would have claimed to be Catholics. Indeed in Haiti the ceremonies ended in time for the worshippers to attend early Mass at 5 a.m. I have been present at Voodoo ceremonies in both countries: they much resembled each other, though perhaps the Cuban ceremony was a bit Low Church, for I don't remember the priest in Cuba biting off the head of a living cock. I wonder whether the drop from 95% of Catholics means a drop in the Voodoo congregation.

I believe that your reference to the Catholic church 'being actively repressed since 1959' should be qualified. Certainly the Papal Nuncio in 1963 and 1966 (the only years I can personally vouch for) was on excellent terms with Fidel Castro to whom he always brought a present of his favourite cheese when returning from visits to Rome.

It must be remembered that practising Catholics (mainly middle class) in Cuba were equally ill at ease under the dictatorship of Batista who sent his henchmen to beat up the Archbishop of Havana in his own palace, *The Tablet*, 8 February 1986.

'TACTICAL ERROR' ON VIET CONG

Surely the refusal of the United States to negotiate with the Viet Cong who control the greater part of South Vietnam is a tactical error of the worst kind . . . As junta succeeds junta in Saigon the claim of the Viet Cong leaders to represent a *de facto* Government becomes stronger. To refuse to negotiate with them is to refuse to negotiate with the future and to repeat the mistakes of the past. But is there another offshore island available for a Vietnamese Chiang Kaishek? *The Times*, 23 June 1965.

POLICY IN VIETNAM

Mr Brian Crozier, except perhaps for Prof. Honey is the most talented and informed British champion of the State Department's policy in South Vietnam. (The Foreign Secretary unfortunately has no personal knowledge of the country and is badly briefed.) Yet I find Mr Crozier's letter disingenuous. Has he any right to assume that for *de facto* recognition an administration must hold *towns*?

He is unable anyway to claim any legal basis for the present Saigon government (I am uncertain, after several days absence from the British newspapers, who at this moment is President of South Vietnam). Even Mr Diem's right to rule depended on the medieval notion that he had been appointed by an Emperor – whom he soon afterwards disclaimed.

Under the circumstances it is wiser in Vietnam to abandon the idea of *de jure* government altogether. The Government of South Vietnam can claim *de facto* to represent a few principal towns; the *de facto* Government of the Viet Cong can claim to administer three-quarters of the countryside. American – and not Vietnamese – air-power sees to it that the Viet Cong administration works from deep shelters and not from conventional offices.

Would Mr Crozier argue that, if German air-power had been sufficient in 1940 to establish a German base and a collaborating government in London and to drive the resistance into shelters and trenches near Edgware, Epping, East Grinstead and Colchester, a resistance which none the less made it impossible for the government conscripts to control the countryside around London, General This and Air Marshal That and a Mr Jones could have legally declared themselves to be the *de facto* government of Great Britain? . . . Mr Crozier need not remind me that the geographical differences are very great – we both of us know Vietnam. The moral parallel is not so far astray . . . In any case Mr Crozier's argument is really an argument against negotiations with any local Communist government and for negotiation only with the Soviet Union or China. Thus the monolithic nature of Communism would be firmly established by our own actions, *The Times*, 7 July 1965.

WAR IN VIETNAM

I objected (February 17) to General Lord Bourne's lack of precision when he spoke of South Vietnam having 'once' suffered under communism. This use of words gave his letter a sense that he may not have intended. Mr Herb Greer (February 19) shares his imprecision and tries to justify it.

Of course areas of South Vietnam, like Hué, have suffered from communist offensives in a civil war which unike the Spanish has been supported on one side only by foreign troops. No one will dispute that, and probably unlike Mr Herb Greer I have been caught up myself in a similar offensive. Incidentally why do supporters of the Pentagon always write of men, women and children being 'butchered' in a Communist offensive, and yet the poor victims of an American offensive become only 'casualties'? *The Times*, 23 February 1971.

EUROPE'S RELATIONSHIP WITH THE USA: IMPLICATIONS OF VIETNAM

A few reflections on your sad issue of January 3.

1. The Prime Minister, at the rather sombre celebration of Britain's entry into the European Community, said: 'Our aim must be that Europe can emerge as a valid partner of the United States in strengthening the prospects for peace and prosperity across the world.' I am sure he was heard in respectful silence, but perhaps there would have been a few half-suppressed laughs if he had read the equally absurd statement that: 'Our aim must be that Europe can emerge as a valid partner of the USSR in strengthening the prospects for the liberties of all small nations on our Eastern borders.'

To associate the United States Government this Christmas in particular, with the idea of peace is surely more than a little misjudged. The B52 bombing of North Vietnam has for the moment ceased, but the indiscriminate bombing of the South continues. To defend an ally now can be defined as killing his population and devastating his country.

2. Sir Edwin Leather (Letters, January 3) seems to share a rather common ignorance of Vietnamese geography and of the way in which this war began. The North Vietnamese differs from the South Vietnamese perhaps as much as a man of Yorkshire differs from a man of Sussex. The Geneva Conference of 1954 had no intention of permanently dividing the country. Elections were to be held both in the North and the South and President Eisenhower foresaw a large majority in the South for President Ho Chi Minh – in spite of the million Catholic refugees who had been told by the 'fighting Bishops' of Phat Diem and Bui-Chi that the Virgin had fled south.

It was President Diem, the favoured child first of the French and then of the American colonialists, who refused to hold elections and began the policy, referred to by Sir Edwin Leather, of 'abductions and assassination' directed against Southern nationalists in the countryside who with the communists had fought the French for the liberation of their country. 'Tyrant elimination' was practised first by Kennedy's advisers with great efficiency, when President Diem, much to American embarrassment, turned against the Buddhists as well as the nationalists and the communists. It isn't whatever one may think of Diem (and on the occasion in 1955 when I took tea with him I had the impression of a near-madman), a very honourable episode in American history. . .

5. I abhor the Czechoslovak invasion (I was in Prague both during the communist take-over in 1948 and during the Russian occupation in 1969) but I doubt if it can compare in horror and immorality with the indiscriminate bombing by napalm and fragmentation bombs of South and North Vietnam, not to speak of the only publicised massacre of women and children in My Lai.

How heartening it would have been if the new Europe of Nine had celebrated January 1 by a common statement that no visit from President Nixon would be welcomed by any member country before the American intervention in Vietnam ended, *The Times*, 6 January 1973.

OPEN DOOR POLICY

I am surprised that Russia has not taken advantage of the strange moral position over Vietnam taken by the Western governments and their odd interpretation of the Helsinki Agreement. Western governments protest against the USSR for refusing to let certain of their people immigrate; they protest against the Vietnamese Government allowing 'the boat people' to go. They even demand that Vietnam close its frontiers. (And of course they protest against the invasion of Cambodia which put an end to the genocidal regime of the Khmer Rouge. Apparently it would have been acceptable if Hitler had confined his massacres to Germany and not crossed the frontier.)

Why hasn't Russia taken this superb opportunity to grant visas to the West to anyone who asks for one? It is highly unlikely that there would be a mass immigration of the proletariat – and that in itself would be a good propaganda point. As for the intellectual dissidents, many like Solzhenitsyn have complained at being forced to leave their country, so perhaps the exodus of the middle class would not be very spectacular. But even supposing the exodus were spectacular . . . the Security Services of the West would be overwhelmed by the numbers they had to vet; our unemployment figures would soar, and what a triumph for the USSR when the Western governments very soon had to plead to Russia to close her frontiers as now they plead to Vietnam? *The Spectator*, 22 September 1979.

Is there not a simple explanation for the policy of Fidel Castro who is allowing those Cubans who wish – for various reasons – to leave their country to do so. I have always believed there is a certain hypocrisy, in view of the Helsinki Agreements, in the attitude of the West towards the boat people of Vietnam . . . when the boat people became too much of a good thing, the governments who had been signatories of the Helskinki Agreements protested against a State which let its people go. One wondered, if Russia should learn that lesson, what would happen if she opened her frontiers to all who wished to leave. The Western security services would certainly be unable to cope. (Who is a genuine refugee for political reasons, who is a criminal, who is a KGB agent?) It wouldn't be very long, in spite of the Helsinki Agreements, before Western governments protested to the Soviet at this appalling freedom of movement.

Cuba perhaps is giving a dress rehearsal of what would happen. We accept a few well-known dissidents, but would we in the West, any more than Peru, be able to receive thousands of 'refugees'? At the next Helsinki follow-up in Madrid who would be accused then of closing their frontiers to free movement, Russia or the West? *The Times*, 12 April 1980.

THE CASE OF MISS WILSON

So we are selling arms to Pinochet and normal diplomatic relations have been resumed, and we can laugh off Miss Wilson's case with reference to 'the Chicago boys' and Pinochet's economic policies. When I was young Zaharoff was regarded with disfavour for his trade in arms. There was even a Royal Commission on private arms traffic – not that it came to any useful conclusions. Now the arms traffic is nationalised and Mrs Thatcher has taken on the role of Zaharoff. The State sells arms to make a profit as Zaharoff did. No moral principles are involved.

Why does Pinochet need arms? Is he threatened by any of his neighbours – Argentina, Bolivia or Peru? If he were threatened, Zaharoff–Thatcher would have found a yet more profitable market for arms by selling to all four. Pinochet needs the arms to support his internal control which involves the torture of his opponents . . . Your contributor, Mr Douglas-Home, in his article on the 'Chicago Boys' seems to excuse Pinochet's 'intervention' (a cosy word for armed rebellion) because of the very high rate of inflation under President Allende. But who caused the high rate? How much of it was caused by the transport strike now admittedly engineered by the CIA? A little patience – for Allende was determined to play the constitutional game – and the Christian Democrats would have been back in power in a couple of years. 'Yes if there's an election', the leader of the Christian Democrats commented to me at the time. 'It's not Allende's intention which I doubt, but I repeat *if* there is an election.' Of course there was no election, and the then leader of the Christian Democrats is in exile. Pinochet's rebellion was not so much against Allende's government as against the continuation of any constitutional government, *The Times*, 15 September 1980.

LIBERATION THEOLOGY

One supposes that if Catholic bishops, like Anglican bishops, were made members of the House of Lords, the present Pope, if he proved logical, would tell them either to refuse their seats or cease to fulfil their priestly functions, especially if they supported the governing party with their votes. But in fact would he? Unlike John XXIII he himself seems to take a political and partisan line. To him, as to President Reagan, Marxism is the great enemy, black against white, and the word Marxist becomes more and more a vague term of abuse. Is anyone completely Marxist any more than any one is completely Christian? Doubt, like the conscience, is inherent in human nature (perhaps they are the same thing) but one might expect the Pope to remember that Marx as a historian condemned Henry VIII for closing the monasteries, *The Times*, 8 September 1984.

THE POPE AND NICARAGUA

The Pope when he speaks of religious persecution in Nicaragua seems to be lamentably ill-informed. I have just returned from that country, and I can only speak of what I saw – big placards displayed on the roads marked 'Revolution Yes. But Christian', the open churches and the traditional celebrations on the eve of the feast of the Immaculate Conception held in the cities and villages. I walked between six and eight in the evening along the streets of Leon in the *barrios* of the poor. Every little house stood open to the crowds and displayed altars decked with flowers and the image of the Virgin. The crowd would shout 'Who has brought us happiness?' and the answering cry was 'Mary the Immaculate' while the host of each house distributed sweets, if he could afford or find them, or cheap jewellery or in one case small home-made brooms. This may be described as Mariolatry but hardly religious persecution, nor were those celebrations a protest against the government. My companion that night in the streets of Leon was my friend Tomas Borge, the minister of the Interior, whom no security guard could possibly have protected in those crowds, *The Tablet*, 4 January 1986.

NICARAGUA

Isn't it about time that a very big question mark was aimed at President Reagan?

'Why do you persist in calling the Nicaraguan government a communist government? Wouldn't it be equally true, or equally false, to call it a Roman Catholic government? I can understand and even sympathise with the objections you might have to a Catholic government, but, of course, the support you give the terrorists would be less excusable in the eyes of your countrymen.'

How can the Nicaraguan government be classified simply as communist? The key positions of Foreign Affairs, Health and Education and Culture are all held by Catholic priests. The official in charge of economic research is a priest. An English priest is organising Rural Libraries in the countryside.

It is true that the Archbishop is opposed to the present government but the Church does not belong to the Archbishop, it belongs to the Catholic people, and I watched last December how the population celebrated with a faith and a fervour which I wish I could have fully shared the Feast of the Immaculate Conception. There are Marxists in the government, yes, but Marxism is an economic theory not a heresy. President Ortega has visited Moscow, yes, and Mrs Thatcher, we are told, also hopes to visit Moscow, *The Times*, 20 March 1986.

The *Sunday Telegraph* reacted to this letter with what amounts to a broadside – an article in the news columns by William Buckley, editor of the *National Review* and Norman Podhoretz, editor of *Commentary* entitled 'Where Graham Greene went astray in Nicaragua' and with a leading article entitled 'Why Mr Greene never sees Red' (23 March 1986). Graham Greene's response:

Nicaragua and the Church

I have no wish to be unpleasant in dealing with Mr William Buckley, perhaps the most extreme Right-wing spokesman in the United States outside the White House, for he has always to me been an endearing figure of fun. English humour is often puzzling to Americans and Mr Buckley hasn't realised that my suggestion that President Reagan might well call the Nicaraguan Government Roman Catholic was not seriously meant.

Alas, these English jokes! I must try to avoid them. My main point that there is no religious persecution in Nicaragua remains unanswered. Mr Buckley should visit Nicaragua and see for himself as the North American bishops have done and fairly reported.

Your editorial with its attack on the political role of the Catholic Church requires a more serious reply (by the way there are three, not two, Catholic priests in the Government). You write 'so far as politics are concerned Catholic priests are very poor judges as to rights and wrongs, since they tend for good reasons to want to be on the winning side'.

Was Archbishop Romero who was murdered in El Salvador at the altar by those in power trying to be on the winning side? Is Archbishop Damas who has followed on the same lines in bravely condemning the death squads trying to be on the winning side? And the Archbishop of Santiago in his courageous opposition to Pinochet? True enough many Church authorities in the Thirties were fellow-travellers with Fascism, but we must remember that even then the voice which spoke out loudest in Spain against Franco after his victory was the voice of Archbishop Segura of Seville, *The Sunday Telegraph*, 30 March 1986.

CATHOLIC DEBATE

You report (September 7) that in an appeal for harmony in the Roman Catholic Church Bishop Harris said: 'Christ came to reconcile'. Isn't this rather unorthodox? In my copy of the New Testament Christ said: 'I came not to bring peace but a sword', and spoke of new wine having to be put in fresh wineskins and cursed Capharnaum. If Christ had come to reconcile would he have been crucified? *The Times*, 10 September 1971.

A DAMNABLE DOCTRINE

I ought not to complain of being called a Jansenist by the amiable Mr Burgess since it has been doubted whether even Jansenius himself was a Jansenist. Mr Burgess, cradle-Catholic though he is, or perhaps because he is, seems rather wobbly in his theology or he would realise that my novels which cast doubt on the doctrine of damnation are tinged with the very opposite of Jansenism, with what he might well consider to be the damnable doctrine of hope. Saint-Simon who was no Jansenist wrote well on the loose use of the term: 'I think that the terms Jansenist and Jansenism are like pitch, used as a convenient method of blackening people's characters, and that out of a thousand so dubbed, less than two merit the name.' *The Tablet*, 12 April 1975.

Notes

To avoid duplication of material full publication details are only given in these notes if the work mentioned is not included in the Bibliography, or, in the case of Greene's own work, if the reference is to the Collected Edition.

Introduction

1. 'I am more a political writer than a Catholic writer. But I prefer to be called a writer who happens to be a Catholic.' 'Graham Greene Takes the Orient Express', Interview with Christopher Burstall, *The Listener*, 21 November 1968.

> I'd be too afraid of being labelled a 'political author' . . . just as I've been labelled a 'Catholic writer', because I don't think that my way of writing or my attitude to writing has been in the least determined by events. Events have merely had an occasional influence on my choice of subject. I suppose I can be called a political writer when I tackle political subjects; but politics are in the air we breathe, like the presence or absence of a God. Marie Françoise Allain, *The Other Man*,
> p. 87.

> He has always been a political writer interested in the larger movement of events. Before the war the frontiers were European. Now these lines of anxiety run everywhere . . . He is an expatriate, but feels very English. And though there are moments when he regrets the passing of Victorian peace, he wishes . . . to remain committed to the whole world. V. S. Naipaul, *The Telegraph Magazine*, 8 March 1968.

2. G. Lukács, *Studies in European Realism*, p. 9.
3. There are of course, exceptions to the general trend of discussing the novels as 'Catholic', 'thrillers' and 'entertainments'. David Lodge writes perceptively and suggests that Greene's work 'does not fit into the categories that orthodox literary criticism has evolved in its appraisal of serious modern fiction'. He argues persuasively that critics have been 'tempted to abstract from the fiction the author's version of reality, measuring this against a supposedly normative version, rather than assessing the persuasiveness with which the novelist realises this version'. Although he concludes that Catholicism 'as a public system of laws and dogmas is far from being an adequate key to Greene's fiction', he endorses the view which ascribes an innate pessimism to Greene and that 'there flows in his work the current of antihumanism'. D. Lodge, *Graham Greene*. Miriam Farris, who with Kenneth Allott wrote the first major critical book *The Art of Graham Greene*, updates their work:

it seems extraordinary not to have seen earlier how arresting a product of the man and the moment [his] achievement really is . . . Criticism . . . has often been content to take a narrower view, encouraged by Greene's Roman Catholicism and its accompanying anhedonia, for some readers the most haunting aspect of his creative sensibility. Discussion frequently modulates into engagement with the hugely paradoxical question of his enormous success. No really good or serious writer, it has at times been felt, could possibly be as popular as *that* . . . I have already indicated briefly in this essay that his Catholicism is not necessarily at all an appropriate starting-point for comprehending the nature of his imaginative achievement' *Critical Quarterly*, vol. 20, no. 3, Autumn 1978, p. 9.

See also 'The Strength of Uncertainty' in which Julian Symons writes of the 'progress' from 'Catholicism to humanism,' but persists in calling Greene's world of struggle 'the world of the Manichee', *The Times Literary Supplement*, 8 October 1982, pp. 1089–90.

4. See Raimundo Pannikar, 'Non-dualistic Relation between Religion and Politics', paper presented at the Annual Colloquium of Philosophers, Instituto di Filosofia, Rome.
5. Claud Cockburn, *I, Claud* (Penguin, 1967) p. 29.
6. E. M. Forster, *A Passage to India* (Penguin, 1983).
7. George Woodcock, *The Crystal Spirit. A Study of George Orwell*, p. 189.
8. Katherine Bail Hoskins, *Today the Struggle, Literature and Politics in England during the Spanish Civil War*, p. 36.
9. '*The Times* was the only national daily to print throughout the 1926 General Strike . . . On Wednesday someone tried to set fire to the paper stocks. But infinitely more damaging was the decision of Winston Churchill as Chancellor to commandeer a quarter of *The Times*'s precious newsprint on which to print his propagandist official sheet, the *British Gazette*.' (4 May 1926). From *The Times: Past, Present, Future* published to celebrate 200 years of publishing, 1 January 1985.
10. Interview – M. C., August 1986.
11. Bergonzi describes Greene as belonging to a category of writers who were 'apolitical or right-wing, like . . . Anthony Powell or Evelyn Waugh' in the opening section of his book and then devotes a whole chapter (Auden/Greene) to a discussion of the influence of Auden on Greene. He tries to cover the contradictions by suggesting that the comparison is purely in relation to style. Interestingly, he consigns even Greene's novels of the 1930s to the familiar 'salvation damnation' catalogue: 'his paradigm is an idiosyncratic Catholic one, based on a polarity between salvation and damnation, rather than the Marxism model that was, for a time, favoured by Auden and his followers. But the difference in ideology hardly affects the quality of the observation, or the stylistic or formal modes of categorising it' B. Bergonzi, *Reading the Thirties*, p. 54.
12. Graham Greene, 'Alfred Tennyson Intervenes', *Spectator* CLIX, no. 5711, 10 December 1937.
13. *Authors Take Sides on the Spanish War* (*Left Review*). This was the result of

poll of 148 British writers organised by Nancy Cunard.

14. I am completely against the intervention of the United States in Vietnam. I see no excuse whatever for the presence of foreign troops on the soil of this country. The excuse of containing Communism assumes that Communism is everywhere an evil. Anyone with experience of Vietnam knows this is not the case. Anyway most of us would prefer rule by our countrymen even though Communist, than by a foreign power.
The conflict in Vietnam can only be resolved by the complete and unconditional withdrawal of American troops. If Britain had intervened in the American Civil War on the side of the South – at one time it seemed possible – would Abraham Lincoln have agreed to negotiate the future of his country with a *British* government? Hanoi is just as close in blood to Saigon as New York to Richmond. The presence of foreign troops prevents negotiations between North and South. Graham Greene in Cecil Woolf and John Bagguley (eds) *Authors Take Sides on Vietnam* (New York: Simon & Schuster, 1967).

15. *Collected Essays* (Penguin, 1970) p. 334.
16. George Orwell, *The Collected Essays, Journalism and Letters*, edited by Sonia Orwell and Ian Angus, vol. III, p. 63.
17. Ibid.
18. Interview – M.C., August 1986.
19. George Orwell, *Collected Essays*, vol. IV, p. 437.
20. Ibid, p. 153.
21. 'Greene: Four Score Years and Then?', *The Times*, 7 September 1984.

1 Explorations

1. Epigraph, *The Lawless Roads* (Penguin, 1971).
2. Samuel Hynes, *The Auden Generation*, p. 218.
3. Evelyn Waugh, *Ninety-Two Days* (Duckworth, 1934) p. 13.
4. *Journey Without Maps* (Penguin, 1971) p. 21.
5. S. E. Ogude, 'Graham Greene's Africa', p. 43.
6. S. E. Ogude, 'In Search of Misery: A Study of Graham Greene's Travels in Africa', pp. 46–7.
7. Interview – M.C., August 1986.
8. Interview with Christopher Burstall, 'Graham Greene Takes the Orient Express', *The Listener*, 21 November 1968.
9. *Journey Without Maps* (Penguin, 1971) p. 19.
10. Paul Theroux, Introduction to Barbara Greene, *Too Late to Turn Back*.
11. Interview – M.C., September 1986.
12. Christopher Sykes, *Evelyn Waugh, A Biography* (Collins, 1975) pp. 183–4.
13. Ibid, p. 188.
14. *The Lawless Roads* (Penguin, 1970) pp. 169–80.
15. John Henry, Cardinal Newman, *Sermons on the Theory of Religious Belief*, pp. 347–8.
16. *The Collected Essays*, p. 13.
17. Martin Green, *Dreams of Adventure, Deeds of Empire*.
18. Martin Green, *The English Novel in the Twentieth Century (The Doom of Empire)*, pp. 108–9.

19. *The Spectator*, 6 November 1942.
20. Christopher Sykes, *Evelyn Waugh*, p. 328.
21. Ibid, p. 326.
22. *Conradiana*, vol. XIV, no. 3, 1982; also 'The Colonialist Bias of Heart of Darkness', Frances B. Singh, *Conradiana*, vol. X, 1978, pp. 41–53; Chinua Achebe, 'An Image of Africa', *Massachusetts Review*, 18:4, Winter 1977, pp. 782–94.
23. Raymond Williams, *The Long Revolution*, p. 278.
24. Ibid, p. 281.
25. Ibid, p. 283.

2 The Intimate Enemy

1. Irving Howe, *Politics and the Novel*, p. 24.
2. Ibid, p. 21.
3. Greene, *Ways of Escape* (The Bodley Head, 1980) p. 34.
4. D. A. Willis, 'New Life for the Novel', *Viewpoint* 1 (April–June 1934) p. 14; also Samuel Hynes, *The Auden Generation*, p. 138.
5. George Orwell, *Collected Essays*, vol. IV, p. 153.
6. *Why Do I Write?* p. 32.
7. Richard Johnstone, *The Will to Believe*, p. 3.
8. Ibid.
9. Ibid, p. 5.
10. *Brighton Rock*, Collected Edition (Heinemann/The Bodley Head, 1970).
11. *Why Do I Write?* pp. 47–8.
12. Richard Johnstone, *The Will to Believe*, pp. 66–7.
13. *The Lawless Roads; A Sort of Life; Lost Childhood and Other Essays.*
14. John Spurling, *Graham Greene*, p. 75.
15. *Ways of Escape*, p. 16.
16. Ibid, p. 17.
17. *Rumour at Nightfall* (Doubleday, Doran & Company, 1932), p. 44.
18. Interview – M.C., May 1984.
19. *Ways of Escape*, p. 29.
20. Harold Fisch, *The Dual Image*, p. 87.
21. Ibid, pp. 88–9.
22. The biennial Jerusalem Prize for the writer who in his writing 'supported best the freedom of the individual in society, to the international personality who best worked for the liberty of man', was awarded to Graham Greene. Previous recipients include Bertrand Russell, Jorge Luis Borges, Ignazio Silone. Graham Greene's speech on the occasion dwelt on the fact that power is a term that is common to politics as well as religion, and concluded thus: 'As a Roman Catholic I thank God for the heretics. Heresy is only another word for freedom of thought.' For the full text see *The Spectator*, 18 April 1981.
23. *Ways of Escape*, p. 70.
24. *A Gun for Sale*, Introduction, The Collected Edition (Heinmann/The Bodley Head, 1973).
25. *It's a Battlefield* (Penguin, 1980).

26. This is a point of view shared by Orwell who writes in 'Shooting an Elephant': 'I did not even know that the British Empire [was] dying, still less did I know that it [was] a great deal better than the younger empires that [were] going to supplant it.' *Inside the Whale* (Penguin, 1981) p. 92. 'I had a great deal of sympathy for the French in Vietnam, but I swung back, and with the American intervention I became even more a Communist sympathiser. On the other hand the combat with Russia even post-Stalin, has made me dislike that form of Communism.' (Graham Greene: Interview with Alex Hamilton, *The Guardian*, 11 September 1971).
27. *A Gun for Sale* (Penguin, 1974) p. 129.
28. *Brighton Rock* (Penguin, 1977) p. 6.
29. Marghanita Laski, *The Times*, 1 February 1966.
30. George Orwell, 'The Sanctified Sinner' in S. Hynes (ed.) *Graham Greene: Twentieth Century Views*, p. 108.
31. Angus Wilson, 'Greene: Four Score Years and Then', *The Times*, 7 September 1984.

3 The Religious Sense

1. *The Power and the Glory*, Introduction, Collected Edition (Heinemann/ The Bodley Head, 1971).
2. *The New Statesman*, 25 March 1939.
3. *Collected Essays* (Penguin, 1970) pp. 91–2.
4. *A Burnt-Out Case* (Penguin, 1977) Dedication.
5. Ibid.
6. Anthony Burgess, 'Politics in the novels of Graham Greene', *Journal of Contemporary History*, vol. 2, no 2, 1967, p. 95.
7. John Henry, Cardinal Newman, *The Idea of a University*, p. 61.
8. Ibid, p. 62.
9. Ibid, p. 64.
10. Ibid, p. 62.
11. Free translation by M.C. of the following extract:

> *Ce que je trouve d'authentique dans les romans de Greene, c'est la Grâce . . . . . la vérité que le monde ne connaît pas . . . . Et cette vérité lui apparaît à lui, anglais d'éducation et de tradition protestante, dans un tout autre éclairage que celui qui nous est familier à nous, catholiques français de tradition janséniste. Nous redécouvrons la foi chrétienne à travers lui; ses réponses touchant la Grâce et le salut échappent aux classements rigides de nos théologiens et de nos casuistes. Il rend à Dieu à notre égard une liberté à la fois terrible et rassurante, parce que finalement Dieu est amour et que si rien n'est possible à l'homme, tout est possible à l'éternel amour.* François Mauriac, *D'autres et moi* (Paris: Bernard Grasset, 1966) p. 61.

12. Graham Greene insists that he does not believe in hell. nor is he fascinated by sin:

I find it difficult to believe in sin. Reviewers talk about my sense of sin but doesn't that belong to my characters? Personally I have very little sense of sin. What it really adds up to is that I write novels about what interests me . . . And the thing which interests me most is discovering the humanity that exists in apparently inhuman characters.'

Interview with Philip Toynbee, 'Literature and Life', *The Observer*, 15 September, 1957.

13. Anthony Burgess, 'Politics', p. 93.
14. Interview – M.C., May 1984.
15. *The Listener*, 20 June 1948.
16. Anthony Burgess, 'Politics', p. 95.
17. George Woodcock, *The Writer and Politics*, p. 143.
18. Terry Eagleton, *Exiles and Emigrés*, p. 109.
19. *The Power and the Glory*, Collected Edition (Heinemann/The Bodley Head, 1971) Introduction.
20. *The Power and the Glory* (Penguin, 1979) pp. 14–15.
21. *The Heart of the Matter* (Penguin, 1971). Greene restored to the British Collected Edition an added scene eliminated from the original manuscript and from all editions until 1971.
22. R. D. Smith, *The Spectator*, 4 June 1948.
23. Introduction to Collected Edition (Heinemann/The Bodley Head, 1971).
24. Ibid.
25. *The End of the Affair* (Penguin, 1966) p. 120.
26. *Collected Essays*, p. 40.
27. *A Burnt-Out Case* (Penguin, 1971).
28. Philip Stratford (ed.) *The Portable Graham Greene* (Penguin, 1977) p. 93.
29. S. E. Ogude, *Graham Greene: Africa*, p. 53.
30. Terry Eagleton, *Exiles and Emigrés*, p. 122.
31. Ibid, p. 137.
32. 'Mau Mau, the Black God', *The Sunday Times*, 4 October 1953.

4 England, My England

1. George Woodcock, *The Writer and Politics*, p. 143.
2. Samuel Hynes, *The Auden Generation*, p. 229.
3. Martin Green, *Children of the Sun*, p. 69 and 381.
4. *England Made Me*, Introduction to the Collected Edition (Heinemann/The Bodley Head, 1970).
5. Ibid.
6. Claud Cockburn, *I, Claud* (Penguin, 1967) p. 26.
7. *The Confidential Agent*, Introduction to the Collected Edition (Heinemann/The Bodley Head, 1971).
8. 'Myth, Reality and Fiction' broadcast by the BBC on 2 April 1962. Conversations with novelists, compiled by Frank Kermode. Greene suggests that the representation of reality, of the real truth about the world is primarily the burden of 'myth': 'my own wish always is to produce a central figure who represents some idea of reasonable

simplicity – a mythical figure, if you like. And the simplicity often gets damaged by plot making'. As example of overloading the plot he cites *The Heart of the Matter* – 'one began to overload the plot and I felt the impulse given by the character was whittled away'. Complex plots, he says, are in opposition to myth, and need to be controlled so as not to damage the mythical centre.

9. Anthony Burgess in 'Man of Mystery: the Enigma of Graham Greene' *The Listener*, vol. 102, no. 2631, 4 October 1979.
10. Kim Philby, *My Silent War* (London: Panther, 1969).
11. John Le Carré in 'Man of Mystery: The Enigma of Graham Greene' *The Listener*, vol. 102, no. 2631, 4 October 1979.
12. *Ways of Escape*, p. 91.
13. Interview – M.C. May 1984.
14. John Le Carré, 'Man of Mystery'.
15. Ibid.
16. George Orwell, *Inside the Whale* (Penguin, 1981) p. 79.
17. Marie Françoise Allain, *The Other Man*, p. 94.
18. V. S. Pritchett in A. F. Cassis (compiler) *Graham Greene, An Annotated Bibliography of Criticism*, (London: The Scarecrow Press, 1980).
19. *The Ministry of Fear* (Penguin, 1972).
20. John Le Carré, 'Man of Mystery'.

5 *Colons*, Intermediaries and Exiles

1. Graham Greene explains: 'It's a restlessness that I've always had to move around and perhaps to see English characters in a setting which is not protective to them, where perhaps they speak a little differently, a little more openly.' Interview with Christopher Burstall, *The Listener*, 21 November 1968.
2. Edward W. Said, 'Reflections on Exile', *Granta*, 13, Autumn 1984.
3. Edward Said writes: 'for the first time in modern history, the whole imposing edifice of humanistic knowledge resting on the classics of European letters, and with it the scholarly discipline inculcated formally into students in Western universities through the forms familiar to us all, represents only a fraction of the real human relationships and interactions now taking place in the world . . . [There is now] diminishing acquiescence and deference accorded to what has been called the Natopolitan world long dominating peripheral regions like Africa, Asia, and Latin America. New cultures, new societies, and emerging visions of social, political, and aesthetic order now lay claim to the humanist's attention, with an insistence that cannot long be denied.' *The World, the Text and the Critic*, p. 21.
4. Michael J. C. Echeruo, *Joyce Cary and the Novel of Africa*, pp. 1–3.
5. E. M. Forster, *A Passage to India* (1924) (Penguin, 1983).
6. Joyce Cary, *Aissa Saved* (1931) (Michael Joseph, 1952); *The African Witch* (Victor Gollancz, 1936); *Castle Corner* (1939) (Michael Joseph, 1932) (1952); *Mister Johnson* (1939) (Michael Joseph, 1947).
7. George Orwell, *Burmese Days* (1934) (Penguin, 1980).
8. Samuel Hynes, *The Auden Generation*, pp. 228–9.

9. Michael J. C. Echeruo, *Joyce Cary*, p. 147.
10. E. M. Forster, *A Passage to India*, p. 58.
11. S. E. Ogude, 'Graham Greene's Travels in Africa', p. 50. The quotation is from *Journey Without Maps*, p. 34.
12. George Orwell, 'The Sanctified Sinner' in S. Hynes (ed.) *Graham Greene*, p. 106.
13. T. Eagleton, *Exiles and Emigrés*, p. 81.
14. Ibid, p. 78.
15. Ibid, pp. 118–19.
16. See *The Heart of the Matter*, pp. 244–5. Greene is critical of the novel, except for one character: 'The scales to me seem too heavily weighted, the plot overloaded, the religious scruples of Scobie too extreme . . . All this said there are pages in *The Heart of the Matter* (and one character, Yusef) for which I care' *Ways of Escape*, pp. 120–1.
17. *In Search of a Character* (Penguin, 1968) p. 106.
18. *Journey Without Maps*, pp. 165, 199.
19. S. E. Ogude, 'Graham Greene's Africa'.
20. 'There had never been a home . . . Home lay like a picture postcard on a pile of other postcards.' *The Power and the Glory* (Penguin, 1979) p. 11.

6 Hegemonies

1. George Orwell, *Collected Essays*, vol. IV, pp. 408–9.
2. Raymond Williams, *Orwell*, p. 35–6.
3. *Collected Essays*, p. 43.
4. Philip Stratford (ed.) *The Portable Graham Greene* (Penguin, 1978) pp. 586–7.
5. Ibid, pp. 608–9.
6. Interview with Philip Toynbee, *The Observer*, 15 July 1957.
7. *What I Believe*, p. 48.
8. 'Malaya, The Forgotten War', *Life*, 30 July 1951.
   Kenya:
   'Kenya As I See It': I. 'Mau Mau – The Terror by Night', *The Sunday Times*, 27 September 1953; II. 'Mau Mau, The Black God', 4 October 1953.
   Indo-China:
   'Return to Indo-China', *The Sunday Times*, 21 March 1955; 'Refugees and Victors', *The Sunday Times*, 1 May 1955; 'The Man as Pure as Lucifer', *The Sunday Times*, 8 May 1955; 'Indo-China', *The New Republic*, 5 April 1954; 'To Hope Till Hope Creates', *The New Republic*, 12 April 1954; 'Last Act in Indo-China', *The New Republic*, 16 May 1955. 'Great Blunders of the 20th Century' (series), 'Decision in Asia: The Battle of Dien Bien Phu', *The Sunday Times*, 3 March 1963.
   Poland:
   'The Half-Defeated', *The Sunday Times*, 8 January 1956; 'Between "Pax" and Patriotism', *The Sunday Times*, 15 January 1956.
   Cuba:
   'Return to Cuba', *The Sunday Telegraph*, 22 September 1963: 'Fidel: An Impression', *The Telegraph Magazine*, 2 December 1966.

Haiti:
'Nightmare Republic', *The Sunday Telegraph*, 29 September 1963.
Chile:
'The Dangerous Edge', *The Observer Magazine*, 2 January 1972.
Paraguay:
'The World Inside the Lotus Blossom', *The Telegraph Magazine*, 3 January 1979.
Panama:
'The Country with Five Frontiers', *New York Review of Books*, 17 January 1977; 'The Great Spectacular', *The Spectator*, 28 January 1978.

9. *The Sunday Times*, 21 March 1954.
10. *The New Republic*, 16 May 1955.
11. *New Statesman*, 22 May 1954.
12. 18 May 1954.
13. *The Sunday Times*, 8 May 1955.
14. *The Sunday Times*, 1 May 1955.
15. *The Sunday Times*, 8 May 1955.
16. *The Sunday Times*, 1 May 1955.
17. *The Sunday Times*, 8 May 1955.
18. 'Our man in Antibes', Gloria Emerson, *Rolling Stone*, 9 March 1978.
19. *The Sunday Times*, 4 October 1953.
20. *The Sunday Times*, 27 September 1963.
21. *The Sunday Times*, 4 October 1953.
22. *The Sunday Times*, 22 September 1963.
23. Ibid.
24. *The Sunday Telegraph*, 29 September 1963.
25. *The Telegraph Magazine*, 2 December 1966.
26. Greene writes:

> There is no inherent opposition between Marxist economics and Catholicism, and in Cuba coexistence with the Church has proved easier than in Poland (Cuba is less strictly Catholic than Poland, just as Marxism here is less philosophical). On a recent anniversary of the attack on Batista's palace by a handful of young men led by José Antonio Echeverria the chairman read out the political testament of the dead leader and omitted a sentence: 'We are confident that the purity of our intentions will bring us the favour of God, to achieve a reign of justice in our land'. Castro leapt on the omission and based his whole speech upon it.' Can we be so cowardly, so mentally crippled, that we have the moral poverty to suppress three lines? What kind of concept is this of history? Can such cowardice be called "the dialectical concept of history?" Can such a manner of thinking be called Marxist? We know that a revolutionary can have a religious belief. The Revolution does not force men, it does not intrude into their personal beliefs. It does not exclude anyone'.

These are not empty words . . . This is a new voice in the Communist world' *The Sunday Telegraph*, 22 September 1963.
27. *The Telegraph Magazine*, 2 December 1966.

28. See Margaret E. Crahan, 'Cuba: Religion and Revolutionary Institution-alization' *Journal of Latin American Studies*, vol. 17, part 2, November 1985, pp. 319–40.
29. *The Observer Magazine*, 2 January 1972.
30. *The Telegraph Magazine*, 3 January 1969.
31. *Saturday Review*, BBC 2, 28 September 1985.
32. *Revolution*, BBC Radio 3, 22 March 1987; third documentary in a series by Lord Rawlinson on the political influence across the world of the Society of Jesus.
33. *The Guardian*, 24 April 1987.
34. See Conor Cruise O'Brien, 'God and Man in Nicaragua', *Atlantic Monthly*, Boston, Massachussetts, August 1986, pp. 50–72. Also see Salman Rushdie, *The Jaguar Smile* (Picador, 1987).
35. Greene writes: 'it is absurd to speak of my friend, Omar Torrijos of Panama as "right wing" . . . "Left wing" certainly, social democrat perhaps, but the 19th century term which suits Torrijos best is the one we apply to men like San Martin and Bolivar, "patriot" ', letter to *The Spectator*, March 1979.
36. Terry Eagleton, *The New Left Church*, p. 2.
37. Anthony Burgess, 'Politics', p. 99.
38. Kim Philby, *My Silent War*, Introduction, p. 7.
39. Ibid.
40. Claud Cockburn, *I, Claud*, p. 26.
41. Kim Philby, *My Silent War*, Introduction, p. 7.
42. In the introduction to the Collected Edition Greene describes his meetings with those involved with the movement: 'All they were concerned with now were the jet planes which the British were preparing to sell Batista – they were better informed than the British Government, in this house in San Francisco Street, for when, after my return to England, a Labour MP, at my request, asked a question on the subject he was assured by the Foreign Secretary, Mr Selwyn Lloyd, that no arms at all were being sold to Batista. Yet some months later, a week or two before Castro entered Havana, the Foreign Secretary admitted that an export licence for some out-of-date planes had been granted. At the time he had granted the licence he had no information – so he said – that a civil war was in progress in Cuba.'
43. M. M. Mahood, *The Colonial Encounter*, p. 131.
44. Marie Françoise Allain, *The Other Man*, pp. 160–1.
45. David Hare, 'Nicaragua: An Appeal', *Granta*, 16, Summer 1985.
46. *The Comedians* (Penguin, 1979) p. 286.
47. *The Honorary Consul*, p. 16.
48. Letter to M.C., 7 May 1979.
49. *The Other Man*, Conversations with Marie Françoise Allain, pp. 160–1.
50. Barbara Rogers and Zdenek Cervenka, *The Nuclear Axis* (New York: Times Books, 1978).

Conclusion: Face to Face

1. Kenneth Tynan, 'An Inner View of Graham Greene', *Harpers Bazaar*, February 1953.

2. Letter to M.C., 1 April 1985.
3. Letter to M.C., 6 June 1980.
4. One cannot resist a comment on Greene's prescience in 1980 of events in 1986 when Reagan's USA clandestinely sold arms to Khomeini's Iran.
5. *Collected Essays*, p. 106.
6. See Interview, p. 213–14.
7. Letter to M.C., 4 March 1987. See also *The Tablet*, 21 February 1987.
8. *Collected Essays*, p. 83.
9. Edward W. Said, *The World, the Text and the Critic*, p. 224.
10. Ibid, p. 225.

Interview

1. *Did You See?*, BBC 2, 10 January, 1984, when some of the programmes on Orwell were discussed. Kenneth Tynan writes:

> Greene's Oxford years had proved to him that the best of English literature, from Shakespeare to James Joyce, had always been produced from the Christian standpoint. It infuriated him to hear men like Stephen Spender deploring the death of politically conscious novelists in England. Political novelists said Greene in the course of a public wrangle with Spender, aimed at an attainable objective, and once that objective had been gained, all passion died. Look, he exhorted his audience, at the later Russian cinema. Religious novelists on the other hand, could never gain their objective, and accordingly their care and passion never diminished. Greene has always preferred a sense of passionate inadequacy to a sense of fulfilment.
>
> (*Harper's Bazaar*, 'An Inner View of Graham Greene', February 1953)

2. Interview with Norman Lebrecht, *The Sunday Times*, 1 April 1984.
3. Joseph Cardinal Ratzinger is Prefect of the Sacred Congregation for the Doctrine of the Faith, Rome.
4. Interview with J. Maclaren Ross, *Memoirs of the Forties* (Alan Ross, 1965).

Bibliography

WORKS BY GRAHAM GREENE

Page references in the chapters for quotations from Graham Greene's books are to the Penguin editions, unless otherwise stated. All books Graham Greene has chosen to reprint are available in the UK in the hardback Collected Edition (London, Heinemann/The Bodley Head) and in Penguin unless otherwise stated. Roman numerals refer to the numbers of the volumes in the Collected Edition. The American Uniform Edition is published by Viking Press, New York. Greene's works are listed below with date of first publication. The place of publication is given only where this is outside the UK.

Novels

The Man Within (Heinemann, 1929) XV.
The Name of Action (Heinemann, 1930; Garden City, NY: Doubleday, 1931).
    Not reprinted and not in paperback.
Rumour at Nightfall (Heinemann, 1931; Garden City, NY: Doubleday 1932).
    Not reprinted and not in paperback.
Stamboul Train (Heinemann, 1932) XII
It's a Battlefield (Heinemann, 1934) II
England Made Me (Heinemann, 1935) III
A Gun for Sale (Heinemann, 1935) IX. American title *This Gun for Hire*
Brighton Rock (Heinemann, 1938)
The Confidential Agent (Heinemann, 1939) VII
The Power and the Glory (Heinemann, 1940) V. American title *The Labyrinthine Ways*
The Ministry of Fear (Heinemann, 1943) X
The Heart of the Matter (Heinemann, 1948) VI
The Third Man and *The Fallen Idol* (Heinemann, 1950) XVI
The End of the Affair (Heinemann, 1951) XII
The Quiet American (Heinemann, 1955) XI
Loser Takes All (Heinemann, 1955) XVI
Our Man in Havana (Heinemann, 1958) IV
A Burnt-Out Case (Heinemann, 1961) XIV
The Comedians (The Bodley Head, 1966) XVII
Travels with my Aunt (The Bodley Head, 1969) XX
The Honorary Consul (The Bodley Head, 1973) XXI
The Human Factor (The Bodley Head, 1978) XXII
Doctor Fischer of Geneva or *The Bomb Party* (The Bodley Head, 1980)
Monsignor Quixote (The Bodley Head, 1982)
The Tenth Man (The Bodley Head/Anthony Blond, 1985)

Short Stories

Twenty-one Stories (Heinemann, 1954. First published in 1947 as *Nineteen Stories*)
A Sense of Reality (The Bodley Head, 1963)
May We Borrow Your Husband? (The Bodley Head, 1967)
Collected Stories (The Bodley Head, 1972)

Plays

Three Plays (Heinemann, Mercury Books, 1961). The plays are *The Living Room* (1953), *The Potting Shed* (1958), and *The Complaisant Lover* (1959)
Carving a Statue (The Bodley Head, 1964)
The Return of A. J. Raffles (Bodley Head, 1975)

Travel and Autobiography

Journey Without Maps (Heinemann, 1936)
The Lawless Roads (Heinemann, 1939)
In Search of a Character: Two African Journals (The Bodley Head, 1961)
A Sort of Life (The Bodley Head, 1971)
Ways of Escape (The Bodley Head, 1980)
Getting to Know the General (The Bodley Head, 1984)

Film Reviews

The Pleasure Dome: The Collected Film Criticism 1935–1940, edited by John Russell Taylor (Secker & Warburg, 1972); paperback (Oxford University Press, 1980)

Essays

The Lost Childhood and Other Essays (The Bodley Head, 1969)
Collected Essays (The Bodley Head, 1969)
British Dramatists (Collins, 1942). Not in paperback. Reprinted in *The Heritage of British Literature* (Thames & Hudson, 1983).

Interview and Letters

Why Do I Write (Percival Marshall, 1948)
The Other Man: Conversations with Graham Greene, Marie Françoise Allain, translated by Guido Waldman (The Bodley Head, 1983)

Pamphlet

J'Accuse – The Dark Side of Nice (The Bodley Head, 1982)

Biography

Lord Rochester's Monkey (The Bodley Head, 1974); paperback (Futura, 1976)

Greene has also published four books for children with the London publisher Max Parrish: *The Little Fire Engine* (1950), *The Little Horse Bus* (1952), *The Little Steam Roller* (1953), *The Little Train* (1957).

BIBLIOGRAPHY

Vann, J. Don, *Graham Greene: A Checklist of Criticism* (Kent, Ohio: Kent State University Press, 1970)
Cassis, A. F., *Graham Greene: An Annotated Bibliography of Criticism* (London: The Scarecrow Press, 1980)

SELECTED CRITICISM OF GRAHAM GREENE

Allott, Kenneth, and Farris, Miriam, *The Art of Graham Greene* (Hamish Hamilton, 1951)
Atkins, John, *Graham Greene* (Calder & Boyars, 1957; revised edn, 1966)
Boardman, Gwenn R., *Graham Greene: The Aesthetics of Exploration* (Gainesville, Florida: University of Florida Press, 1971)
Burgess, Anthony, 'Politics in the Novels of Graham Greene', in *Urgent Copy: Literary Studies* (Jonathan Cape, 1968); also in *Journal of Contemporary History*, April 1967
Chapman, Raymond, 'The Vision of Graham Greene' in Nathan A. Scott (ed.) *Forms of Extremity in the Modern Novel* (Virginia: Chime Paperbacks, 1965)
De Vitis, A. A., *Graham Greene* (New York: Twayne, 1964)
Duran, Leopoldo, 'A Priest reads *The Honorary Consul*', *The Clergy Review*, September, 1976; also an article on *Doctor Fischer of Geneva* in *The Clergy Review*, 1980
Evans, Robert O. (ed.) *Graham Greene: Some Critical Considerations* (Lexington, Kentucky: University of Kentucky Press, 1963)
Greene, Barbara, *Too Late to Turn Back* (Settle & Bendall, 1981)
Hynes Samuel (ed.) *Graham Greene: A Collection of Critical Essays* (Englewood Cliffs, NJ: Prentice-Hall, 1973)
Johnstone, Richard, *The Will to Believe: Novelists of the Nineteen Thirties* (Oxford University Press, 1984)
Kulshrestha, J. P., *Graham Greene: The Novelist* (New Delhi: Macmillan, 1977)
Kunkel, Francis L. *The Labyrinthine Ways of Graham Greene* (New York: Sheed & Ward, 1959)
Lewis, R. W. B., *The Picaresque Saint: Representative Figures in Contemporary Fiction* (New York: Barnes & Noble, 1959)
Lodge, David, *Graham Greene* (New York and London: Columbia University Press, 1966)
Madaule, Jacques, *Graham Greene* (Paris: Editions du Temps Present, 1954)

Mesnet, Marie-Beatrice, *Graham Greene and the Heart of the Matter* (Cresset Press, 1954)

Ogude, S. E. 'In Search of Misery: A Study of Graham Greene's Travels in Africa', *ODŪ* 11, January 1975 (Ile Ife, Nigeria: University of Ife Press)

Ogude, S. E., 'Graham Greene's Africa', *ODŪ* 14, July 1976 (Ile Ife, Nigeria: University of Ife Press)

Poole, R. C., 'Graham Greene's Indirection' in Harry Cargas (ed.) *Graham Greene* (St Louis, Missouri: Herder)

Pryce-Jones, David, *Graham Greene* (Oliver & Boyd, 1963, 1973) 2nd edn.

Sharrock, Roger, *Saints, Sinners and Comedians* (Notre Dame, Indiana: University of Notre Dame Press, 1984)

Smith, Grahame, *The Achievement of Graham Greene* (Harvester Press, 1986)

Spurling, John, *Graham Greene* in Contemporary Writers series (Methuen, 1983)

Stratford, Philip, *Faith and Fiction: Creative Process in Greene and Mauriac* (Notre Dame, Indiana: University of Notre Dame Press, 1964)

Wolfe, Peter, *Graham Greene the Entertainer* (Carbondale and Edwardsville, Illinois: Southern Illinois University Press, 1972)

Woodcock, George, *The Writer and Politics* (Porcupine Press, 1948)

Wyndham, Francis, *Graham Greene* (Longmans Green, 1955)

OTHER SOURCES

Bergonzi, Bernard, *Reading the Thirties* (Macmillan, 1978)

Bayers, Robert, *Atrocity and Amnesia: The Political Novel since 1945* (New York, Oxford University Press, 1985)

Bradbury, Malcolm, *The Social Context of Literature: Texts and Contexts* (Oxford University Press, 1974)

Coburn, Claud, *I, Claud* (Penguin, 1967)

Dawson, Christopher, *Religion and the Rise of Western Culture* (Sheed & Ward, 1950)

Dawson, C., *The Spirit of the Oxford Movement* (Sheed & Ward, 1945)

Eagleton, Terry, *Exiles and Emigrés* (Chatto & Windus, 1970)

Eagleton, Terry, *The New Left Church* (Sheed & Ward, 1966)

Echeruo, Michael, J. C., *Joyce Cary and the Novel of Africa* (Longman, 1973)

Fisch, Harold, *The Dual Image: The Figure of the Jew in English and American Literature* (World Jewish Library, 1971)

Garaudy, Roger, *The Alternative Future: A Vision of Christian Marxism* (Penguin, 1976)

Green, Martin, *Children of the Sun* (Constable, 1977)

Green, Martin, *Dreams of Adventure, Deeds of Empire* (Routledge & Kegan Paul, 1980)

Green, Martin, *The English Novel in the Twentieth Century: The Doom of Empire* (Routledge & Kegan Paul, 1984)

Gutierrez, G., *A Theology of Liberation* (New York: Orbis Books, Maryknoll, 1973)

Hoskins, Katharine Bail, *Today the Struggle, Literature and Politics in England during the Spanish Civil War* (Austin and London: University of Texas Press, 1969)

Bibliography 245

Howe, Irving, *Politics and the Novel* (New Left Books, 1961)

Hynes, Samuel, *The Auden Generation: Literature and Politics in England in the 1930s* (Faber, 1976)

Lodge, David, *The Novelist at the Crossroads and other Essays on Fiction and Criticism* (Routledge & Kegan Paul, 1971)

de Lubac, H., *The Drama of Atheist Humanism* (Sheed & Ward, 1949)

Lukacs, G., *Studies in European Realism* (Merlin Press, 1972)

Mahood, M., *The Colonial Encounter* (Rex Collings, 1977)

Nazareth, Peter, *The Third World Writer and His Social Responsibility* (Nairobi: General Printers, 1978)

Newman, John Henry, Cardinal, *An Essay on the Development of Christian Doctrine* (Penguin, 1974)

Newman, John Henry, Cardinal, *Sermons on the Theory of Religious Belief* (Gilbert & Rivington, 1843)

Newman, John Henry, Cardinal, *The Idea of a University* (Longmans Green, 1912)

Orwell, George, *Inside the Whale and Other Essays* (Penguin, 1981)

Orwell, George, *The Collected Essays, Journalism and Letters*, edited by Sonia Orwell and Ian Angus (Secker & Warburg, 1968) vols III and IV

Parry, Benita, *Conrad and Imperialism – Ideological Boundaries and Visionary Frontiers* (Macmillan, 1983)

Parry, Benita, *Delusions and Discoveries – Studies on India in the British Imagination* (University of California Press, 1972)

Philby, Kim, *My Silent War* (London, Panther, 1969)

Ricoeur, Paul, *The Symbolism of Evil* (Boston, Mass.: Beacon Press, 1969)

Said, Edward W., *The World, The Text and The Critic* (Faber, 1984)

Williams, Raymond, *Orwell* (Fontana/Collins, 1961)

Williams, Raymond, *The Long Revolution* (Chatto & Windus, 1961)

Woodcock, George, *The Crystal Spirit: A Study of George Orwell* (Jonathan Cape, 1967)

Index

Achebe, Chinua 16
Afghanistan 211
Africa 10–19, 88, 111–12, 113–19,
    125–7, 130–1, 132–3, 218, 219,
    222
Allende, Salvador 158, 215, 227
Auden, W. H. 5, 91, 92, 207, 208

Bennett, Alan 176
Borgez, Tomas 202
Bergonzi, Bernard 5, 208
Bowen, Elisabeth 131
Brighton Rock 7, 8, 32, 33, 55–61,
    65, 66, 67, 140, 142–3, 162, 183,
    190, 202
Burgess, Anthony 63, 65–6, 67,
    167–8, 212, 229
Burgess, Guy 176, 209
Burnt-Out Case, A 62, 63, 85–90,
    112, 114, 116, 117, 127–31, 139–
    40, 168, 176

Callaghan, James 210
Camus, Albert 214
Cardenal, Ernesto 179, 202, 213
Cary, Joyce 16, 114, 115–16, 131
Castro, Fidel 21, 152, 156–60, 164,
    209–10, 222–23, 226
Catholic Church
    in Central America 160–3,
        164–6, 183, 202, 215
    in Cuba 158–60, 215, 223
    in Latin America 158–60, 163,
        164, 166, 183, 202
    in Poland 212, 213
    in Vietnam 153–54, 171
Catholic novel/novelist 1, 5, 26,
    32, 57, 59, 91, 119, 167–8, 184,
    185
    Liberation Theology 21, 159,
        213–14, 227
Catholicism 1–2, 4, 7–8, 9, 23–4,
    31–3, 38, 57, 59–61, 62–9, 90,

178, 202, 206, 211–14, 220, 229
Cervantes 24, 201
Cervenka, Zdenek and Rogers,
    Barbara 194, 219
Chamberlain, Neville 104
Chesterton, G. K. 202
Chile 147, 158, 160–1, 202, 209,
    215, 226–7
Churchill, Winston 5, 208, 210
Cockburn, Claud 2, 5, 97, 173–4,
    207, 208
Comedians, The 66, 99, 119, 126,
    134, 138–9, 141, 143, 148, 149,
    176, 177–82, 183, 186
Communism 2, 5, 8, 18, 31, 45,
    103–4, 105, 154, 158–60, 162,
    164, 167–9, 174–6, 178, 179, 183,
    200, 202, 207, 209, 211–12, 213–
    14, 217–18
Conference of Latin American
    Bishops 163
Confidential Agent, The 8, 91, 97–
    105, 174
Conrad, Joseph 10, 14, 16, 27, 37,
    112, 113, 126, 219
Cuba 112, 147, 157–60, 176, 178,
    179, 190, 215, 217, 222–3, 226
Czechoslovakia 210, 211, 225

Depression, the 25, 137
Doctor Fischer of Geneva 26, 141,
    186, 197–200

Eagleton, Terry 68, 87–8, 120, 165
Echeruo, Michael 114, 116
EEC 136, 225
Eliot, T. S. 5, 7
Emerson, Gloria 154–5
El Salvador 164, 229
Empire, The (British) 8, 9, 11, 14,17,
    18, 20, 23, 25–6, 27, 31, 32, 45–8,
    49, 91, 96–7, 109–10, 115, 118,
    124–5, 127, 174–6, 218, 220–1

End of the Affair, The 62, 63, 69, 74, 81–4, 138, 197
England Made Me 8, 91, 92, 93–7, 143–4
Escoto, Miguel d' 202, 213

Falklands, The 210
Fisch, Harold 41–2
Forster, E. M. 3, 13, 25, 62, 114, 117, 118, 122–6, 183, 216
Fyvel, T. R. 7

Gaulle, General Charles de 213
General Strike, The 5, 207–8
Getting to Know the General 21, 149, 164–5, 209
Green, Martin 25–6, 92–3
Greene, Barbara 14, 136
Greene, Charles 174
Greene, Graham, Works by
   Brighton Rock 7–8, 32, 33, 55–61, 65–7, 140, 142–3, 162, 183, 190
   Burnt-Out Case, A 62, 63, 85–90, 112, 114, 116, 117, 127–31, 139–40, 168, 176
   Comedians, The 66, 99, 126, 134, 138–9, 141, 143, 148, 149, 176, 177–82, 183, 186
   Confidential Agent, The 8, 91, 97–105, 174
   Doctor Fischer of Geneva or The Bomb Party 26, 141, 186, 197–100
   End of the Affair, The 62, 63, 69, 74, 81–4, 138, 197
   England Made Me 8, 91, 92, 93–7, 143–4
   Getting to Know the General 21, 149, 164–5, 209
   Gun For Sale, A 8, 33, 41, 42–3, 44, 52–5, 98, 140
   Heart of the Matter, The 7, 62–3, 66, 74–81, 84, 112, 114, 117, 119–27, 130, 131, 138, 171, 208, 218
   Honorary Consul, The 26, 67, 71, 112, 126, 135, 138–9, 149, 159, 161, 163, 166, 172, 183–90, 196, 202
   Human Factor, The 26, 48, 97, 103, 114, 124, 138, 140, 142–3, 149, 172, 173, 190–6, 197, 218
   It's a Battlefield 15, 25, 30–1, 33, 45–52, 100–1, 142, 147, 167, 183, 219
   J'Accuse 57
   Journey Without Maps 10–19, 97, 111, 115, 117–18, 126, 136, 143, 145, 218–19
   Lawless Roads, The 10, 15, 20–3, 111, 145, 159, 162–3
   Man Within, The 24, 26, 33–8, 58
   Ministry of Fear, The 91–3, 97, 105–9, 177
   Monsignor Quixote 24, 67, 131, 136, 145, 163, 166, 197, 200–3, 214
   Name of Action, The 33, 38–9
   Our Man in Havana 26, 85, 92, 141, 149, 157, 176–7
   Power and the Glory, The 33, 56, 62–3, 66, 69–74, 84, 111, 141, 162–3, 166, 202
   Quiet American, The 5, 85, 138–9, 147, 153–4, 166–76, 188
   Rumour at Nightfall 33, 38–9
   Sort of Life, A 5, 137, 214
   Stamboul Train 30, 33, 39–44, 97
   Tenth Man, The 198
   Travels with my Aunt 112, 117, 121, 124, 126, 131–6, 176, 198, 201, 220–21
   Gun for Sale, A 8, 33, 41, 42–3, 44, 52–5, 98, 140

Haggard, Rider 25, 34, 115, 127
Haiti 112, 147, 178, 190, 215, 217, 223
Hare, David 184–95
Heart of the Matter, The 7, 62–3, 66, 74–81, 84, 112, 114, 117, 119–27, 130, 131, 138, 171, 208, 218
Ho Chi Minh 21, 151–3, 156, 209, 217
Honorary Consul, The 26, 67, 71, 112, 126, 135, 138–9, 149, 159, 161, 163, 166, 172, 183–90, 196, 202
Howe, Irving 30

Human Factor, The   26, 48, 97, 103,
    114, 124, 138, 140, 142–3, 149,
    172, 173, 190–6, 197, 218
Hunger Marches, the   9, 208–9, 216
Hynes, Samuel   115

India   156, 178, 217–18
Independent Labour Party (ILP)   5,
    18, 174, 206
International Forum for a Nuclear
    Free World   202
It's a Battlefield   15, 25, 30–1, 33,
    45–52, 100–1, 142, 147, 167, 183,
    219

J'Accuse   57
James, Henry   10, 27, 37, 62,
    146–7, 220
Jansenism   24, 65–6, 190, 212, 229
Johnstone, Richard   31–2, 33
Journey Without Maps   10–19, 97,
    111, 115, 117–18, 126, 136, 143,
    145, 218–19

Kenya   147, 149, 155–6, 218, 222
Kenyatta, Jomo   155–6
Kipling, Rudyard   25, 92, 115, 145,
    165, 204, 220

Laski, Marghanita   56
Latin America   135, 136, 154, 157,
    158, 159, 160, 179, 183, 189, 204,
    220
Lawless Roads, The   10, 15, 20–3,
    111, 145, 159, 162–3
Le Carré, John   103–4, 110
Liberia   10–19, 21, 114, 132, 215,
    219, 220
Low, David   4

Malaya   116
Mahood, Molly   179–80
Man Within, The   24, 26, 33–8, 58
Marcel, Gabriel   212
Martin, Kingsley   62, 151–2
Mau Mau   116, 149, 155–6, 222
Mauriac, François   62, 65–6, 149,
    168, 183, 212
Mexico   10, 19–23, 56, 62, 111, 147,

    158, 159, 185–6, 215, 220
Ministry of Fear, The   91–3, 97,
    105–9, 177
Monsignor Quixote   24, 67, 131, 136,
    145, 163, 166, 197, 200–3, 214
Munich Agreement, The   97

Name of Action, The   33, 38–9
Newman, John Henry
    Cardinal   10, 23–4, 32, 64–5,
    220
Ngũgĩ Wa Thiong'O   16
Nicaragua   147, 160–3, 165–6, 183,
    185, 202, 211, 213, 215, 227–9

Ogude, S. E.   11, 87, 118, 132–33
Orwell, George   4, 5, 7–8, 10, 13,
    31, 56, 59, 97, 104–5, 114, 117,
    119–26, 145–6, 201, 206–8
Our Man in Havana   26, 85, 92, 141,
    149, 157, 176–7
Oxford Movement, the   27

Painter, George, D.   66
Panama   147, 163–5
Paraguay   112, 136, 147, 160, 184,
    190, 215
Philby, Kim   92, 102–3, 174–6, 196,
    209
Pinochet, General   202, 209, 215,
    226–7
Pinter, Harold   161
Poland   154, 212–13
Pope John XXIII   159, 176, 227
Pope John Paul II   162, 212–13,
    227–8
Power and the Glory, The   33, 56,
    62–3, 66, 69–74, 84, 111, 141,
    162–3, 166, 202
Pritchett, V. S.   106

Quiet American, The   5, 85, 138–9,
    147, 153–4, 166–76, 188

Ratzinger, Cardinal   212
Read, Herbert   5
Reagan, Ronald   227, 228
Rogers, Barbara and Cervenka,
    Zdenek   194, 219

Rumour at Nightfall 33, 38–9
Russia 159, 164, 168, 193, 202–3, 211, 218

Said, Edward 113, 203–5
Sandinistas, the 103, 156, 164, 179, 209
Sheen, Bishop Fulton 159
Sierra Leone 12, 131, 134, 190, 218, 219
Sort of Life, A 5, 137, 214
South Africa 193–5
Spanish Civil War 4–6, 9, 97, 103, 207–8
Spellman, Cardinal 159
Spender, Stephen 206–7
Spurling, John 37
Stroessner, General 160, 215
Stamboul Train 30, 33, 39–44, 97
Stevenson, R. L. 25, 216
Sykes, Christopher 19–20, 26–7
Symons, Julian 7

Tenth Man, The 198
Thirties, the 4, 6, 29, 30, 96, 103–4, 113, 115, 154, 201, 206, 207–8, 216, 229
Thatcher, Margaret 210, 227, 228
Times, The 5, 56, 207, 208

Tito, Marshall 4
Torres, Camilo 161, 186, 214–15
Torrijos, General Omar 221, 152, 156, 163–5, 209
Travels with my Aunt 112, 117, 121, 124, 126, 131–6, 176, 198, 201, 220–1
Tynan, Kenneth 198

United States of America 150, 158–9, 164, 166–7, 194, 208, 209, 211, 217, 218

Videla, General 209
Vietnam 5, 6, 20, 112, 150–5, 169, 178, 190, 216–17, 223–6

Waugh, Evelyn 4, 5, 7, 11, 19–20, 26–7, 32, 115, 168, 212, 215
William, Raymond 28–9, 146
Wilson, Angus 8, 59–60
Wilson, Harold 174, 210
Woodcock, George 66, 91
Woolf, Virginia 62–3, 183
World War
First 2–3, 9, 30, 91–2, 115, 143, 215
Second 3, 9, 19, 93, 105, 113, 143, 215